This book provides two important theoretical contributions to existing theories within the innovation literature. First, it extends the existing literature on financial innovation to a completely new field and construct which is based on a religious imperative as a framework within which financial innovation and engineering are constrained. It explains how an innovation in Islamic financial institutions (IFIs) can be directed within religious rules, which indicates that innovation in IFIs is a learning philosophy. Secondly, the book introduces and examines the analytical process, of assessing the suitability and acceptability of a financial innovation from a Shariah perspective, as a conceptual and practical framework.

Finally, before I leave the reader to explore my work, I would like to thank and acknowledge every person who helped and provided support to me in achieving this objective and writing this book. My thanks also go to all those who read this book and make use of it and its findings.

Birmingham, UK Samir Alamad
23 March 2017

Contributions to Management Science

More information about this series at http://www.springer.com/series/1505

Samir Alamad

Financial Innovation and Engineering in Islamic Finance

Springer

Samir Alamad
Al Rayan Bank
Birmingham, United Kingdom

ISSN 1431-1941 ISSN 2197-716X (electronic)
Contributions to Management Science
ISBN 978-3-319-52946-2 ISBN 978-3-319-52947-9 (eBook)
DOI 10.1007/978-3-319-52947-9

Library of Congress Control Number: 2017936952

Printed on acid-free paper

This Springer imprint is published by Springer Nature
The registered company is Springer International Publishing AG
The registered company address is: Gewerbestrasse 11, 6330 Cham, Switzerland

I dedicate this work to my wife Lara and our two daughters Faith and May, my mother and my late father who always encouraged me and to those who seek knowledge.

Preface

This book was motivated by the desire to further the evolution of Islamic finance and banking in the field of social sciences. The book was based on the findings of my doctoral research and a robust research process that took over 6 years. This project covered the practices, processes and structures of financial product development of Islamic finance and banking over five continents. This book is not merely an academic work, nor is it a pure practitioner guide; rather, it is a robust work that combines both. It marries rigorous academic research and theories with practical industry experiences. It is a condensed account of my own practical experience, which covers working in Islamic financial services, setting up a Shariah governance system from scratch, developing a unique product portfolio for the first Islamic bank in Western Europe and advising the UK government and other national and international institutions.

It is important to understand that religious ethical values can mesh with finance for a better financial outcome that benefits all involved stakeholders in society and minimises undesirable harmful consequences of the banking system. I have been asked in various forums what Islamic finance is. My answer was Islamic finance is not what you think. If you think Islamic finance is only about providing financial products based on Islamic finance principles that ape the interest-based products offered by conventional banks, it is not. Islamic finance is much more than that; it is an all-encompassing approach to financial matters.

There are a lot of steps that Islamic finance should undertake to deliver its aspirations and reach its potential to live up to the teachings of Islam and the requirements of Islamic commercial law, rather than just meeting the minimum Shariah requirements and being labelled as 'Shariah compliant'. It is with regret that there remains a lot of work to be done by the players in this industry. There are already many breaches, exceptions and diversions by the Islamic banking industry to mimic conventional banking, except for some who steadfastly implement a robust Shariah governance. This concern is manifested in the processes and procedures of developing new financial products.

There is little in the literature about financial product development or financial innovation and engineering in Islamic finance. Similarly, nothing exists from a practice perspective, as this aspect is very secretive within Islamic financial institutions, and therefore, there is no cohesive streamlined approach within the industry.

Therefore, it was very important for my work to address this gap and set down the first building block outlining the correct Islamic financial engineering process. During my academic career and research, I have developed my analytical and critical skills and research rigour that helped me see things through a different lens. As a passionate expert involved in Islamic finance and banking, who fears it being hijacked by conventional banking practices and demolished, this book was planned as a bulwark against such hijacking to inform and inspire the reader.

However, I am sure you are keen to know more about the content of this book. Drawing from work found in the financial innovation literature, the main objective of this book is to explore the effect of religious rules on financial innovation and engineering in Islamic Finance. The book also examines what constitutes Shariah-compliant financial innovation and how it is enacted in the innovation process. Islamic rules in financial innovation are conceptualised and defined, as a system, in this book.

In order to achieve this objective, I employed multiple theoretical perspectives to develop its conceptual framework. It combines traditional innovation theories with the theories of economic thought in Islam in order to explore the role of religion in the financial innovation processes in Islamic finance. Financial innovation and engineering and the role of Shariah are portrayed as a multidimensional knowledge and philosophical structure.

The book is designed to be suitable for all readers whether they possess an advanced knowledge of Islamic finance and banking or none at all, for academics, students or practitioners. The first three chapters of this book provide the context and important details that help the reader understand what Islamic finance and banking are and their building blocks. Chapters 4 and 5 provide a historical analysis of financial innovation and engineering and their development over 14 centuries up to the modern day. Chapters 6 and 7 analytically discuss conventional and Islamic theories of financial innovation, respectively. Chapters 8–10 provide a working practical guide explaining the thought process in initiating and examining financial innovation and engineering from an Islamic finance perspective. Chapter 11 illustrates a case study that follows a documentary analysis process to examine existing financial products according to certain criteria. Finally, building on the empirical results and findings, the book illustrates the practical implications of collaboration and develops a novel analytical framework for understanding financial innovation in Islamic finance. This practical contribution concludes by noting the policy and managerial implications of the findings of the book and presents a new Shariah-compliant financial innovation and provides directions for further research in Chapter 12.

Acknowledgement

First and foremost, I would like to thank my family, my wife Lara for standing beside me throughout my career and writing this book. Also, my two daughters Faith and May have always been there for me with support, love and endless patience with my busy schedule.

To my beloved parents, I owe a debt of gratitude for their love, enduring support and prayers for me. It was my father who inspired me to follow this path; although he is no longer with us, his belief in me has motivated me and continuesly fueled my work. It is to him that I dedicate this book.

I would like also to thank my friends, who always supported me, many individuals from the community and the Islamic finance industry. My thanks are extended to all Islamic banks around the world who contributed to this book with data and information too.

Contents

List of Figures

List of Tables

List of Common Abbreviations

A.H	After the Hijra: referring to the migration of the Prophet Muhammad to Madina from Makka. The Islamic lunar calendar starts from this event
AAOIFI	Accounting and Auditing Organisation for Islamic Financial Institutions
FCA	Financial Conduct Authority, UK
GCC	Gulf Cooperation Council (Saudi Arabia, Kuwait, Bahrain, United Arab Emirates, Qatar and Oman)
IB	Islamic banking
IFI	Islamic financial institution
IFSB	Islamic Financial Services Board
NPD	New Product Development
OIC	Organisation of Islamic Cooperation
PBUH	Peace Be Upon Him
PRA	Prudential Regulatory Authority, UK
RA	Blessing Upon Him, short for the Arabic 'radi Allah anhu'
SSC/SSB	Shariah Supervisory Committee/Board

Chapter 1
Introduction

1.1 Background

Since the global financial crisis of 2008, interest in the Islamic banking and financial system has sharply increased. After the near collapse of the world financial system and the bankruptcies and government bailouts of several long established financial institutions (see e.g. Plosser 2009; Poole 2011; Duska 2009; Jameson 2009), attention has shifted to the newly emerged Islamic banking system. The focus of examination is whether Islamic banks have been impacted by the financial crisis in a similar manner to the conventional banking system.

The question always asked was how Islamic banking and its financial products were and are different from its conventional counterpart. Also, what underpins the financial innovation and engineering processes to make this banking system immune, to some extent, from the recent financial crisis?

Comparisons between Islamic and conventional banking have also surfaced in other arenas. In Anti-Capitalist protests around the world, there was considerable anger towards the conventional financial institutions.

These events were thought provoking and raised many questions about Islamic finance and banking that need to be seriously considered. Does the Islamic financial system really hold a solution, or at least a partial solution, to our financial problems for people who have lost faith in capitalism and the current practices of the financial system and its institutions? What shielded the Islamic financial and banking system from the financial storm that destroyed significant parts of our conventional financial and banking system? How did the Islamic financial system develop its principles and foundations in relation to financial innovation and engineering, where did Islamic finance come from and what are the characteristics that this system represents?

We aim in this book to answer the above questions as possible and shed the light in a robust academic manner on the system of financial innovation and engineering in Islamic finance and banking. Recent academic research (Plosser 2009; Poole

S. Alamad, *Financial Innovation and Engineering in Islamic Finance*,
Contributions to Management Science, DOI 10.1007/978-3-319-52947-9_1

2011; Duska 2009; Jameson 2009) has suggested different reasons for the failure of the financial and banking systems that triggered the financial crisis in 2008. Kling (2010) summarises that the main focus was on two competing narratives: moral failure and cognitive failure. The capital regulations played a fundamental role in fostering the behaviour that created the financial crisis. Occurring in parallel to this under-regulation were subprime mortgages, underwriting criteria, the sophisticated financial innovation and engineering, principles of financial product development and debt securitisation.

These dual processes combined to trigger the 2008 financial crisis, which is still affecting the economy and society as a whole (Plosser 2009; Poole 2011; Duska 2009; Jameson 2009). Yet the role of banks and their practices in causing the current financial crisis is underplayed and under analysed. This lack of scrutiny has occurred in spite of a colossal sum of taxpayers' money being injected to save banks, which themselves have played crucial part in the current financial crisis.

By examining the banking practices that were the root cause of the recent financial crisis as outlined in the literature, they all lead to two intertwined, overriding concerns, namely cultural and behavioural failures. These failures impacted the processes of initiating new financial innovation, financial engineering, the new financial product development (NPD) and the way these products were introduced and sold in the market by circumventing legal rules and regulations.

New, light touch regulatory changes, according to Turner (2012), were introduced by financial regulators into banks in order to address this issue. As an example, the UK government has introduced the separation of commercial and investment banking functions, which will come into effect around 2019. However this does not represent any real reform of the financial system and banking system, because it does not fully address the working culture underpinning banking practices.

This research, therefore, adopts the view that the cultural and behavioural failures are the overriding concerns, as the basis for exploring and explaining these issues in the context of the Islamic finance and banking. The behavioural approach and culture of the financial innovation and engineering processes are crucial elements to be assessed in order to explore what constitutes a religiously guided process towards financial innovation and engineering.

1.2 Importance of Financial Innovation: Realising the Potential

Growth of the Islamic finance is in progress with key players pioneering new ways for consumers to generate a profit from their wealth in a Shariah compliant way. However, the challenge does not end here. Whilst product innovation needs to keep pushing the boundaries, consumer education and awareness must also be increased to drive product take-up for an increased market share. The industry's success so far proves that this is not mission impossible (Iqbal 1999).

Rapid surge of financial innovations in international financial markets was witnessed in the 1980s. Financial innovations transformed the traditional financial and banking markets into highly sophisticated markets featuring high degrees of liquidity and a wide-array of instruments to share and transfer various sources of risk. Such financial instruments are believed to be contributable factor to the recent global financial crisis (Philippe and Da Silva 1995: 5). The bank for International Settlement (BIS 1986) identifies three types of financial innovation activities with the most significant impact on the markets innovations to enhance liquidity, to transfer risk (price and credit), and to generate revenues (from credit and equity).

Financial engineering can be viewed as a process of building complex instruments utilising basic building blocks or unbundling and repackaging different components of existing financial instruments, e.g. return, price risk, credit risk etc. Most of financial innovations today are financial ideas that are engineered to incorporate highly liquid instruments and derivatives that are nothing but a structure based on simple and basic set of instruments (Iqbal 1999).

A close scrutiny of instruments underlying Islamic financial system reveals that such instruments have similar characteristics of many of today's basic building blocks. It is a matter of designing more complex instruments without violating any of the boundaries defined by Shariah rules (Iqbal 1999). Therefore, based on the above discussion and for the purpose of defining key terms used in this book, this book adopts the following meaning when referring to, financial innovation, financial engineering and new product development (NPD):

(a) Financial innovation is the generation of new idea for a financial product with the objective of securing market competitiveness, addressing risk, generating revenue or enhancing liquidity.
(b) Financial engineering, on the other hand, is the process of employing basic financial tools to build what may appear as a complex structure in order to provide a suitable design for the new financial innovation.
(c) New product development process (NPD) is the overall process that sets the steps for taking a new financial innovation from the concept or initiation phase, through the financial engineering and design phase, by following the different phases and governance controls. This would lead to a complete financial product that complies with all applicable Shariah rules, in order to be introduced in the market. This involves taking into account all operational, market, system and distribution channels and sales requirements. The requirement of a financial engineering would determine whether the NDP requires such phase or not, if it is designed on a simple single financial instrument.

The above technical meaning and definition of the three identified terms that this work revolves around, would be the approach used herein and throughout this book when referring to any of them. The Shariah principles, rules and ethics that should be observed are incorporated into the processes of those technical terms in this book.

1.3 What Makes a Bank Islamic

The basis for Islamic finance lies in the principles of the Shariah, or Islamic Law, which is taken from the Qur'an and from the example of Prophet Muhammad (peace be upon him). The Islamic form of finance is as old as the religion of Islam itself (Visser 2009: 34).

Central to Islamic finance is that money itself has no intrinsic value. As a matter of faith, a Muslim cannot lend money to, or receive money from someone and expect to benefit from this alone. This is why interest (known as *riba*) is not allowed and is considered effortless profit (Ahmed 1976; Siddiqi 1981). Therefore, the exclusion of interest from its activities is the founding principle of an Islamic bank.

Instead, according to Islam, money must be used in a productive way and wealth can only be generated through legitimate trade and investment. It is also essential that all parties share the business risk involved in the activity. As a result, the parties concerned are each entitled to a share in the profits that are generated (Iqbal 1999).

Islamic banking therefore uses various principles recognised as Shariah compliant such as *Ijara* (leasing), *Musharaka* (partnership) and *Mudaraba* (profit sharing agreement), full explanation of all common principles is provided in Chap. 2, Sect. 2.4. Islamic banks use these, and other, Islamic finance principles to develop Shariah compliant financial products, such as savings accounts, investment, commercial and development finance and home finance, which allow Muslims to conduct their finances in an Islamic and ethical way.

1.4 Values Embedded in the Islamic Banking Products

Islamic banking and conventional banking are based on different values and the absence of interest in Islamic banking is one of the key differentiators. However, there are other important differences:

(a) Islamic banking (IB) is asset-backed (Ahmed 1976; Siddiqi 1981); which means that Islamic banking should not conduct business unless it has the funds or assets to back the transaction. As a result, Islamic banking should avoid putting its customers' assets at risk through the use of sophisticated financial instruments (used in the conventional banking system) that involve speculation.

So, for home finance e.g., Islamic banks use their own funds, or the savings deposits from their customers, to provide finance (Al Zarqa 2012: 48–51). The customer and the bank buy the property jointly under one of the financing structures (this structure is based on a diminishing co-ownership with lease) used by Islamic banks for that purpose. The monthly payment increases the customer's share in the property and includes rent on the share that the IB owns. At the end of the finance term the customer will own the property outright and the IB will transfer the legal title to the customer.

For savers, Islamic banks invests their depositors' money in low risk commodities trade in inter-banking deposits placements with counterparty Islamic banks, or conventional banks with an Islamic trade desk, and in the IB's assets products. The return received from both of these activities is shared and distributed as profits to savings customers. By following this asset-backed system (as there must be an underlying asset for any financial transaction), Islamic banking as a whole, is not exposed to the same risks as conventional banks.

(b) The values underpinning Islamic banking stipulate that the source of funding, profits and business investments cannot be in/from businesses that are considered unlawful under Shariah, such as companies that deal in interest, gambling, pornography, speculation, tobacco, arms and other commodities contrary to Islamic values (Visser 2009: 34).

(c) The principles of fairness and transparency play a large role in Shariah compliant banking, although it might not be fully implemented in practice. For customers this translates itself in different ways. For example, a customer taking out a home finance product would only be charged a fee that reflects the administrative costs the bank incurs to arrange the finance. Small print of associated risks, extra terms and conditions that shift risk unfairly to customers and hidden charges that are not clear upfront are practices against Islamic teachings for financial transactions (Iqbal 1999).

(d) The whole premise of Islamic banking is to provide a way for society to conduct its finances in a way that is ethical and socially responsible. Interest is forbidden in Islam because it is considered effortless return that does not serve the real economy (Al Zarqa 2012: 36). Conventional financial instruments, for example short-selling, futures and options contracts and derivatives, are also not permitted as they would create risks that do not promote the financial well-being of the parties involved, and society as a whole. In addition to, some of those financial products lack certain requirements to be acceptable as Shariah compliant financial products (Al Zarqa 2012: 36).

However, trade, entrepreneurship and risk and profit sharing activities are encouraged, and these are the financial principles that underpin the products and financial innovation offered by Islamic banking. These are complemented by ethics and values such as inclusivity, transparency, integrity, respect and fairness. The two are combined to offer a banking system that is built on a different and possibly more ethical footing, than conventional banking.

1.5 If All Banks Adopted Islamic Values, Would There Have Been a Banking Collapse?

The principles of Islamic banking, is believed to have been designed to, promote a stable economic environment (Wilson and El-Ashker 2006: 38; Green 1993). Importantly, speculation is not permitted and all activities must be asset-backed. Further, the replacement of trade over interest as the founding principle in Islamic banking introduces a level of equity between the customer and the bank. Therefore, Islamic banking was better protected from the credit crunch crisis affecting mainstream banks in 2008. Essentially, as an asset-backed structure, it is believed that Islamic banking was not impacted by its root cause, i.e. 'toxic assets' (Al Zarqa 2012: 48–51).

In contrast to the conventional banking sector today, Islamic banking is claimed to be based on traditional values and is very prudent in its approach to managing its risks and its customers' assets. If lessons are to be learned by the conventional banking sector from the 2008 financial crisis, then the principles of Islamic banking would, perhaps, be a good place to start. They would possibly provide a useful framework to establish a resilient process for the development of financial innovation in banking system that could sustain and minimize the effects of future financial crises (Al Zarqa 2012: 48–51). Thus, this research aims to explore what constitutes a religiously guided process towards financial innovation and engineering.

1.6 Significance of this Book

The issue of financial innovation and engineering in the product development process in Islamic banking and the basis that it should be built on to be fully compliant with Shariah is not yet matured and identified. This study explores financial innovation in Islamic finance and the product development process for Islamic financial institutions (IFIs) in order to understand its characteristics and guiding principles. The design of this book aims to explore the current financial innovation and product development process in IFIs, by articulating the financial innovation and engineering constructs and components from an Islamic finance perspective.

This theoretical framework is important because it serves the real economy as described in the classical books of the Islamic Commercial Law. Furthermore, this work also evaluates the current practices of Islamic banks, in relation to financial innovation and engineering, in light of the developed theoretical and practical framework. It also extended the theoretical framework for innovation orientation to another level by identifying and conceptualising religious orientation towards financial innovation and the role of Shariah as a boundary in that process.

The work has not been able to locate, following an extensive literature review, any specific research conducted regarding this very specialised and important subject. Some researchers (see El-Gamal 2006), argue that Shariah compliant financial products offered by IFIs mimic the conventional counterparts and are labelled as Islamic. Therefore, this book attempts to demarcate the boundaries and role of Shariah in the financial innovation and financial engineering process.

Therefore, this work is vital in examining, evaluating and exploring this issue by developing a theoretical and practical framework for Islamic financial innovation and product development process from an Islamic finance perspective. This could ensure that financial innovation and engineering in IFIs is following a robust framework that meets all the Shariah requirements and can be congruent with current financial regulations. This is in order to avoid financial fragility by circumventing these requirements and regulations as happened with its conventional counterpart for various reasons.

1.7 Motivation of the Book

Although Islamic banking has been evolving for the last four decades or so, which is relatively a short period compared to the conventional banking system, there has been a justified increased criticism from some Islamic academia. These critiques relate to the issue of whether the Islamic finance industry has gone off course from its original principles, and started mimicking the conventional banking system and products. The Islamic finance industry is also criticised for not having a framework for financial innovation and engineering or structure that is rooted in the Shariah principles and objectives, which will protect the characteristics and identity of Islamic finance and banking. Being an interest-free financial and banking system, Islamic banking products have a different structure than those in the conventional banking system.

However, the literature review revealed that the issue of financial innovation and engineering, as part of the overall product development process, for Islamic banking and finance and its Shariah roots has not been adequately researched or addressed. What would constitute a good financial innovation and engineering that meets all Shariah requirements and objectives as far as Shariah is concerned. This is a question that does not currently have any answer and would require one. In contrast, conventional financial innovation and engineering, as argued in the literature (Plosser 2009; Poole 2011; Duska 2009; Jameson 2009; Mullineux 1997; Persons and Warther 1997) has been the cause of financial fragility and eventually, the trigger of financial crises.

Nevertheless, this subject is a cornerstone for the Islamic finance industry's growth and for it to be a sustainable system that offers a model of an alternative, ethical, faith-based approach for banking and finance. Therefore, this book aims to address this problem and offer a possible insight that could address this gap in the literature by developing a conceptual and practical framework for financial innovation and engineering as theorised by Shariah. It would be rooted in the core principles and spirit of Shariah, while also meeting the higher Shariah objectives.

1.8 Objectives of this Book

Bearing in mind the discussion above, the literature review shows that there are hardly any studies that address the phenomena of religious orientation towards financial innovation and engineering as prescribed from an Islamic perspective. This is the main objective of this book from which the objectives below are derived. Therefore, the book has the following two key objectives:

1. To explore and explain the dynamics of what constitutes a religious orientation towards financial innovation and engineering in the Islamic finance industry.
2. To identify the basis of how a theoretical and practical framework for financial innovation and engineering from an Islamic finance perspective could be constituted.

1.9 Contribution of the Book

This book offers an opportunity to develop theoretical, empirical and practical contributions that demonstrate the novelty and validity of the underlying study. The underlying theoretical framework of what constitutes Shariah-induced financial innovation and engineering is the primary theoretical contribution of this research study. It provides a conceptualised framework to understand the nature of what constitutes religious orientation towards financial innovation and the dynamics of its implementation in the Islamic finance industry.

The concept of religious orientation helps to explain the empirical consequences of the absence of a clear definition of religious orientation towards financial innovation in the existing context of the Islamic finance industry. It also addresses the challenge to have a clear concept of what constitutes a religious orientation towards financial innovation as a new phenomenon within the innovation orientation field. Therefore, the main contribution of this work could be outlined as follows:

(a) The book extends the existing literature of innovation orientation to a completely new field and construct that is based on a religious imperative as a framework within which financial innovation is constrained. It explains how an innovation orientation in IFIs can be directed within religious rules.
(b) The research introduces and examines the role of Shariah as a key construct and its dynamic role in managing tension and conflicting values in the financial innovation process.

Furthermore, building on the empirical results, the book illustrates the insights that the theoretical lens affords into practices of collaboration and develops a novel analytical framework for understanding religious orientation towards financial innovation. The conceptualised framework provided here would help IFIs to formally identify and develop organisational conditions and competencies needed to fulfil their objectives as guided by their faith. This practical contribution provides an evaluative and measurement tool, provided by the research findings and the developed framework, to examine existing financial products on offer. The findings of this research study would enable IFIs to reflect on their current practices, processes, Shariah compliance framework for financial innovation and engineering and NPD.

1.10 Potential Implications of this Book

As Islamic finance and banking continues to develop rapidly in many countries, the main implication of this book is that it would shed light on the financial innovation and product development process. Thus, helping to create a theoretical framework and identify some areas for future research. If this proves to be the case, greater scrutiny and analysis of the financial product development and financial engineering would ensure that IFIs, in particular, and conventional financial institutions at large could be following the ethical Shariah practices when introducing a new financial innovation or developing financial products. Hence, this would reflect on the whole financial system resulting in a more sustainable and stable financial system in the face of future harmful financial crises.

1.11 Outline of the Book Chapters

In pursuit of the objectives of this book and in order to answer the above posed questions, the book is made up of the following chapters:

Chapter 1: Introduction
As detailed in this chapter, Chap. 1 provides an overview and background of the book, its objectives, motivation and contribution. It also provides an outline of the book chapters and briefly describes their contents.

Chapter 2: The Context of Islamic Banking and Finance
The objective of this chapter is to outline and discuss the underlying context of this book. It addresses the nature and characteristics of Islamic finance and banking, and the core principles which underpin their operation. It shows the comparison between Islamic banks with their conventional counterparts, the differences of principles, products, services, governance structure and the control system. The

chapter focuses in particular on the issues of Shariah governance around financial innovation and engineering in the product development cycle in IFIs.

Chapter 3: Analysis of Financial Innovation and Engineering in the Literature
This chapter provides an understanding of Islamic finance, financial innovation and product development from a research perspective. It analyses the traditional context of innovation and financial product development reflecting on relevant theories and issues. It also discusses various topics related to financial innovation and the subject of financial engineering and product development in Islamic finance in a broad sense. The discussion in this Chapter is divided into different themes to identify theoretical and empirical work on this subject to point out weaknesses and strengths and identify key issues to be considered in the chapters that follow.

Chapter 4: A Historical Analysis of Financial Innovation in Islamic Economics and Finance from Inception to the Sixteenth Century
This chapter provides an analysis of financial innovation and engineering as part of the historical development of Islamic finance from its inception as a concept over 1400 years ago. It then describes the main influencing factors and elements that played a critical role in its development. The history of innovation in Islamic finance is discussed and is divided into eight phases. This Chapter discusses the phases of innovation in Islamic finance up to the sixteenth century. Each phase covers a critical period of the history of Islamic finance and its financial innovation in the context of economic, social, political, regional and global influencing factors. Thus, it is very important, as this chapter concludes, to study Islamic finance in its historical context in order to have a correct understanding and appreciation of its history and the different development phases that it has gone through.

Chapter 5: A Historical Analysis of Financial Innovation in Islamic Economics and Finance from the Sixteenth Century to Present
This chapter starts with phase five from the sixteenth century that covers an important phase of innovation in Islamic finance as it reflects an era of stability and prosperity in the historical context of Islamic finance. This scene changes then in phase six due to important historical events and takes another turn in phase seven. The historical analysis, in this chapter, shows that the more powerful economy usually prevails over others and dictates the rules of economic and financial engagement in relation to structure and practices. This was obvious during certain phases of the Islamic finance history, when the state was politically and economically stable and strong. However, this factor changed later in recent history, with the domination of interest-based capitalism on the financial system worldwide enforcing its rules on the financial sphere. Hence, Islamic finance has had to make some concessions and compromises in its modern history to create its own space in the new global economic order.

Chapter 6: Traditional Theory of Financial Innovation
This chapter aims to explore financial product innovation from a conventional perspective and its consequences that are often ignored, by highlighting three Schumpeterian schools of innovation. In order to do so, it approaches this goal by

focusing first on the role played by financial innovation in creating financial crises. This will provide a theoretical understanding of what would have caused the current (i.e. 2008) and previous financial crises and their effects. Most of the analyses conducted have focused on the nature of financial innovations with exploring and contrasting the current financial system with the Islamic financial system, and extracting some lessons to be learned. This chapter further explains what would happen following a financial crisis, and brings to light that the resilience of the banking system is a crucial element for a strong financial system. It also argues that there is an innovation bias across the academic research and that financial market is under regulated, and more robust regulations are required. It also critically discusses financial innovation, its theory, schools and its impact on society through uncalculated risks.

Chapter 7: Financial Innovation Theory from an Islamic Perspective
This chapter attempts to articulate the distinctive features and characteristics on which a financial innovation theory, from an Islamic economic thought perspective, could be developed and built. This theory then will be the cornerstone for the cycle of any financial engineering and product development in the financial system. This chapter endeavours to set the foundations for financial innovation and engineering concepts as rooted in the traditional Economic thoughts in Islam. It links the religious compliance in observing an overall divine power as guided in Islamic finance to the application of normativity through social practices theory as articulated by Bourdieu. It, further, articulates the thoughts of the Islamic school in relation to innovation as an addition to the three Schumpeterian schools of innovation that were discussed in Chap. 6.

Chapter 8: Futures Contracts as an Underlying Product of Financial Engineering in Islamic Finance
This Chapter analyses futures contracts as a derivative product in the financial market and the possibility of engineering this product to be compliant with Shariah requirements. The analysis carried out in this Chapter would be complemented with a further analysis undertaken in Chap. 9 regarding another derivative product (options contracts). The combined analysis of both chapters would portray a full picture for a framework for financial innovation and engineering in Islamic finance and sets out the thinking process in order to reach a conclusion regarding the contemplated financial innovation. This analysis of the thinking process would set the structure of a framework for financial innovation and engineering in Islamic finance. A further analysis is then presented to ensure that such engineered structure and the combination of various Islamic finance principles does not breach any Shariah rules or requirements. This process does not always mean that an acceptable Shariah engineered solution for the financial product can be achieved though.

Chapter 9: Options Contracts as an Underlying Product of Financial Engineering in Islamic Finance
This Chapter complements the analysis undertaken in Chap. 8 regarding futures contracts. The analysis of options contracts, as a derivative product in the financial

market and the possibility of engineering this product to be compliant with Shariah requirements, is provided in this Chapter. The analysis carried out in this Chapter would further outline the building blocks for a framework for financial innovation and engineering in Islamic finance and continues to establishing the thinking process in order to reach a conclusion regarding a contemplated financial innovation. This analysis of the thinking process regarding options contracts would provide further insights for financial innovation and engineering in Islamic finance.

Chapter 10: Outlining a Framework for Financial Innovation and Engineering in Islamic Finance
The analysis carried out in this Chapter builds on the discussion in the previous two chapters in order to demark the framework of engineering Shariah compliant solutions for a financial innovation to be offered by IFIs. The thinking process carried out in this Chapter is to explore whether such a financial innovation can be structured in a Shariah compliant way by engineering various solutions or combining more than one Islamic finance instruments. This Chapter is organised in a logical way that ensures the flow of the analysis provided in the previous chapters and is divided into sections. Some sections identify Shariah prohibitions associated with options and futures, others explain the logic behind the Shariah prohibitions and the analysis of the role of options and futures in the financial market. The Chapter then concludes by attempting to adjust such derivative products on possible engineered solutions and how this process is structured and rationalised from a Shariah juristic perspective.

Chapter 11: Case Study: Analysis of Selected Shariah Compliant Financial Products
This Chapter presents the findings of a practical analysis of a case study. This analysis is based on the discussion in the previous chapters and the framework we established in Chap. 10 in terms of the considerations and steps that should be followed by IFIs in the financial innovation and engineering process. The documentary analysis method, undertaken in this Chapter, complements the analysis conducted in Chaps. 8, 9, and 10 for more robustness and rigorous findings.

It examines current practices in the Islamic finance industry as a whole and IFIs, by analysing existing financial products and innovation in the market against the framework that has been outlined in the earlier chapters. This framework takes into account the philosophy and objectives of the Islamic economic thought and the Shariah requirements for financial innovation and engineering as conceptualised in the process of analysing futures and options from an Islamic finance perspective. The documentary analysis covered a wide range of existing financial products, for a representative view of the existing practices in the Islamic finance industry.

Chapter 12: Discussion and Conclusion
This chapter presents a discussion and conclusion of the findings of the data collected. As part of the discussion, this chapter describes the research policy and managerial implications and suggests avenues for future research. It also states parsimoniously the contribution of this study to relevant theory and draws a

conclusion. It demonstrates the theoretical, empirical, and practical contributions of the research and presents a new financial innovation that was developed to address a serious social and financial problem in the UK. It concludes with a reflection on the whole research process, and the resulting analysis with suggestions for future research topics.

Chapter 2
The Context of Islamic Banking and Finance

2.1 Introduction

The previous chapter (Chap. 1) provided an overview of this book setting out its objective, contribution and outlines of the book chapters. This chapter, however, aims to provide the underlying context, nature and basic understanding of Islamic finance and banking, and its financial principles. It explores the main differences between Islamic banks and their conventional counterparts.

In addition, the role of Shariah governance and an overview of the role of the Shariah Supervisory Committee (SSC), in the innovation and financial engineering process, are discussed. It also provides a definition of Islamic finance and explains the prohibition of usury. It goes further, then, to explain the main classical modes of Islamic finance highlighting the major differences with conventional banks. Financial innovation and engineering in Islamic finance are also discussed to provide a brief context to this book.

2.2 Defining Islamic Finance

It is known that Islamic finance revolves around the prohibition of usury (Qur'an, 2: 275), however, that is not the only reason for avoiding conventional finance products. Islamic finance provides a comprehensive approach to undertake financial activities that are linked to the overall religious philosophy in Islam (Visser 2009: 26). Therefore, it is useful to start with defining Islamic finance. Definitions of Islamic finance range from the very narrow definition of 'interest-free banking model' to the very broad one of 'financial operations conducted by Muslims'. Warde (2010) suggested the following definition: 'Islamic financial institutions are those that are based, in their objectives and operations, on Qur'anic Principles'.

S. Alamad, *Financial Innovation and Engineering in Islamic Finance*,
Contributions to Management Science, DOI 10.1007/978-3-319-52947-9_2

They are thus set apart from 'conventional' institutions, which have no such preoccupations.

This definition goes beyond simply equating Islamic finance with 'interest-free' banking. It allows taking into account operations that may or may not be interest-free, but are nonetheless imbued with certain Islamic principles: the avoidance of *riba* (in the broad sense of unjustified increase) and *gharar* (uncertainty and speculation). Although Warde stated that this definition is for Islamic finance, but he started the definition defining Islamic banks. Therefore, his definition could be accepted for Islamic banking, but not for Islamic finance.

This is because, simply, Islamic finance goes beyond the boundaries of banking operations as financial intermediaries and providers of financial products and services. It includes all financial institutions and transactions, such as *takaful* (Islamic insurance) operators, *zakat*, (alums giving) fiscal policy and endowments. Another issue is noted with the definition suggested by Warde is that, he limits the operations of IFIs to be only based on the Qur'anic principles, rather than Shariah (see Fig. 2.1 below for illustration about the sources of Shariah and what it includes), which includes the *Sunnah* as well. It is known that most of the issues related to Islamic finance are founded and illustrated in the *Sunnah* of the Prophet.

Thus, we suggest the following definition for Islamic finance, 'it is an approach to finance and undertaking financial activities as founded, governed and illustrated under Shariah'. This definition combines the principles of Islamic finance and associated ethics, excludes all prohibitions under Sharia, includes all possible forms of finance whether practiced on a state, organisational or individual levels. Figure 2.1 above illustrates the main sources of Shariah that Islamic jurists and scholars employ to reach an opinion about the compliance of a financial innovation or product and their processes.

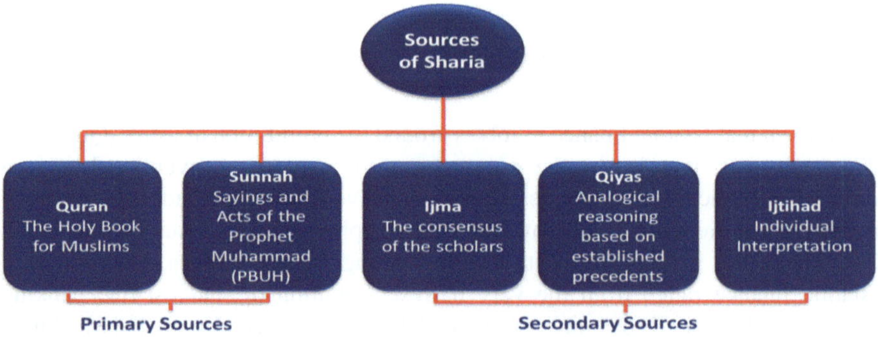

Fig. 2.1 Main sources of Shariah. *Source*: Based on Al-Bouti 2005

2.3 The Prohibition of *Riba* in Islamic Finance

This specific prohibition in Islamic finance has been singled out as being the distinguishing element of the Islamic finance. Any financial transaction that leads to *riba* would be rendered impermissible. The ban on *riba* is based on a number of verses of the Qur'an, such as 2:275–278, 3:130, 4:161 and 30:39. Therefore, all forms of interests are prohibited without any question.

This Islamic view on *riba* was observed in the early days of Islam and was taken for granted by medieval Islamic scholars, such as Al Ghazali (Ghazanfer and Islabi 1990). According to Lisan Al Arab (Ibn Mandhur 2009), *riba* means 'increase or addition'. In Shariah it means an addition to the principal, which implies a monetary, or any other benefit, payment for the use of money which has been fixed at the outset. It is a form of excess of unjustified portion of income, and thus, it at variance with the principle of *tawheed* (monotheism), brotherhood and Islamic concepts of income distribution (Choudhury 1986: 11).

2.4 The Ethical Basis of Islamic Finance

Islam is both a religion and a civilization that spans over fourteen centuries of human history, and a geographical presence in vast areas stretching over the Asian and African continents and even parts of Europe. It is also a spiritual and metahistorical entity that has transformed the inner and outer life of numerous human beings in very different temporal and spatial circumstances. Around 1.6 billion people from different racial and cultural backgrounds identify themselves as Muslim (Nasr 2003).

Historically, Islam has played a significant role in the development of certain aspects of other civilizations, especially Western civilization. Not only is Islam a major presence in today's world, but its influence is also evident in the history of the Christian West, not to mention that of India and other regions of Asia and Africa. This influence posits Islamic finance as a somewhat new financial model in undertaking finance and business activities (Nasr 2003).

The appropriate development of human life, as articulated in Islamic economics, requires two things: (1) the resources needed to maintain life and fulfil the material needs of both the individual and society; (2) the individual's knowledge of the principles of individual and social behaviour to allow individual self-fulfilment Islamic finance: on the one hand and the maintenance of social justice and tranquillity on the other (Ahmad 1971). Islam emphasises the need for balance between the demands of this world and the demands of the afterlife (Chapra 1992). However, worship is not confined to these since worship also requires that Muslims serve God through good behaviour in all aspects of their daily life, even in their financial activities, work and business life. Many passages in the Qur'an encourage commercial and economic activity (Lewis 2001).

2.5 The Concept of Growth and Purification in Finance

As part of the Islamic teachings, every individual is required to work (Rahman 1994). However, any work or activities should follow clear guidelines for the benefit of all stakeholders in the society. The concept of *Tazkiyah* (growth and purification) requires active participation in the material world in order to build the earth and innovate to satisfy worldly needs (Gambling and Karim 1991: 33).

However, all forms of productive work can be considered as an act of worship, provided that they are accompanied with pure intention to fulfil God's instructions, and that material enhancement and growth leads to social justice and spiritual enhancement. According to Al Ghazali (1987), 'Shariah as a law and code of conduct aims to improve the welfare of individuals in society, and adherence to this law will benefit people and the whole society, not only in this life, but also in the Hereafter'.

Therefore, it is very important that social welfare and the intention and motive of any financial innovation are for the greater good and benefit of individuals and society. If so, (Williams and Zinkin 2010) they are performed in accordance with the injunctions of God. Thus, the concept of worship, in Islam, is defined very broadly and recognises that mankind can be rewarded by performing both ritual acts and daily works.

However, for daily actions to be regarded as part of worship there are three conditions: (1) the action must be undertaken wholeheartedly for the sake of God, and not for another reason (e.g. the love of money or profit maximisation), although achieving worldly ends and making money in accordance with the guidance of Shariah is legitimate and the person would be rewarded for that, however, it has to be primarily for the sake of God; (2) the action must be in accordance with the Shariah (the Islamic Law), thus, the role of a religious body as a part of the governance of IFI; (3) it must not cause a Muslim to neglect existing obligations (Williams and Zinkin 2010). Also this act should not cause harm to others in the society (e.g. financial innovation that does not comply with Shariah or result in financial fragility and harm to the economy and society).

2.6 Islamic Finance Instruments

Islam is not only about prohibitions, it also provides alternatives that would have a better impact on society as a whole. Islamic finance is based on financial principles that promote partnership and risk and reward sharing instruments. Some of those instruments are briefly outlined below (Visser 2009: 54).

Mudaraba is a profit sharing contract, also known as *qirad* and trustee finance. The capital provider would provide the entire capital to the trustee who will provide labour and expertise to invest the capital in approved and acceptable investments under Shariah. A profit sharing ratio is agreed at the outset and the capital provider would bear the risk of any loss in the capital (Visser 2009: 54).

Musharaka, is a profit and loss sharing agreement that is based on a partnership financing, it is a form of equity participation agreement. Profit is shared according to a pre-agreed ratio and losses are shared according to the capital ratio of each participant. *Musharak* has different forms, it can be amortised as a reduced equity over time or open-ended partnership.

Murabaha is a cost plus profit or mark-up contract. *Murabaha* is a trade contract which stipulates that one party buys a commodity for its own account and sells it on to the other party at the original price plus a mark-up. The mark-up is considered as a payment for the services provided by the financier and a guaranteed margin of profit (Abu Zaid 2004: 23). The sale price is paid then according to the agreed intervals, in most cases over a period of time, as agreed between the parties to the agreement. This form of finance is very popular currently and heavily used by Islamic banks, thus we are going to elaborate more on it herein. A sub-contract of *Murabaha* called *Tawarruq*, which is translated as monetisation, is also used by Islamic banks. Under this contract the Islamic bank sells the commodity to the client on a *Murabaha* basis who then, sells it in the market on the spot price to generate the required cash (Visser 2009: 57).

Islamic finance has developed different techniques that are rooted in Shariah to offer Shariah compliant financial products. The most common techniques that are used frequently by Islamic banks are *mudaraba* (profit sharing agreement), *musharaka* (partnership agreement), *wakala* (agency agreement) and *ijarah* (lease agreement). However, Abu Zaid (2004) discusses specifically the *murabaha* (cost plus profit or credit sale agreement) technique in details, due to its widespread use in IFIs, and its applications in contemporary financial transactions as practised by Islamic banks. He argues that as the *murabaha* technique is widespread and used by Islamic banks as a tool for liquidity and inter-banking placements, it was very important to discuss *murabaha* in detail. He discusses the critiques of this type of sale among jurists and the Shariah adjustment to the simple *murabaha* transaction and the newly devised version of it, *murabaha* for the purchaser order, which is practised widely in Islamic banking.

Abu Zaid (2004) suggests that a bilateral promise between the Islamic bank and the client in the *murabaha* for the purchaser order is acceptable under Shariah as it forms the introduction to a valid sale contract. A bilateral promise in this case is where the bank promises the client that it will sell the commodity to the client; in return, the client will promise the bank that he/she will buy the commodity from the bank on a *murabaha* contract after the bank purchases it from the supplier. This is something that many Shariah jurists disapprove of, as a mutual bilateral promise is considered a binding forward sale contract which is not permissible under Shariah. Shariah may only permit a unilateral (one-sided) promise in the case of the *murabaha* for the purchaser order agreement.

Ijara is a lease agreement, under which the financier purchases the required commodity and leases it to the other party, in this case, the client of the Islamic bank. On expiry of the lease term, the commodity could be sold to the lessee with the transfer of the legal title (El-Gamal 2006: 67). This would be subject to the agreed terms between the parties.

Wakala is an agency agreement for a fee. The capital provider (*Muwakkil*) would provide the entire capital to the trustee (*Wakeel* or agent) who will provide labour and expertise to invest the capital (Ramadan 2009: 86). The realised profit will be then paid to the investor i.e. the capital provider. The *Wakala* fee is agreed between the parties in advance as a flat fee and paid regardless of the generated profit from the investment.

Bai' al Salam is a sale contract where the buyer pays in advance for the goods for a future delivery. The goods do not need to exist at the time of the contract as long as it is described exactly and known as to both quality and quantity (Al-Bouti 2005: 134). The exact date and place of delivery should be also known. If the seller is unable to deliver, they may agree to postpone or the seller may provide the same goods as specified from another supplier for the same agreed price. This contract is, usually, applied to agricultural products or fungible manufactured goods that could be financed by an Islamic bank (Visser 2009: 58).

Istisna', is a contract of manufacturing with progressive financing or a contract of ordering specified goods where the price is paid progressively according to delivery. Under this contract Islamic banks provide finance to a client by commissioning a supplier to manufacture the goods or complete a building work that is already specified and agreed with the bank's client. Payments are paid according to the progress of the job. This type of contract is also used for development finance products.

Qard hasan is a beneficence loan, on which no financial payment or otherwise is charged (Visser 2009: 62). This principle is used, usually, by Islamic banks to provide current accounts where the client would deposit their money in the current account as a loan to the Islamic bank. The account does not pay any return or interest to the client.

Based on the above main principles of Islamic finance, many products and financial innovations are engineered and developed. This could be achieved by using one single principle or a combination of two or more in order to reach the desired outcome that complies with Shariah. However, in order to do that, Islamic financial institutions would require guidance from scholars and experts in Islamic commercial law and Shariah. This leads us to the next section that explains Sharia governance.

2.7 Shariah Compliance and Governance (SCG) of Islamic Financial Institutions (IFI)

The organisational structure of the Shariah supervision is formalised in various forms in different IFIs, we can assign the SCG as the generic framework for, the Shariah Control Committee (SCC), Shariah Supervisory Board (SSB) or Shariah

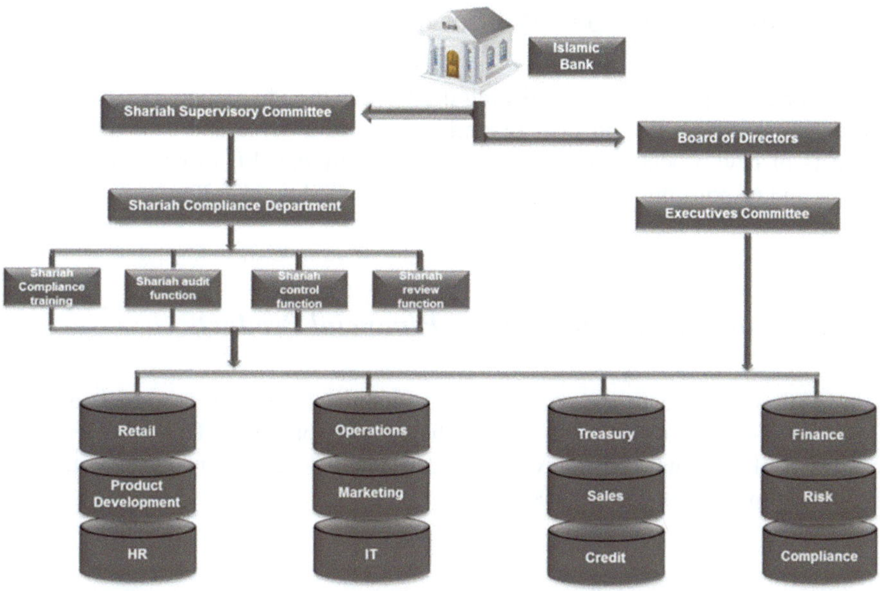

Fig. 2.2 Shariah compliance governance and structure in IFIs. *Source*: Based on AAOIFI 2014 Governance Standards

Supervisory Committee (SSC). Different names, but the role is the same. The work of the SSC, which is chosen here as the most common name, includes all the supervisory elements and activities that are used to ensure the compatibility of IFIs with Shariah. The SSC ensures that the operations and all activities of an IFI are in accordance with Shariah requirements and rules according to the accredited and agreed legal opinions (*fatwa*), (Qattan 2006: 273).

The SSC is an independent body that does not report to the board of directors or management of the IFI. The members of the SSC are appointed by a general meeting of the shareholders of the financial institution. This is in order to maintain their independence and credibility in supervising the IFI in its activities. They have the power to block any attempt to develop or launch a financial product that would be considered harmful to the society or not compliant with Shariah. Figure 2.2 below illustrates the Shariah compliance governance and structure of an IFI.

Figure 2.2 above shows the typical Shariah compliance governance structure in an IFI, and its independence as a supervisory and audit function in order to maintain its credibility. Due to the relatively small size of most IFIs, they may not all have the sub-functions of the Shariah compliance department, as shown in Fig. 2.2 above.

2.8 Duties and Responsibilities of the SSC

The primary objectives of establishing the SSC as the Shariah governance framework are to advise IFIs in their operations, and to analyse and evaluate Shariah aspects of new products and services submitted by the IFI. In general, the main duties and responsibilities of the SSC can be summed up as follows.

2.8.1 Concept and Structure of Financial Products

The SSC will evaluate the concept and structure of the new proposed financial innovation or product and will review the existing products. This would include approval of the financial innovation and product development cycle with their associated processes (Qattan 2006: 273).

2.8.2 Documentation

The Shariah governance does not stop at the concept stage of the new product, it extends to its documentation as well. The SSC will vet meticulously and endorse all documents involved and these include the terms and conditions contained in the proposal, contracts, and agreements or other legal documentation used in executing the transactions. This would also include the product manual, marketing advertisements, sales illustrations and brochures used to describe the product. In doing that, the SSC is supported and assisted by a Shariah compliance department or internal adviser who will monitor the daily activities. They will, then, give their comments in order to ensure the compliance with the Shariah principles.

2.8.3 Shariah Advisory

The SSC is required to advise the IFI on all Shariah related issues to concerned parties. This would entail detailing the Shariah position and formally communicating their opinion to the IFI (Qattan 2006: 273).

2.8.4 Providing Shariah Legal Opinion

The SSC role is to provide their formal opinion as to matters of Shariah, or when approving new financial products, which can be made public for customers and the general public, who wish to know the basis of this Shariah opinion (Rammal 2006).

2.8.5 Undertaking Shariah Compliance Audit

The SSC is responsible for undertaking a regular Shariah compliance audit that covers all operational and business activities in the IFI. They could do that themselves or by appointing someone else with the required qualifications to perform this task (Rammal 2006). This task is, usually, fulfilled by the internal Shariah compliance department or adviser, the findings of the audit review will be reported to the SSC, who then provide their report to the shareholders and the board of directors of the IFI. This report is then made publicly available.

2.9 Major Differences Between IFIs and Their Conventional Counterpart

Table 2.1 below summarises the main differences between Islamic banking and traditional banking as shareholder-owned for profit financial institutions. It does not aim to provide an exhaustive list or compare different structures of financial institutions, such as mutual institutions. It rather explains the major basic differences in relation to the approach of operations between Islamic banking and its counterpart, as commonly referred to, conventional banking, for a reader who does not know anything about Islamic banking or know very little.

As we have seen in Table 2.1 above, there are key differences between Islamic and conventional banks in terms of governance structure, product design and structure, profit, risk and transparency. The above table does not aim to provide a detailed list; it rather highlights the key differences.

2.10 Financial Innovation and Engineering

As the operations and financial products offered by IFIs are different to those of conventional banking, it is also the same regarding financial innovation and engineering. The processes and cycle of which might overlap and have common grounds with conventional innovation cycle, however, it differs and would undertake some additional processes and requirements to the traditional innovation and

Table 2.1 Main differences between IFIs and conventional financial institutions

Conventional banking	Islamic banking
Generation of profit	
Generates its income and profits from interest-based and speculative products. Has been criticised for not monitoring the effects of its activities and their effects on the customer and/or society as a whole.	Generates money in a productive way using trade, entrepreneurship and investment. Works in partnership with the customer and its activities help to promote economic growth and stability for society as a whole.
Speculation and risk	
Uses speculative instruments which can encourage excessive risk-taking. This can promote a culture of greed and creates 'toxic assets' where the value of the end commodity is not clear or has been over-valued. The result of these activities recently de-stabilised the global financial system, during the 'sub-prime'/credit-crunch crisis, putting consumers, businesses and the global economy at risk (Plosser 2009).	Avoids toxic assets and speculation by being asset-backed, resulting in a more stable financial system that was relatively unaffected by the recent credit-crunch crisis. Deposits are managed in a prudent way with investments only taking place in stable commodities and assets, such as property.
Transparency	
Has been criticised for not being transparent enough about its business and does not always explain to the customer how its money is being used by the bank.	Is committed to transparency and fairness, integrity and respect, putting the customer at the heart of its business. To illustrate: 1. IFI customers are made aware that savings accounts offer 'expected profits' and that the IFI uses their money in trades of low risk commodities (metals) and in the property finance products. 2. The whole premise of Islamic banking is that the customer and bank work together as trading partners towards a mutually profitable end. This is monitored by an expert independent body, the Sharia Supervisory Committee (SSC), to ensure that the IFI's activities do not only serve its own purposes but benefit the customer as well.
Use of customers' deposits	
Uses deposits in a range of activities that are not always in the interest of society. For example, it may fund a casino or betting shop even though this may be of detriment to the people that it serves.	Considers the impact of its activities on society and does not permit investment in certain industries such as tobacco, alcohol, pornography, gambling and arms.
Regulation	
Does not have a system of independent internal regulation to ensure that its products and activities meet minimum moral and ethical standards. Does not go above and beyond industry regulation to ensure that it is 'doing the right thing' for its customers and the society in which it operates. As a result, conventional banks may develop a culture that principally considers their own needs rather than those of their customers too.	Acts in a socially responsible way and, in general, has a culture of 'doing the right thing'. This is monitored by an independent panel of Sharia Scholars and an internal Shariah officer. Their work is similar in nature to an ethics committee/officer. Together they ensure that the IFI's operations, products and structure meet strict standards and its activities are genuinely 'good', not just for customers but for society as a whole.

development concept. This is, clearly, due to the nature of the IFIs financial products and the required Shariah compliance structure and governance that they adhere to, as explained above.

IFIs have to meet the demands in the market and maintain their competitiveness by innovating and developing new financial products. This, however, has to be subjected to rigours processes to ensure any new financial innovation or new product idea fits with the framework of Shariah. The processes and framework for that would differ from an IFI to another. The aim of this study is to explore the current practices of IFIs regarding financial innovation and new product development and the Shariah governance around it.

This governance and control, as discussed above, could be the answer to many loopholes in the current practices of the conventional system, as discussed in Chap. 6, in relation to financial innovation and engineering. Financial innovation and engineering, therefore, is driven by three things: changes in demand conditions, changes in supply conditions and changes in regulatory requirements. Such changes promote financial institutions, in general, to devise innovative new products that would allow them to remain in the market and be profitable. This process is called financial innovation or engineering (Iqbal and Khan 2005: 2).

2.10.1 Scope of Financial Innovation and Engineering

Financial products offered by IFIs have, so far, been substantially limited to the classical principles of Islamic finance that were developed over 1400 years ago. While they have been very useful and have provided the foundations for IFIs, there is not any reason for the Islamic finance industry to be restricted to those principles (Iqbal and Khan 2005: 11). Shariah provides the flexibility for more innovation and engineering of new financial contracts that meet the market demands, such instruments are e.g. *ijtihad* (scholarly interpretation and efforts) analogy and other possible instruments (see Fig. 2.1 for the sources of Shariah and methods used to interpret Shariah rules).

2.10.2 Innovation and New Product Development in Finance

Financial innovation surged in the 1970s, as a result of consistent global economic growth, and since then has transformed the dynamics of the financial industry (Podolski 1986: 105); see Chap. 3, Sect. 3.7 for more details. The stream of innovation increased post a long period of stagnation, which started during the great depression and stayed until 1950s (Miller and Friesen 1982). Factors determining innovation in Islamic finance would be similar to those of the conventional system; however the nature of innovation could be more complex due to the Shariah requirements.

As Islamic banking is relatively new, innovation in functional terms would take two forms, the inert type and the creative innovation type. The former implies that the industry has to provide an array of products to fulfil financial functions, such as mobilising resources, allocating capital and managing risks. These products already exist in conventional forms and inert innovation helps IFIs to catch up with their conventional counterparts. This is in order to meet the existing market needs, that already created by conventional banks, in a Shariah compliant way. The latter would enable the Islamic finance industry to develop new innovative products (Ahmed 2011: 9) that are unique to the financial market.

2.11 Conclusion

This chapter provides the context for the subject matter of this book by explaining key aspects related to the phenomenon in question. Providing the context of the research would pave the way for simplifying the complexity of the phenomenon and put the reader on a smooth path to facilitate easy understanding of the chapters that follow.

Islamic finance is unique in its characteristics and nature as it provides a new approach to finance and undertaking financial and banking operations. Financial products offered by Islamic banks should be asset-backed and generated from trading rather than a lending/borrowing transaction. This approach and the Shariah governance, which regulates the financial innovation and engineering cycle, would offer an insight that could be very valuable. It provides a new perspective and conceptual framework to the existing financial innovation literature.

Current financial products of IFIs can be one of two types, existing conventional products that were reengineered and structured to meet Shariah requirements, which is the dominant type, or new innovation that does not have precedence. This process is still ad hoc and would require a clear theoretical framework and processes, which this study has attempted to achieve. The next chapter (Chap. 3) provides the relevant review and analysis of financial innovation and engineering in the academic literature, highlighting various theories, concepts and issues raised by key economists.

Chapter 3
Analysis of Financial Innovation and Engineering in the Literature

3.1 Introduction

The previous chapter (Chap. 2) provided the context for the subject of this book by discussing issues related to Islamic finance, its definition, governance in IFIs, main differences with traditional banks and the role of the SSC. Having established the context of this research domain, this chapter reviews and analyses the existing theoretical and empirical works on Islamic finance and banking, reflecting on conventional theories in relation to financial innovation and engineering, product development, Islamic commercial law and other related topics. The aim is to highlight the positives and weaknesses of existing work, with a view to highlighting various theories, concepts and issues raised by key economists.

It is important, however, to recall here a brief explanation about what Islamic finance is as a starting point and a reminder to the reader. Islamic finance is a way to put Islamic principles and teachings about the economy into practice. It attempts to develop a specific Islamic version of economics, which is based upon the precepts of the holy book of Muslims, the Qur'an, and on the *Sunnah*[1] (Visser 2009: 1).

This chapter is divided into themes, each theme concentrates on a particular issue within the field of Islamic finance and banking as a whole and financial innovation. Themes covered in this Chapter are: product development, financial engineering and innovations and its relation to financial crisis, regulatory implications, risks, corporate governance, Islamic financial principles and techniques, structuring Islamic financial transactions, usury (*riba*), critics and defenders of Islamic finance and banking, the emergence of Islamic finance, Islamic economics and ethics, legal stratagems and financial exclusion.

[1]The *Sunnah* is the practice and sayings of Prophet Muhammad (peace be upon him) and is the second source of authority and legislation in Islam after the Qur'an.

S. Alamad, *Financial Innovation and Engineering in Islamic Finance*,
Contributions to Management Science, DOI 10.1007/978-3-319-52947-9_3

Therefore, the above themes are believed to be related to this subject directly or indirectly. Hence, it was important to critically review previous work in this domain.

3.2 Differences Between Islamic and Conventional Banking

Ahmad (1993) argues that Islamic banks, like all conventional banks, are in the business of financial intermediation to perform a socially useful role in managing financial resources. The difference is conventional banks carry out these functions on the basis of interest. Unlike conventional banks, Islamic banks seek to perform the same functions by developing a new relationship with their clients, without indulging in interest baring transactions which are prohibited in Islam. Wilson (2010) has argued that the Islamic financial system is not simply about prohibitions, it provides guidance on how to do business in line with religious teachings, which can be considered positively from an ethical perspective.

It is important, however, to mention that commercial activities under Shariah are subject to the ban on *riba* (interest) in addition to other restrictions. These other restrictions include, but are not limited to, the ban on *gharar* (uncertainty) and *maysir* (gambling and speculation) in financial transactions (Obaidullah 2005: 29).

Visser (2009: 81) further argues that when discussing what makes Islamic banking different from its conventional counterpart, we should discuss the financial instruments offered by Islamic banks, their funding and their sources of funds. As Islamic banks have to follow the teachings of Shariah for Islamic finance, this requires that not only their financing (lending) but also their funding should be from Shariah compliant sources and transactions. Return cannot be guaranteed on money deposited with Islamic banks as savings account are based on profit sharing instruments, unlike conventional banks. Islamic banks are, therefore, permitted to issue shares, but not conventional interest bearing debt.

3.3 The Difference Between Usury (*Riba*) and Interest

Mews and Abraham (2007) discuss the concept of usury; they argue that in the Christian tradition, usury always meant the concept of extra money demanded in excess of a loan. Whereas, interest is perceived as a just compensation to the lender for the loan. They tried to draw a distinction between usury as illegitimate predatory lending and interest as an acceptable compensation in order to form a common ground between this distinction and the ethical financial principles in both Islam and Christianity. Mews and Abraham (2007) argues that this is an old argument dressed in a contemporary way to legitimise interest as a compensation payment to the lender. This argument has been clearly rejected by the majority of Muslim scholars and jurists, such as Al-Zuhayli (2002) who argued that usury and interest is the same thing and is prohibited in Islam.

Hassan (1992: 107) defines usury as a return that someone gets from another which is not a gift and not a compensation of work performed, without facing any risk for the money invested. This definition is very broad and does not reflect the definition in the classical books of jurisprudence (*fiqh*) that define usury or interest as any benefit (this includes money and otherwise) received by the lender over the loan or for an extension of time for the payment of the owed sum. According to Mujahid (d. 722 C.E), *riba* of the pre-Islamic period was that "if a person took a loan from another he or she would say: I would give you so such money if you grant me extension of time" (Mannan 1980).

Arrif (1982) clarifies that the argument concerning the distinction between interest and usury in the late middle ages in Europe had its impact on some writers, who applied it as it is to make a distinction between *riba* and interest on the basis that interest is not regarded as *riba* as long as its rate is not usurious. There is a controversy over the differences between '*al riba*' or usury and 'interest'. Khan (1995) makes it clear that there is no difference between forbidding *riba* and interest, and they are the same thing. He defines interest simply as "it is any increase (large or small, nominal or real) received on a loan".

Mannan (1980) has explained that if the meaning of *riba* is viewed in its correct historical perspective, there appears to be no difference between *riba* and interest. An overall view of all modern theories of interest has revealed that the economists have failed to discover a clear answer as to why interest is paid, on the other hand, the Islamic theory of capital does recognise the share of capital in national wealth only to the extent of its contribution, to be determined as a variable percentage of profits rather than the fixed percentage of capital itself (Khan 1995).

Concerning this issue, Khan (1994) has argued that this claim does not deserve serious attention, because it is clearly stated in the Qur'an that at the expiry of the time limit of a loan, the lender is only permitted to receive his principal without any addition. Actually, this distinction does not have any theoretical base; however, it is more or less a pragmatic attempt to 'Islamize' the un-Islamic situation existing today in Muslim countries.

3.4 Emergence of Islamic Banking

It has been argued in the literature whether the restrictions in Islamic finance on some financial activities, such as derivatives, options and future contracts would enable Islamic finance to provide a wide spectrum of financial instruments that sufficiently serve the needs of a developed, or even at least developing, economy without compromising its principles. Visser (2009: 140) suggests that a country considering the adaptation of Islamic finance, across-the-board, and the operation of the economy exclusively according to its principles, might be condemned to permanent low growth rates.

Visser (2009: 5), controversially, attributes the origins of Islamic finance as known and applied to Abu Al A'laa Al Mawdudi in 1941, which most of the Arab writers would strongly disagree with. Smith (2006) has addressed this issue by conducting a case study on three Gulf States tracing the origins of Islamic finance and the pioneering Arabs behind its emergence. Al Qaradaghi (2010) also disagrees with Visser's claim as he discusses in his work this argument by stating that the beginning of Islamic economics in the modern days is attributed to the pioneering Arabs in setting up Islamic banks, its theories, system and its relationship with the conventional economic system.

Visser (2009) argues that the efforts by Muslims to establish a well-recognised Islamic economics system have been a frustrating experience with little success even across other religions. He asserts that Islamic finance is a mere facet of important Islamic teachings, with implications for finance. It is something that he shares with Ramadan (2009) who argues that there is nothing called Islamic economics or Islamic finance as an actual system rather; it is a set of ethics that govern the conduct of business transactions.

Smith's (2006) study has developed an analytical framework to explain the emergence of Islamic banking. She argues that her approach in conducting the study cannot be fully understood without recognising Islamic finance as a constructivist project. Then she builds on this argument by studying Islamic banks, their origins and development in the Gulf States, their negotiation with the global conventional finance and their relationship to political Islam. The author employs multi case studies method in collecting her data, the three Gulf Countries included as case studies are Saudi Arabia, Bahrain and Kuwait.

She defines Strategic Constructivism as the act of making an institution work towards alternative political objectives via symbolic action. Conceptually, the study tries to introduce a framework for incorporating symbolic power into the study of institutions with the aim to generate a political theory of institutional change.

Smith (2006) implies that the emergence of Islamic banking enabled the Islamists to put capital in this industry and use it with a hidden agenda for political gains. The study ignores the fact that the Islamic finance principles and techniques existed over 1400 years ago and developed over time to accommodate different commercial needs (El-Gamal 2006; Visser 2009). The study focuses on the post-colonial period of the history of the Gulf States, it was very normal, after having gained their independence, to develop their financial system in a way that complies with Shariah and is compatible with the existing conventional finance and banking system. However, the author believes that this development was for political reasons with ulterior motives.

This shows that the study was heavily subjective rather than objective as it ignored some facts in the development of the Islamic banking, as mentioned above, which would argue against the author's theory. This view would imply that this argument permeate Western studies of Islamic finance. A counter argument would state that there is, generally, a strong link between politics and financial policies.

Moreover, countries have the right to determine their own political ideologies and destinies without needing the approval from their colonial rulers, hence, to suggest otherwise it would imply a colonial attitude.

Hence, Smith (2006) in her study addresses the political motive in the development of Islamic banking and the relationship between petro-dollar industry in the Gulf States and the emergence of Islamic banking.

3.5 Islamic Banking and Finance: Critics and Defenders

Al-Bouti (2005), Al-Zuhayli (2002), and Usmani (2005) discuss different financial transactions, sales and other financial activities in Shariah in a generic way, but do not go into details with their current application in Islamic banks. They do not offer any sort of Shariah framework for Islamic financial engineering, this is understandable and expected from such writings as they do not draw on the practical banking and finance expertise. They offer glimpses of different juristic opinions of the four schools of thoughts with regards to sale contracts and other financial transactions. However on the other hand, Abdul Rahman (2005) and Dwabeh (2004) have tackled the issue of Islamic financial transactions in general, they discuss them from their applications in Islamic banks such as basic savings accounts, letter of credits and insurance.

It is worth mentioning that Al-Zuhayli's (2007a) work has discussed all financial transactions that are addressed in the classical books of *fiqh* (jurisprudence). It discusses different juristic opinions on wide variety of financial transactions. This, however, could be a critique at the same time of his work as not being specialised and does not focus in-depth on specific pressing issues in Islamic finance and banking. Furthermore, Al-Zuhayli (2007b) discusses the differences between Islamic and conventional interest-based banks and suspicions surrounding Islamic banks and their operations. He, as an advocate of Islamic banking, analyses their functions, objectives and role in social growth and development.

El-Gamal (2006), on the other hand, has been a voice of criticism and suspicion of current practices of Islamic banks. He argues that Islamic banks have diverted from the objectives of Islamic finance and the ultimate aim of the Islamic banking pioneers. He correctly points out that Islamic banks are mimicking the financial products offered by conventional banks by labelling it as 'Shariah compliant' or Islamic; rather than creating a distinctive Islamic financial products that serve the real economy. In his opinion, Islamic banks are driven by profit maximisation in focusing more on the legal form of the financial transactions instead of following the spirit of Shariah in ensuring that these transactions are just and fair. He continues criticising financial institutions for using the designation of 'Islamic' in branding their financial products, which are normally more expensive than their conventional counterparts, to create a monopoly in a competitive market.

Kamali (2000) raised the issue of permissibility of options in Islam whilst discussing the opinion of mainstream scholars. His argument states that in the light of Shariah rule of permissibility which renders all commercial transactions permissible in the absence of a clear prohibition. This is the opinion of the Mecca-based *Fiqh* Academy and also of many Islamic scholars who have proscribed futures trading and declared it totally forbidden. This body of opinion is founded on the analysis that futures' trading does not fulfil the requirements of Islamic law of sale contract.

This opinion, according to Kamali, did not give a due consideration to the fact that futures trading are a new phenomenon which has no parallel in the conventional Islamic code of transactions. Therefore, it should be governed by a different set of rules. This approach also fails to relate the issue at hand to the normative guidance of the Qur'an and *Sunnah*, which can support different calibre research and an affirmative ruling on the subject.

Alchaar et al. (2009) has also contributed with selected subjects of Islamic financial transactions including financial techniques, *sukuk, takaful*, corporate governance and financial reporting, without a clear and informative focus on the issue of financial innovation and engineering. Al-Barwari (2005), on the other hand, discusses analytically the financial market from an Islamic perspective. He discusses the nature and functionality of the financial market analysing its activities in line with Shariah, and how some unacceptable transactions can be adjusted to meet Shariah requirements. He attempted to offers a brief vision on how the financial market can interact with Islamic finance and investment approach.

Although the above literature offers a wide variety and understanding of the Islamic financial transactions, it is still very similar to some extent and does not tackle the issue of financial innovation and product development and the role of Shariah in setting its requirements. There is clearly a gap in the literature in dealing with the subject of Islamic financial engineering from both commercial and Islamic jurisprudence perspectives that deal with the issue in detail incorporating the higher Shariah objectives.

3.6 Innovation

3.6.1 Definition of Innovation

Innovation is defined as a management process that is extremely driven by the organisational structure and context, in addition to, the influence of the macro system in which the organisation exists (Trott 2008). However, Kumar and Phrommathed (2005) are of the view that 'innovation' is a repeated process which is commenced by the perception of a new market or service opportunity for technology-based innovation, which results in development, production and marketing tasks in hunting for commercial success. This definition includes two distinctions: the innovation process comprises technological development combined with the market introduction, and the innovation process is iterative. Freeman

(1982) put it clearly that the survival of the financial system is by keeping innovating financial products that are compatible with the new economic and financial changes in the world. To not innovate is to die.

Academic research has explored the design of financial innovations and their impact on the financial system in recent decades, see e.g. Allen and Gale (1988, 1994), Bahattacharyya and Nada (1996), and Duffle and Rahi (1995). However, according to Boot and Thakor (1997), this academic research tackled the issue from three perspectives; the first is the research in addressing financial innovation which attempted to explain factors that motivate financial innovation and structuring securities. The second perspective in the literature has addressed the question of the functionality of the banking system, and whether we should look into separating banking functionality, i.e. investment and commercial, or not.

Finally, as Boot and Thakor (1997) summarise that, others looked into it from a more generic perspective with a focus on financial system design, which leads us to the third perspective in the literature. The key parts of this literature, which adopted a more holistic approach are markets, institutions, how risk-sharing ventures are affected by the design of financial system, corporate governance, the structure of a financial system, cost of funds and structure of financial contracts.

Hence, Frame and White (2010: 3) define financial innovation as: something new which helps reduce costs, risks or provide an improved product, service or instrument that better meets the satisfaction of participants in the financial system. Financial innovation can be categorised as new products (e.g. subprime mortgages), new services (e.g. internet banking), new production processes (e.g. credit scoring) or new organisational forms (e.g. internet only banks).

3.6.2 Nature and Theory of Financial Innovation

Anderloni et al. (2009: 4) argue that financial innovation is a reflection, and partly a cause, of structural changes evident in many financial systems since the early 1990s. During this period a general trend towards securitisation (financial intermediation with a counterpart of tradable financial assets) has emerged, and the use of derivative, instruments and contracts. Product innovation, as a type of innovation, is the creation of new financial instruments, techniques, contracts and markets.

Innovation has been a subject of debate for many years; Schumpeter (1934, 1939, 1942) was the first economist among others to highlight the necessity for new product development as stimuli to economic growth. According to Trott (2008) the cyclical innovation view can be traced to Marx who was the first to mention that innovations could be related to waves of economic growth. This is because; early observations concluded that economic growth does not take place in a regular manner. It seems to happen in waves of activity, signalling the critical impact of external elements on economic development.

Thereafter, others like Schumpeter (1934, 1939), Kondratieff (1935/51), and Abernathy and Utterback (1978) have debated the long-wave theory of innovation.

A number of studies (see e.g. Simon 1957; Woodward 1965) of innovation were conducted that focused on the internal features of the innovation process within the economy.

These studies aimed to look at economics, organisational behaviour and business management. This has included the generation of new knowledge, the application of this knowledge in the product development processes and the commercial exploitation of these products in relation to the generation of financial return. A new theoretical framework was developed as a result of these studies with the objective of understanding how organisations managed the features above and why some of them seemed to be more successful.

3.6.3 Three Schumpeterian Schools of Innovation

The literature on innovation, according to Tzeng (2009), is not limited to the Schumpeterian tradition. There are other important schools as well that established their theories on classical sociologists, philosophers, and the natural sciences. The configuration school (e.g., Miller and Friesen 1982), derived from the Weberian tradition of ideal type, provides efficient ways to help classify innovative organisations.

The knowledge management school (e.g., Nonaka 1994), based on Polanyi's theory of personal knowledge, explores the conversion process between tacit and explicit knowledge. The cluster school (e.g., Porter 1990), for its part, draws from Marshallian externalities to study how geographical proximities between firms and its suppliers, customers, and competitors can lead to more innovative products (Tzeng 2009).

Moreover, the complexity adaptive systems school (e.g., Anderson 1999), which originated from physical science, aims to better understand the nonlinear and dynamic relations between the innovative agent and its environment. The population ecology school (e.g., Aldrich and Martinez 2001), which is built on biological science, researches on the process of variation, selection, and retention to calculate the aggregate survival rate of firms in the evolution of technological innovation (Tzeng 2009).

Since Schumpeter's work the debate has evolved with more recent studies (Chandler 1962; Nelson and Winter 1982; Cohen and Levinthal 1990; Prahalad and Hamel 1990; Pavitt 1990; Patel and Pavitt 2000) with relation to what enhances innovative performance, which also offered a better understanding of innovative management.

Financial innovation has been a concomitant of economic development from the beginning of the modern financial system. Economists failed to isolate financial innovation as a subject deserving serious attention (although they were aware of it), until it started to be blamed for causing parametric instability in the demand for money function. The topic of financial innovation was neglected up to 1970s, and more concerted consideration to this subject did not develop until after the mid-1970s (Podolski 1986: 105).

Pawley (1993: 2), argued the issue of whether financial regulations are driven by financial innovation as responding to the changes in the financial and banking system or *vice versa*. He discusses the issue of financial innovation and offshore banking transactions as an objective for avoiding regulations. Sinkey (1992) also argues that product innovation is driven by the desire of circumventing prudential and monetary regulations imposed by financial authorities and central banks.

This argument is worth researching its applicability on financial innovation in Islamic finance and banking system. Innovations in Islamic finance are meant to follow the principles of Shariah and Islamic business ethics to be acceptable as Shariah compliant financial activities. Moreover, in the case of Islamic finance, new taxation and financial regulations have played a vital role in the development of Islamic financial innovation by responding to this change in order to create a level playing field for Islamic finance. This has resulted in a regulatory-induced innovation which is all about adhering to regulations and Shariah law rather than circumventing them, as the case may be with its conventional counterpart.

3.6.4 Innovation Orientation

Few studies within the large spectrum of the innovation literature have addressed the concept of innovation orientation. This research did not find, as far as it is aware, any study in the innovation literature that addresses a religiously-oriented innovation concept. The earliest of these articles, that addressed innovation orientation as a concept, is from Manu (1992: 334), who explains innovation orientation as encompassing "the total innovation programmes of companies and is strategic in nature because it provides direction in dealing with markets". Manu and Sriram (1996: 81) conceptualise innovation orientation as a multicomponent construct (see also: Worren et al. 2002: 1127; Amabile 1997; Keller and Warrack 2002: 18). A further dimension of innovation orientation is the social impact. This poses potential difficulties of supporting a social issue that organisations identify with a desire to support it, but they do not always act on that desire (Sonenshein et al. 2014).

Berthon et al. (1999: 37) define innovation orientation in relation to technological superiority: firms that "devote their energy toward inventing and refining superior products." This conceptualisation consists of both openness to innovation (Zaltman et al. 1973) and a capacity to innovate (Burns and Stalker 1977). This latter perspective of innovation orientation, according to Siguaw et al. (2006), overlaps Hurley and Hult's (1998: 44) conceptualisation of innovativeness as "the notion of openness to new ideas as an aspect of a firm's culture" and Hult et al.'s (2004: 430) view of innovativeness "as the capacity to introduce some new process, product, or idea in the organisation." Innovation requires, according to Scarbrough, et al. (2015), collaboration among groups possessing specialised expertise in order to coordinate the innovation process, which poses a real challenge for the organisation.

3.6.5 The Relation Between Innovation and Financial Crisis

Academic research has also explored the main causes of financial crises in recent decades, (see e.g. Persons and Warther 1997; Bhattacharyya and Nada 2000; Finnerty 1992; Duska 2009). However, these researches tackled the issue of financial crises from different perspectives. Some examined separating banking functionality i.e. investment and retail, others looked into it from a financial innovation perspective, for example, competition in the financial market and complexity of this innovation.

Some academic research (see Kaminsky and Reinhart 1999, 2000), states that, there is a major problem with the current financial system in the new capitalist era, namely that this financial system is under regulated and requires a fundamental reform. In contrast, there are some emerging financial systems, such as the Islamic finance and banking system, which has survived the recent financial crisis, in 2008, with minimum effects due to the characteristics of this system.

The empirical literature on banking practices have mainly focused on the U.S. banking system (Berger 1995; Angbazo 1997; De Young and Rice 2004; Hirtle and Stiroh 2007) and other banking systems in the Western and developed countries only, e.g. New Zealand (To and Tripe 2002), Australia (Williams 2003), Greece (Pasiouras and Kosmidou 2007; Kosmidou et al. 2007; Athanasoglou et al. 2008; Kosmidou and Zopounidis 2008). Given the relation between the well-being of the banking sector and the growth of the economy, knowledge of the underlying factors that influence the financial sector's stability is therefore essential not only for the managers of the banks, but for numerous stakeholders such as the central banks, governments, and other financial authorities. Knowledge of these factors would also help the regulatory authorities and banks formulate policies going forward for improved stability of the banking sector and financial innovation.

Overall in the literature, both interpretive and positivist epistemologies were adopted, qualitative and quantitative methods were employed with dominance of the latter, and data collection involved case studies, financial sampling, surveys, financial reporting and official statistics. Kling (2010), however, argues that the main focus in the literature was on two competing narratives: moral failure and cognitive failure. The capital regulations played a fundamental role in fostering the behaviour that created the financial crisis, because they discouraged traditional mortgage lending and instead encouraged securitization.

3.7 Product Development

3.7.1 Definition of Product Development

Product development is defined by Smith and Reinertsen (1998: 167), as 'a process of gradually building up a body of information until it eventually provides a complete formula for manufacturing a new product'. However, Ulrich and Eppinger (2008: 2) look at the definition of product development from a market angle and define it as 'the set of activities beginning with the perception of a market opportunity and ending in the production, sales and delivery of the product'.

These definitions outline the product development process in general however; one may say that the development process may differ subject to requirements of different industries. Therefore, product development in financial services has also its requirements and characteristics, which would be different from other industries. The same view would also apply on product development in Islamic finance due to its structure and requirements.

3.7.2 Importance of Product Development

Product development is a key requirement for Islamic banks to compete and offer alternatives to conventional banks. This is because one of the important tactics of product differentiation that many firms in general and banks in particular have implemented in order to have a competitive advantage in the marketplace; is efficient new product development and the successful introduction of new products into markets (Kumar and Phrommathed 2005).

Ahmed (2011) criticises the current practices of Islamic banks, of mimicking the conventional products and labelling them as Shariah compliant products, he quotes authors who have raised the same issue of criticism, such as El-Gamal (2006).

3.7.3 Product Development Process

Ahmed (2011) describes the product development cycle as designed for conventional financial product development, then, he adds the Shariah controls steps in the cycle. He refrains from diving deeper into the tools and techniques of Shariah, mainly the principles of jurisprudence (*usoul al fiqh*). This is essential in extracting new Shariah rulings to address arising issues in Islamic finance. He briefly touched on certain aspects of the objectives of Shariah (*maqased al* Shariah) without clearly incorporating those objectives in the product development cycle.

This is, also, a key and main differentiator of Islamic financial product development process in developing products that meet the objectives of Shariah. The cycle of product development and its different stages should be identified clearly. A stage in product development, as Li et al. (2006) sate, is simply portrayed as a black box, which inputs are built on and flow from the previous stage, and which outputs flow as inputs for the next stage.

Ahmed (2011) divides the process of product development into three phases, idea generation and acceptance, converting concept to product and commercialisation. He shows a good understanding of the product development process when he discusses these three phases. However, one may argue that this division is not accurate and does not reflect the full cycle of product development as there are some other aspects that need to be considered, such as post product launch.

The commercialisation phase does not reflect what it entails. It normally refers to the marketing stage of the product cycle which includes the product management stage. Hence, a clear distinction here with regards to this matter would be helpful. McGrath (1996), in contrast, divides the product development cycle into seven stages; although someone may argue that he combines product development with product management. These stages, as McGrath (1996) argues, are decision making, project team organisation, development activity structure, development tools and techniques, product strategy process, technology management and pipeline management.

3.7.4 Product Development in Islamic Banking

El-Gamal (2006) critically evaluates the expression of "Islamic finance" suggesting two competing forces at work. The noun 'finance' suggests that Islamic financial institutions deal with the allocation of financial credit and risk. Therefore, this means that Islamic finance must be, in essence, similar to other forms of finance. However, the adjective 'Islamic' suggests some fundamental differences between Islamic finance and its conventional counterpart. Commentators on the theory and practice of Islamic finance and the product engineering process sense a tension between being essentially similar to conventional finance (in terms of competitiveness and efficiency) and attempts to preserve its unique Islamic character. One of the key differentiators between Islamic and conventional product development, is that Islamic product development is either asset based or asset backed products, unlike its conventional counterpart.

Katila and Ahuja (2002) argue that a competitive advantage can be obtained by Islamic financial institutions through a process of strategic innovation, which in addition to other factors, will require the development of at least some new knowledge and capabilities. Govindarajan and Trimble (2005) also added that this will have high potential for income growth. Lyons et al. (2007) further discusses that new ideas must be developed, implemented and delivered to customers to create commercial revenue.

There has been a major impact on Islamic financial services industry and its development and challenges that enhanced product development. This impact resulted from globalisation, transparency and capital movement. The main challenge is the Islamic financial services industry's ability to develop financial products that fully comply with Shariah. Therefore, as Islamic finance and banking is a new industry, it is critical that products and services continue to be developed on regular basis. This also will require great emphasis on the quality and diversity of these financial products and services provided by Islamic financial institutions and the challenges that they face in that regard (Al-Salem 2009).

El-Gamal (2006) correctly states that there is a gap in addressing the processes of financial engineering, as the Shariah supervisory committees of IFIs put more emphasis on the wording of the legal contracts, rather than ensuring that these contracts meet the spirit of Shariah.

3.7.5 Islamic Ethics and Financial Product Development and Engineering

There are two primary sources of normative business ethics and code of conduct for financial activities in Islam. These two sources are Qur'an (the Muslim Holy Book) and *Sunnah* (the tradition of Prophet Muhammad [peace be upon him]). When examining financial engineering and product development from Islamic ethical point of view, we should view it from following main criteria, justice and balance, transparency, honesty, trust and benevolence (Beekun and Badawi 2005). With these criteria in mind, Islam permits the contracting parties of a developed financial product to agree on any conditions as long as they are within the tenet of Shariah, and do not violate any Shariah ruling with regards to financial contracts (Iqbal and Khan 2005).

Beekun and Badawi (2005) rightly argue that Islam is a full way of life, not just a religion. Therefore, business ethics and the Shariah objectives cannot be ignored or separated in financial engineering and product development. The Islamic ethical system demands for the rights of both the primary and derivative stakeholders, in the process of developing and offering financial products, to be respected. This approach will not allow exploitation, nepotism and other human ills and unethical business practices. Instead of working towards maximising profits by any means, as an objective of financial engineering, Islam seeks value maximisation within the parameter of ethical principles in Islam as mentioned above.

It is clear from the literature review that Islamic finance is trying to take its place in the global financial market by making some concessions to catch up, to some extent, with its conventional counterpart. This will, essentially, include by default the financial engineering and product development methodology, which may eventually result in Islamic finance losing its identity. Therefore, it is important that Islamic finance emphasises its unique characteristics manifested in its product development approach to preserve its identity.

Hence, it is vital, in order to achieve this objective, to address this identified gap in the literature to structure a possible unified framework for Islamic financial product development. Therefore, this study aims to address this gap in the literature by developing a framework for financial innovation and engineering that incorporates both Shariah and business requirements. This framework will help forming the basis in standardising the process of Islamic financial product development across the industry. It will further protect Islamic banking and finance from losing its unique identity and going astray from its main objectives and role; providing financial stability as a model for resilient financial system.

3.8 Regulatory Challenges

One of the key challenges for financial innovation and engineering in Islamic finance and banking is the existing regulatory framework, which does not accommodate the nature of Islamic financial products. Archer and Abdel Karim (2007) argue that this challenge is wider than what the regulators would expect, which is to some extent a slight exaggeration, if we take e.g. the case of the UK and the regulatory adjustments that were issued to accommodate Islamic banking. They, rightly, highlighted the challenge that faces the experts in the Islamic commercial jurisprudence to raise awareness of the requirements for a viable legal and regulatory structure for Islamic finance.

Alexakis and Tasikouras (2009) state that the main regulatory issues faced by Islamic financial institutions are due to its unique characteristics compared to conventional financial institutions. They assert that Islamic banks due to their particularities are better to adhere to the existing capital adequacy standards and build on them, adjusting where necessary, rather than adapting the Basel Accord for capital adequacy. This is an approach taken by the Accounting and Auditing Organisation for Islamic Financial Institutions (AAOIFI). This is in addition to, the issues of lack of transparency, consistency and rating agencies.

Archer and Abdel Karim (2007) also argued that one of the main regulatory issues for Islamic banks operating in highly developed financial markets, such as the UK is the treatment of *mudarabah* investment accounts as deposit accounts. Banks are defined in these markets as “deposit-taking financial institutions”, whereas from banking regulatory perspective and legal status deposits are considered debt and being ‘capital certain’.

Islamic banks take deposits on a profit sharing basis, where the bank invests the available deposits in the investment accounts and then shares the generated profit with the depositors. The profit sharing contracts do not guarantee the capital as this will render the contract non-Shariah compliant. However, this issue is not new with regards to Islamic banks as deposit-taking, and was dealt with before in different writings (see Kamali 2000). So, the authors did not provide any new contribution or possible solution rather than articulating an existing concerns for deposit-taking in Islamic banks which could be the first step towards a possible solution.

3.9 Risks in Islamic Banking

There are various considerations of risks associated with the development and introduction of a new financial innovation in the market. Some of these risks are shared between conventional banking and IFIs and others are unique to the operations and structures of financial products of IFIs. Greening and Iqbal (2007) focused on extra risks that Islamic banks have to consider due to the nature of their operation and products. They state that a financial review would take into account a review of financial conditions and certain issues with regards to the bank exposure to risk and the management of this risk.

The main technique used to analyse financial risk is by undertaking a robust review of a bank's balance sheet. This will also include important qualitative factors, and view financial ratios within a wide spectrum of risk assessment, risk management, trends and changes to such risks.

For Islamic banks however, as Greening and Iqbal (2007) state, such assessment must consider the nature of the contracts and principles underlying financial products to understand how risk is shared and allocated. The authors go on in explaining the extra risk analysis required for Islamic banks by focusing on a key contract in Islamic banking. The fund's mobilisation and utilisation in the *mudarabah* contract is based on profit sharing among the parties to this agreement. The authors use a descriptive approach of the risk assessment for Islamic banks. This account is informative in general but lacks flow and coherence and does not offer any new contribution.

Although Sundararajan (2007) agrees in general with Greening and Iqbal (2007) in their approach of analysing risks for Islamic banks, however, he disagrees with the method used. He suggests that a risk measurement framework tailored to Islamic banks should be created. He argues that empirical evidence shows that the sharing of risks model is very limited in practice.

Even though, ideally, well-structured risk sharing contracts for the profit-sharing investment accounts would be a powerful tool for risk mitigation in Islamic banks. Some researchers, who are critical of Islamic banks such as El-Gamal (2006), would disagree with Sundararajan's (2007) statement as they would consider this to contravene with the nature of such contracts and may render them void from a Shariah perspective.

Al-Amine (2008: 1) outlines different risks that need to be managed by financial institutions whether Islamic or not. They include among others market risk, litigation risk, credit risk, operational risk, interest rate risk, liquidity risk and foreign exchange risk. The management of risk in Islamic banking is more challenging due to its peculiar nature and characteristics and the requirements to comply with Shariah.

Al-Amine (2008: 3) argues that the Basil II initiatives on the identification on market, credit and operational risks, can be assimilated into Islamic banking. However, the initiatives have to be complemented with the other dimensions of risks that are inherent in Islamic financial transactions. There is also the need for the

Islamic banking industry to develop a derivative market as a risk management tool. Moreover, there is the risk of maturity mismatch between the assets and liabilities due to a lack of long term funding for Islamic banking. This will require a development of instruments that provide long term funding to match the long term asset, such as home finance, in order to mitigate this risk. Some of these risks are outlined below.

3.9.1 Credit and Market Risks

Haron and Hock (2007) further discuss the credit and market risks for Islamic banks. They are of the view that credit risks with the possibility of counterparties not meeting their pre-agreed financial obligations is something that both Islamic and conventional banks share. They nicely list the most common contracts of Islamic banks and the credit risks they are exposed to.

However, they do not follow on by discussing or offering solutions for how Islamic banks would deal with and address these credit risks. The approach that would be taken by Islamic banks to deal with credit risks is, obviously, different from what would be the process in conventional banks. This is because of the special characteristics of the Islamic banking products. Although, this is an important issue that would benefit Islamic banks greatly, it was not addressed by the authors.

Haron and Hock (2007) also tackled the issue of market risk which is according to them, the risk of losses in on- and off-balance sheet positions caused by market pricing. They correctly assert that conventional financial institutions are, unlike Islamic financial institutions, exposed to market risks due to the various instruments they used for short term profit from price and interest rate variations.

Islamic banks are less exposed to such risks due to Shariah restrictions on such financial instruments. The authors failed to show an understanding in distinguishing between what would be considered speculative instruments that are prohibited and what would be a legitimate profit generating instrument from Shariah perspective.

3.9.2 Operational Risk Exposure of Islamic Banks

Haron and Hock (2007) have addressed the issue of operational risk for Islamic banks in light with the Basel II definition. Basel II defined operational risk as "the risk of loss resulting from inadequate or failed internal processes, people and systems or from external events ... [including] legal risk ... but [excluding] strategic and reputational risk".

Haron and Hock (2007) divide the operational risks that Islamic banks would face into three categories:

(a) operational risks that would result from different sorts of banking activities, and which is shared among all financial intermediaries,
(b) Shariah compliance risk, this would be attributed to non-compliance with Shariah requirements and rules in the bank's operation; and the risk related to the bank's fiduciary responsibilities as fund manager (*mudarib*) towards funds providers in a *mudarabah* contract in the case of misconduct and negligence by the bank,
(c) legal risks, this would arise from the Islamic bank's operations or legal uncertainty related to the interpretation of Shariah related clauses and its enforceability.

The authors missed other contracts that have similar nature to the *mudarabah* contract referred to in the Shariah compliance risk above, such as *wakala* (agency agreement). Further, they also failed to mention some very common operational Shariah compliance risks related to the *murabaha* contract; in terms of, e.g., processing the transaction of buying and selling the commodities in the right sequence.

3.9.3 Impacts of Basel III on Islamic Banks

3.9.3.1 Current Scenario

Basel III concerns approaches to enhance the quality of capital. The enhancement changes the demographic of debt based capital to one of equity. Islamic banks already have a higher proportion of equity as capital. Basel III covers buffer capital ratios introduced via the Capital Conservation Buffer and Counter Cyclical Capital Buffer. The Islamic banks have introduced Investment Risk Reserve and Profit Equalisation Reserve.

3.9.3.2 Capital Impact

Islamic banks are required to hold much more of the best form of capital while some of the existing capital will cease to count. Deductions from capital will increasingly be made from core tier 1. Dividends and bonuses will be constrained to boost core tier 1. Islamic banks will have to hold purer liquidity in larger amount and match closely between their financing and deposit base. A large part of the Islamic banks' profits over the next decade will go into the new standing funds according to these regulations.

3.9.3.3 Leverage Ratio

PSIA (Profit Sharing Investment Accounts) cannot be included in additional Tier1 capital because they do not meet the criteria set out by the Basel III. Assets financed by the PSIAs are excluded from the exposure measure because the PSIAs are not included in the Tier 1 capital. Generally, Islamic banks are not highly leveraged due to the strict prohibition of 33% debt to equity ratio.[2]

In summary, there is no noticeable impact on Islamic banks positions by adapting the requirements of Basel III.

3.9.4 Liquidity in Islamic Banks

According to the Islamic Financial Services Board (IFSB 2012) in Islamic banks (IBs), various types of risks interact with liquidity risk in a variety of ways, both in normal and stressed conditions. Credit risk in an IB can transform into liquidity risk if it faces major defaults in its financing and investment portfolio. Uncertainty about the creditworthiness and quality of an IB's financing portfolio can make it difficult to obtain funding from the market or to resell an eligible asset portfolio to other IB. In many IBs across different jurisdictions, a large part of their financing portfolio consists of *Murābahah* or other debt-based modes of financing.

Hence, this portfolio cannot be re-sold in the market due to Shariah restrictions on the selling of debt unlike conventional banking. The lack of depth in Shariah compliant instruments and Sukūk (Islamic certificates) in many jurisdictions increases the market risk of IBs. During the stressed conditions, the IB may find it difficult to sell or collateralise these assets to generate liquidity.

Further, any reputational problem experienced by an IB due to perceived Shariah compliance or fiduciary risk may result in the withdrawal of funds by the fund providers, resulting in heightened liquidity risk for the IB. The liquidity risk management framework of the IB should factor in these and similar relationships and interactions between liquidity risk and other risks while setting limits, performing stress testing and executing its risk management strategy and policies in its operational environment.[3]

Hence, the issues raised above, regarding unique risks associated with financial innovation and products in Islamic banking, have to be considered in the financial innovation and engineering process as their implication would differ from an Islamic finance principle to the other.

---

[2]Taken from Abdulla Haron, (2010), *Basil III: Impacts on IIFS and the Role of IFSB*, working paper, presented in AAOIFI conference on 23–24 October 2010, Manama, Bahrain.

[3]IFSB (Islamic Financial Services Board—12 Guiding Principles on Liquidity Risk Management (Mar 2012), p. 20.

3.10 Corporate Governance

Corporate governance is about how public companies are structured and directed (Monks and Minow 2011: 1). Greening and Iqbal (2007) argue that corporate governance provides a disciplined structure through which a bank sets its objectives, determines the means of attaining them, and monitors the performance of those objectives. There has been, in the last few years, a growing interest in the corporate governance of banks and more studies have emerged (see e.g. Macy and O'Hara 2003; Caprio and Levine 2002; Levine 2003; Charkham 2003).

However, Levine (2003) questions the need for a separate analysis for corporate governance of banks as this would require justification, as banks like any other organisations have the same corporate structure of shareholders, boards of directors, competitors etc. Caprio and Levine (2002) mention three characteristics of the governance of banks to support the claim that no separate analysis is required for banks. They argue that banks are, in general, more opaque than other financial institutions, which completely intensifies the agency problem.

Second, banks are exposed to very robust regulations in the financially developed countries and, third, the widespread government ownership of banks raises some governance issues. Charkham (2003: 15) argues this point as in his view, banks are different from other companies as their collapse would affect the society, furthermore, it may also impact the financial system with a domino effect to the economy as a whole.

IFIs have a special corporate governance structure represented by the additional layer of governance for Shariah compliance and the role of the SSC, as explained in Chap. 2. This governance structure is very important in the process of financial innovation and engineering in IFIs. Shariah governance plays a key part in determining whether the financial innovation or product is acceptable to be developed and offered in the market by an IFI or not. It plays the role of coordinating the work with all stakeholders in the process and business functions to achieve and engineer the required outcome of the financial innovation.

The debate in the literature about corporate governance has mainly focused on whether corporate governance should concentrate on protecting the shareholders' interests or it should be broader in taking into account the interests of other stakeholders (Macy and O'Hara 2003). Instead of interest-bearing deposits, Islamic banks invest deposits in profit and loss sharing investment accounts.

However, investment account holders lack rights of governance that shareholders enjoy, although they are (legally speaking) a type of equity holder with residual claims to their share of the bank's assets. The law provides a governance structure for debt holders in case of default. While in case of investment account holders in Islamic banks, neither the Shariah nor the secular law makes any such provision according to Archer and Abdel Karim (2007).

Archer and Abdel Karim (2007) further argue that this would raise a possible conflict of interests between the two groups of equity holders. This is because of the type of these investment accounts and the underlying Shariah principle. They also highlighted the risk of available adequate information to the investment account holders about the activities in which their deposits are invested in and the associated level of risk.

Blum (2002) and Cordella and Yeyati (1998) argue that a conventional bank's risk choice will be efficient if the bank deposits are uninsured, because they factor the impact of their risk choice on their depositors. This is because, normally, higher risk is associated with higher return, so, depositors will be demanding higher compensation. However, according to Baumann and Nier (2003) if the bank's risk choice is not observable by depositors or deposits are insured, the bank would choose higher risk at the expense of depositors.

3.11 Islamic Economics and Ethics

Ramadan (2009) discusses three fundamental propositions that the modalities of the reform process should be reconsidered by all Muslims based on the changing world as we know it today. He distinguishes between 'adaptation reform' and 'transformation reform'. His third proposition is that it is not sufficient to rely only on scriptural sources when examining the relationship between human knowledge and applied ethics. He suggests that text and context scholars must work together to achieve the higher objective in combining human knowledge and applied ethics.

Ramadan (2009) argues that there is no 'Islamic economy' and if we look into it differently, we find a set of principles for an ethical framework. These ethics are a general philosophy of the economy's aims, but there is nothing called an 'Islamic economy', it is just mere ethics that govern business transactions. However, the author completely dismisses a whole section in the Islamic classical books of jurisprudence (*fiqh*) called Islamic commercial law (*fiqh al-mu'amalaat*). This section outlines all Islamic contracts, agreements and principles that can be used in structuring financial and business activities. Ethics, as part of Shariah, articulate how business can be conducted in terms of manners when Muslims undertake different activities and interact with each other and with non-Muslims.

There is a clear difference between the principles and contracts such as *Ijara* (lease), *Musharakah* (partnership), which form part of the Islamic economics system and ethics, such as the seller is obliged to disclose all hidden defects in the commodity being sold, not to cheat and not to overstate the benefits of the product being sold. There are other elements, such as *Zakat* (the poor due), taxes, international business principles and the rules that govern the state financial system in deploying the state's income and taxes. All the above and more form the Islamic economy, the Islamic finance and banking system is part of this economy. The author correctly asserts that Muslims should reform the instruments of deducting the legal rulings to address contemporary issues as required. However, it could be argued that his dismissal of the fact that an 'Islamic economy' exists and it is just a mere series of ethics is not supported by Islamic Scriptures.

Tripp quoted the argument by Abd al-Rahman Yusri (Director of the Higher Institute of Islamic Economics in Egypt) who argues that an Islamic economy can be established by inculcating Islamic values into a successful programme of economic development. He cites the fundamental respect within Shariah for capital and its productive use in a market designated as free and competitive, but nevertheless under the moral guidance and supervision of the institution of the *hisbah*: 'all wealth belongs to God and must be spent on whatever can bring a profit for Islamic society'.

3.12 Legal Stratagems (*Hiyal*) in Islamic Commercial Law

Ismail (2010) discusses the issue of legal stratagems (*hiyal*) in Islamic jurisprudence broadly, and then focuses on the *hiyal* used, in an attempt, to legitimise some controversial financial transactions by avoiding the prohibition of usury in Islam. He focuses in his study on the Islamic finance industry and the leading role played by these stratagems in introducing some financial products as Shariah compliant. He argues that the subject of *hiyal* should be examined within its historic context to clarify the role of those *hiyal* as portrayed in the discourse of the classical Islamic jurists. His argument is based on the fact that *hiyal* are envisaged to be established upon a teleology which describes *hiyal* as a way of avoiding controversial matters (*makharij*).

As a follower of the Hanafi school of thought, Ismail (2010) uses this for his advantage in discussing the subject of *makharij* which are limited to the systematic reasoning of the Hanafi jurists, who set out the parameters of its use and its acceptance. He correctly, asserts that the use of *hiyal* has proven to have been mainly applied as an alternative to philanthropy. He draws a historical example from the Ottomans period where the extensive practice of usurious *hiyal* had negative socio-economic effects which are normally associated with interest-based economies.

Ismail (2010) dismisses the idea of an Islamic financial institution that operates with the objective of making profit and tries to compete in a conventional financial system. His work studies the theoretical account of the subject of *hiyal* from the classical point of view of the Islamic Commercial Law, without relating that to Islamic financial sector. It is clear that his religious background limits the scope of his study, he does not reflect on the other side of knowledge i.e. economics in terms of how we may relate this to address the current financial issues and practices.

Balala (2010) argues that as the interpretation of the Quran and *Sunnah* form a central role in Shariah. It is important to be undertaken in accordance with the spirit and principles of the primary sources of so as to uphold the requirements of contractual fairness and bring about social justice. The spirit of equity and justice, as a centrepiece of an Islamic society, necessitates that adherence to the substance of any undertaking to be in the forefront of any form it serves or mimics.

Ismail's (2010) inquiry argues to establish a framework for the *hiyal* as a jurisprudential instrument. It is a good attempt to explain the legitimate remit of using *hiyal*, in order to provide better understanding and prevent its misuse in the Islamic finance sector. The study aimed at answering the question of *hiyal* in the Hanafi school of thought from three perspectives the theory of usury, the concept of usury as a polemic and legal genre and lastly the *hiyal* as a historical practice. The study is rooted in the Islamic jurisprudence dealing with *al-Shaybani* contribution about *hiyal* who was one of the early Hanafi scholars.

The study does not examine the theology as a measure for the current practices of Islamic financial institutions in using *hiyal* to expand and offer more financial products that are compatible with its conventional counterpart. It is also important to highlight that the practical implication of the study would have been better if the study have provided a practical guide for the legitimate use of *hiyal* to address some pressing financial issues.

He concludes by stating that the usage of the *hiyal* was far more extensive during the era of Ottomans, and was even officially endorsed via a royal decree of the Sultan and the *fatawas* (Islamic legal opinions) of the leading Ottoman jurists at that time. This raises a question of 'what' and 'why' that happened, is it possible that the public interest from Islamic perspective at that time required these concessions, and under what circumstances and to what extent? The answer to these questions was clearly provided in the study.

3.13 The Role of Islamic Finance in Tackling Financial Exclusion

According to Sinclair (2001: 9) financial exclusion can be defined in either a narrow or a broad way. It has been defined, in a narrow sense, as exclusion from particular sources of credit and other financial services (including insurance, bill-payment services and appropriate deposit accounts). However, it relates, in broader sense, to elements that result in shutting out of the less well off from mainstream money services. Delving (2005: 30) asserts that financial exclusion is where a proportion of the population has a limited access to the mainstream financial services. It can be manifested in various shapes and forms by different groups.

Hersi (2009) discusses the subject of financial exclusion in the UK and the benefits have been introduced to the financially excluded Muslims by tackling this issue and paving the way for Islamic financial institutions to operate in the UK. According to him, the UK financial system does not cater to the financial needs of the British Muslims. This is because of the religious prohibition on dealing with any type of interest-based financial transactions and the restrictions on dealing with conventional banks.

Hersi (2009) examines the argument that the UK government has addressed the issue of financial exclusion in the UK by encouraging Islamic finance. Hence, this argument implies that the financially excluded Muslims in the UK will be encouraged and by large numbers to take up the Shariah compliant financial products offered by Islamic banks. However, his findings show that this has not been the case, as the actual demand for Shariah compliant financial products is currently not as expected.

There is almost an agreement among experts that financial exclusion is mainly associated with the issue of accessibility, which can be limited by affordability or self-exclusion due to negative perceptions about available services. There were hopes that the authorisation of Islamic banks will address this issue in relation to Muslims. However, it is argued that is not the case and Islamic banks are catering to professional segment of the British Muslims. Hersi (2009) attributes this as revealed in his analysis to many reasons such as lack of awareness of the Shariah compliant financial products, poor demand for such products in the market, lack of trust and scepticism about its compliance with Shariah, financial illiteracy and the affordability and accessibility of such products by the less affluent Muslims in the UK.

The above reasons might be factors that impacted the growth and demand for Islamic financial products. However, Hersi ignored the UK Muslims' religious attitudes towards the Shariah compliant financial products and what would be their main driver in making financial decisions. The UK Muslims' religious attitudes can be divided into three categories: the first is fully practicing Muslims who would take up Shariah compliant financial products only regardless of pricing or other financial aspects. The second category is, practicing Muslims but a bit more lenient, for them the Shariah compliant financial products would be their first choice, then, the conventional financial products with religious commitment to supporting the former. The third category is Muslims who are less practicing and more rate/pricing driven as a determinant element for any financial decision.

A question can be raised here whether Islamic banks are looking to cater for a niche market in order to cater for the demand of Muslims in addressing their financial needs or aim to obtain a share of the market by competing with conventional banks?

3.14 Conclusion

This Chapter attempted to cover key pertinent issues in the literature in relation to financial innovation and engineering in IFIs. The review is divided into different themes to identify theoretical and empirical work on this subject to point out weaknesses and strengths and identify key issues to be considered in the chapters that follow. The review has covered research in both English and Arabic languages. In conclusion, this review shows that the area of financial product development and financial innovation and engineering in Islamic finance and banking is under-researched and under-represented.

Exploring financial innovation and engineering within a religious framework and the role of Shariah in-depth is very important to address this gap in the literature. This is because articulating these Shariah fundamentals and principles in relation to what constitutes religious framework for financial innovation and product development in IFIs would provide a step forward for academic and practical research in that field. Furthermore, the conventional financial system would also benefit from the findings of this work in order to modify their financial innovation and engineering processes, in an ethical way for a more resilient and stable financial system.

We identified a gap in the literature that needs to be addressed adequately in order to close this gap, this book attempts to provide the first building block in addressing this gap. This Chapter has provided an analysis of key points related to innovation and existing debates in relation to Islamic finance, such as usury, corporate and Shariah governance and risks that are very important issues when studying financial innovation and engineering in IFIs. Addressing these issues in this Chapter would pave the way for the coming chapters and would equip the reader with a solid background when we dig deeper in this subject in the coming sections.

The following chapter (Chap. 4) provides an analysis of the history of financial innovation in Islamic finance from its inception as a concept over 1400 years ago in the seventh century up to the sixteenth century. It also studies the main influencing factors and elements that played a critical role in the development of financial innovation and financial products or decline.

Chapter 4
A Historical Analysis of Financial Innovation in Islamic Economics and Finance from Inception to the Sixteenth Century

4.1 Introduction

The previous chapter (Chap. 3) provided an analysis of key points related to innovation and existing debates in relation to Islamic finance. Addressing these issues in Chap. 3 would help the reader in understanding the more indepth discussion in this Chapter and the chapters that follow.

There has been a lack of research into the history and development of innovation in Islamic finance. This is due to the relative deficit of documents and sources that describe the financial activities and instruments used in the early stages and how they evolved during different periods of its history (see e.g. Al Omar 2003; Lewis 1970; Hitti 1963). Historical perspectives of Islamic finance are particularly important in comprehending the new development and concepts that have emerged in recent decades in order to establish the credibility and originality of Islamic finance.

This is carried out with a view to explore Islamic Finance as a potential ethical alternative to traditional financial methods. Most of the current studies, particularly, in the last two decades looked at the subject of Islamic finance from the point of view of the emergence of Islamic banking and the provision of Shariah compliant financial products, which goes back to the 1960s. Such academic research viewed the emergence of Islamic banking in isolation of its historical context which goes back to the birth of Islam as a religion.

This chapter (and the chapter that follows) provides an analysis of the history of financial innovation in Islamic finance from its inception as a concept over 1400 years ago. It then studies the main influencing factors and elements that played a critical role in its development until the modern day. Thus, it is very important, as this chapter concludes, to study Islamic finance in its historical context in order to have a correct understanding and appreciation of its history and the different development phases that it has gone through. Islamic finance as a concept and practice has existed for over 1400 years, however, it has only begun to offer financial products via a banking system, such as savings and investment

S. Alamad, *Financial Innovation and Engineering in Islamic Finance*,
Contributions to Management Science, DOI 10.1007/978-3-319-52947-9_4

accounts, home and commercial finance products, in the last half of the twentieth century.

The importance of studying the history and development of Islamic economics and finance is due to the significant role played by the economic system in building and developing society. It is also vital to explore the main elements that have contributed to the development of Islamic economics and the different phases it has gone through. Therefore, the study of Islamic economics and finance would provide an economic framework from which ethical principles and foundations for establishing a comprehensive Islamic economic and financial system flow.

Thus, one of the most important concepts that this chapter endeavours to demonstrate is that, the principles and foundations of Islamic economics and finance, which were practised through its various historical phases, could provide the basis for a comprehensive economic and financial system which is compatible with modern life.

4.2 Phases of the History of Islamic Finance and Its Innovation

The history of innovation in Islamic finance is discussed in the sections below and is divided into eight phases. This Chapter discusses the phases of innovation in Islamic finance up to the sixteenth century; the other phases (Phase 5 onwards) from the sixteenth century to modern days are covered in the chapter that follows (Chap. 5). Each phase covers a critical period of the history of Islamic finance and its financial innovation in the context of economic, social, political, regional and global influencing factors.

4.2.1 Phase 1: Formation (622–661)

Some of the Islamic finance principles, as known today, existed in the pre-Islamic era in the Arabian Peninsula and practiced by the Arabs. Prophet Muhammad himself traded according to these principles before Islam. Ibn al Atheer and Ibn Hishaam narrated that Khadija, the first wife of prophet Muhammad, used to hire men to travel with her goods and merchandise to Syria to trade there. The contract between them used to be a profit sharing agreement. When she heard about the good characteristics and honesty of Muhammad Ibn Abdullah, she hired him to trade with her goods for a share of the profit (the agreement was based on the Islamic finance principle of *Mudaraba*). His honesty and honourable dealings when trading with her goods, was the reason for her to ask him for marriage (al Bouti 1991: 80).

Fifteen years later, Muhammad (pbuh) received his first revelation to call people to Islam and worship the One and only God. After 13 years of struggle in Makkah,

Muhammad (pbuh) received another revelation instruction to migrate to Madinah where the dawn of the Islamic state started (Al Omar 2003: 100). During that time, usury (interest), which was widely spread in Arabia, was addressed in the Qur'an as an unethical financial practice and as a result was forbidden with very strong wording. The Qur'an says 'Those who swallow usury cannot arise except as one whom Satan has prostrated by (his) touch does arise. That is because they say trading is only like usury; and God has allowed trading and forbidden usury', (Qur'an 2: 275).

Also, 'O you who believe! Be careful of (your duty to) God and relinquish what remains (due) from usury, if you are believers. But if you do (it) not, then be apprised of war from God and His Apostle; and if you repent, then you shall have your capital; neither shall you make (the debtor) suffer loss, nor shall you be made to suffer loss' (Qur'an 2: 278–279). Therefore, the price of capital, in Islam, is not the rate of interest; it is the rate of return generated from the capital as mainly a profit.

The question of interest on theoretical grounds is not a recent concern. Plato considered it as a means whereby the rich could exploit the poor, and Aristotle believed that money was to be 'used in exchange and not to increase at interest'. Prohibitions on usury is manifested clearly in both the *Old Testament* (including Exodus 22:25, Deuteronomy 23:19 and Nehemiah 5:7) and the *New Testament* (Matthew 25:26–27 and Luke 19:23). Many Jews, however, have interpreted the prohibitions as applying only to loans made between Jew and Jew, not between Jew and Gentile (El Diwany 2010a: 25).

The Church's representatives stood firm on the issue of usury. For many centuries a consensus ruled against the practice of usury. Nonetheless, some time before 1220, the canonist Hispanus identified a charge that would be paid by a borrower who did not repay his usury-free loan on time (Noonan 1957: 14–56). This charge was to compensate the lender for the loss of use of his money in between the initial repayment time and the time the loan is actually repaid. It would be called 'interesse', derived from the Latin for 'in between', and was to give rise of the modern term 'interest' as we know it today (Noonan 1957: 14–56).

The main focus of Muhammad (pbuh), and the first caliph his companion Abu Bakr al Siddiq after him, was to establish the social justice and growth of the public resources of the emerging Islamic state on interest-free foundations (Al Omar 2003: 100). The social justice in the Islamic society is backed by religious obligations and Islamic teachings rather than a legal system. Muslims at that time were busy waging wars and fighting battles for the survival of their young state. Therefore, the focus was on the importance of public money, rather than the management of the financial system which started to take its shape during that period (Al Omar 2003: 100). The modern concept of social justice emerged in the West out of the early industrialisation movement in France and Britain in the 1840s. Then, social justice became the rallying cry of social democratic parties everywhere in Europe and backed by the legal system as it has developed (Barry 2005: 5).

During his life, Muhammad (pbuh) was the point of reference to his followers in any financial matters or activities that they faced at that time. He established the foundations for an Islamic economic and financial system and its instruments to address any finance related matters, or otherwise, after his life.

One of the main landmarks established by Muhammad in the new Islamic state is when he planted the seeds of social solidarity in society by establishing the brotherhood concept between the people of Madinah (the original inhabitants of Madinah) and the people of Makkah (the emigrant Muslims, *Muhajireen*) who migrated and left everything behind escaping with their belief from torture (al Bouti 1991: 150–180). The people of Makkah easily assimilated into the new society that became one society working towards one goal. The concept of social solidarity then developed to include even non-Muslims who lived under the umbrella of the Islamic state.

As a result, new financial relationships were created between the people of Makkah and the people of Madinah. Partnerships in businesses, profit sharing agreements and farming contracts. This brotherhood initiative was with the aim to help the people of Makkah settle down in the new society and start their new life. Muhammad did not rely on the social solidarity as the only source of economic and financial stability to meet their financial needs; he also focused on other factors such as labour and production.

The first caliph Abu Bakr al Siddiq focused on preserving and growing the state funding by collecting *zakat* (obligatory alums giving). He also fought the war of *riddah* (apostasy) against tribes who refused to pay *zakat* to the state. He ruled for two and a half years, he then appointed Umar Ibn al Khattab as the second caliph before he died. During his rule, Abu Bakr signed many strategic treaties with tribes in northern Arabia, and hence maintained unity, peace and order in the Islamic state (El Diwany 2010: 4).

During the time of Umar Ibn Al Khattab, the second caliph, the Islamic state expanded as Muslims conquered Iraq, Syria and Egypt and applied fare taxes, which was less than what they used to pay their rulers before the conquest of Muslims, on lands and its resources as a state's revenue (Al Doori 1982: 18). Although, those lands were owned by the state, its return was distributed to the people and from that dual ownership (public and private ownership of resources) concept was established. Trade also flourished with non-Muslim states on the basis of Islamic finance principles (Katibi 1994: 110). This required the development of a comprehensive tax system due to the new finance and trade structures, where a financial management of the generated wealth from trades to the state was required. Therefore, a state treasury (called *bait al maal*) for the management of public money was established, and a record keeping of all financial affairs in relation to its utilisation and distribution was maintained (Katibi 1994: 110).

During the time of the third and fourth caliphs Uthman Ibn ‘Affan and Ali Ibn Abi Talib, they maintained and built on the economic and financial system they inherited. They favoured the public financial interests over private interests; they also developed the financial system with future generations in mind and society as a whole (Al Sawwaf 1989: 249–290). More attention was given to poor people and their financial needs. These caliphs also paved the way for open commercial trade with other nations and developed financial methods and instruments that other nations were more familiar with. They also established the public finances department in the Islamic state's treasury to manage the state's financial matters (Al Sawwaf 1989: 249–290).

The Islamic economy, in this phase, moved from an economic system that relied on livestock to an agricultural system after gaining many lands as a result of conquest of new regions. The income of the Islamic state also shifted from relying on charity collections and spoils of wars, to generating this income from collecting different types of tax and trade (Al Omar 2003: 98). The growth of the economy of the conquered countries in North Africa and Spain (*Andalus*) also contributed to the development of the overall economy of the Islamic state. During this period, laws and rules governing the tax system and the treasury (*bait al maal*) and record keeping of all financial affairs of the state and public ownership were established (Al Doori 1982: 28).

During this phase most of the Islamic financial principles were established, those principles were mainly captured in the Prophetic Sayings, some of which are summarised below.

4.2.1.1 Currency Exchange

Abu Al-Minhal narrated, I used to practice money exchange, and I asked Zaid bin 'Arqam about it, and he narrated what the Prophet said in the following: Abu Al-Minhal said, 'I asked Al-Bara' bin 'Azib and Zaid bin Arqam about practicing money exchange. They replied, 'We were traders in the time of Allah's Apostle and I asked Allah's Apostle about money exchange'. He replied, 'If it is from hand to hand, there is no harm in it; otherwise it is not permissible', (Al-Bukhari 1985, Volume 3, Book 34, Number 276). Abu Al-Minhal narrated that: I asked Al-Bara' bin 'Azib and Zaid bin Arqam about money exchanges. Each of them said, 'This is better than I,' and both of them said, 'Allah's Apostle forbade the selling of silver for gold on credit', (Al-Bukhari 1985, Volume 3, Book 34, Number 387).

4.2.1.2 Credit Sale and Mortgage

'Aisha narrated that: The Prophet purchased food grains from a Jew on credit and mortgaged his iron armour to him, (Al-Bukhari 1985, Volume 3, Book 34, Number 282). Hakim bin Hizam narrated that: Allah's Apostle said, 'The seller and the buyer have the right to keep or return goods as long as they have not parted or till they part; and if both the parties spoke the truth and described the defects and qualities (of the goods), then they would be blessed in their transaction, and if they told lies or hid something, then the blessings of their transaction would be lost', (Al-Bukhari 1985, Volume 3, Book 34, Number 293).

4.2.1.3 *Murabaha* Sale

Tawus narrated that: Ibn ‘Abbas said, ‘Allah’s Apostle forbade the selling of foodstuff before its measuring and transferring into one’s possession.’ I asked Ibn ‘Abbas, ‘How is that?’ Ibn ‘Abbas replied, ‘It will be just like selling money for money, as the foodstuff has not been handed over to the first purchaser who is the present seller’, (Al-Bukhari 1985, Volume 3, Book 34, Number 342).

4.2.1.4 Forward Sale (*as-salam* Contract, Sales in Which a Price Is Paid for Goods to be Delivered Later)

Ibn ‘Abbas narrated that: The Prophet came to Medina and the people used to pay in advance the price of dates to be delivered within 2 or 3 years. He said (to them), ‘Whoever pays in advance the price of a thing to be delivered later should pay it for a specified measure at specified weight for a specified period’, (Al-Bukhari 1985, Volume 3, Book 35, Number 443).

4.2.1.5 Transference of a Debt from One Person to Another (*Al-Hawaala*)

Abu Huraira narrated that: The Prophet said, ‘Procrastination (delay) in paying debts by a wealthy man is injustice. So, if your debt is transferred from your debtor to a rich debtor, you should agree’, (Al-Bukhari 1985, Volume 3, Book 37, Number 486).

4.2.1.6 Representation, Authorisation and Business by a Proxy Via Agency (*Wakala*)

Ali narrated that: Allah’s Apostle ordered me to distribute the saddles and skins of the *budn* (camels) which had been slaughtered, (Al-Bukhari 1985, Volume 3, Book 38, Number 496). Abu Musa narrated that: The Prophet said, ‘An honest treasurer who gives what he is ordered to give fully, perfectly and willingly to the person to whom he is ordered to give, is regarded as one of the two charitable persons’, (Al-Bukhari 1985, Volume 3, Book 38, Number 512).

4.2.1.7 Partnership

Jabir bin ‘Abdullah narrated that: The Prophet established the right of *Shu’fa* (i.e. Pre-emption) in joint properties; but when the land is divided and the ways are demarcated, then there is no pre-emption, (Al-Bukhari 1985, Volume 3, Book 44, Number 675). Anas narrated that Abu Bakr As-Siddiq wrote to him the law of

Zakat which was made obligatory by Allah's Apostle. He wrote: 'Partners possessing joint property (sheep) have to pay its Zakat equally', (Al-Bukhari 1985, Volume 3, Book 44, Number 667).

Those financial principles were practiced in their simple forms as we would expect in that era and its lifestyle regarding financial transactions. Other contracts that we discussed during this period were also established such as profit sharing and lease of services. The use of the above financial principles and contracts has evolved and expanded in the phases that followed.

4.2.2 Phase 2: Growth and Stability (Seventh–Tenth Century)

This period was a time of political stability (the Islamic state had established itself as a very powerful state among other nations at that time and the ruling system was very stable) and economic growth. It covers the Omayyad era and the first Abbasid era and the beginning of the second Abbasid era until the rule of the Abbasid caliph Almuttaqi Billah.

The Islamic economic and finance system was largely dependent on agriculture and its produce during this phase. The private ownership of the conquered farming lands was a clear landmark during the Omayyad era. Muslims kept people of the lands and gave them the same status they held before the conquest in order to maintain and grow the lands for an agreed share of the production (Al Omar 2003: 104). The methodology followed by the Islamic state, at that time, was to make political treaties with other nations when possible to avoid a war if a nation showed hostility towards the Islamic state.

This approach enhanced the continued economic growth. The Omayyads also maintained the *al kharaj*[1] (land tax) system that was established by Umar Ibn Al Khattab with some amendments that were required due to changes in the circumstances and time, such as allowing the collection of *al kharaj* in the form of money rather than a proportion of the same production of the lands. They also standardised the system of *al kharaj* in all cities of the Islamic state (Al Omar 2003: 104).

The Abbasids however, realised the necessity to review the system of calculating *al kharaj* to be based on the amount of production instead of the size of land. This is due to the important role of *al kharaj* as an income to the state and *bait al maal* (Katibi 1994: 197). The Abbasid caliph Haroon al Rasheed (170–193H, 786–808 CE) asked the judge Abu Yousuf (a *Hanafi* jurist and judge) to write a book to address the issues of the state finances and the issue of *al kharaj*. Abu Yousuf in his

[1]***Kharàj***: land tax. *Kharàj* tax was introduced by Caliph Umar to replace the system of distributing conquered land among Muslim warriors, and became the first tax to be introduced to the Islamic tax system outside those stipulated in the Qur'an and the Sunnah. The tax was imposed on land, not individuals, with the tax base being the cultivable land and a proportional tax rate.

book supported the approach of taking a share of the production of the land in either form money or crops, as he deemed this better for the volatility in the market prices (Abu Yousuf 1985: 49–50).

A big role was played, in this phase, by natural disasters, such as the Plague of Basra in 684 CE which killed a large number of people and farmers. Such disasters affected economic growth and political instability on labour which became a dear need. The need to ensure security and safety in the state required the establishment of a police force that was formed from non-local foreign people who were brought from other states (Shalaq 1997: 270). A big number of those foreigners were Turkish slaves who assumed security jobs during the eighth to the tenth centuries. Growth in agriculture pushed the rulers to import labour force from Africa. Nevertheless, there was not a huge dependence on slaves in the agricultural sector as it was still managed by local farmers (Shalaq 1997: 270).

One of the main features in this phase is growth in the export of local goods and the wide expansion of commercial dealings and trades with other nations that was based on different Islamic finance principles. This generated a huge wealth and prosperity to the Islamic state with the exception of very short periods of political instability (Al Omar 2003: 105).

In Central Asia, the expansion of Islam from the seventh century onward brought a stop to Chinese expansion towards the West following the Battle of Talas in 751. Further expansion of the Muslim Turks in Central Asia from the tenth century brought an end to disrupting trade in that part of the world. For much of the Middle Ages, Islamic Caliphate (in the Near East) often had a monopoly over much of the trade conducted across the Old World including the Silk Road routes as shown in Fig. 4.1 below (Bentley 1993: 32).

This map shows the Silk Road routes and other trade routes used at that time (Katibi 1994).

During this phase Muslims were able to conquer and take control of many strategically important trade routes as shown in Fig. 4.1 above. They fully conquered North Africa after they built a huge fleet of ships that successfully pushed the Byzantines out of the Mediterranean Sea (Katibi 1994: 192). They kept control of the Mediterranean Sea for many centuries and their ships dominated the sea trade routes and transport until the twelfth century. They also started to expand their trade with China since the middle of the ninth century (Shalaq 1997: 270).

This expansion in trade and the use of different financial transactions played a big role in the development of Islamic finance and its instruments such as *Istisna'*[2] and *Suftajah*[3]

[2]***Istisna'***: an order to manufacture. A purchase order contract of assets whereby a buyer places an order to purchase an asset that will be manufactured and delivered in the future. In other words a buyer will require a seller or a contractor to deliver or construct the asset that will be completed in the future according to the specifications given in the sale and purchase contract. Both parties to the contract will decide on the sale and purchase prices as they wish and the settlement can be delayed or arranged based on the schedule of the work completed.

[3]***Suftajah***: money order. A credit instrument issued to a creditor to enable him to use it or cash it at another predetermined venue and at the future date. Also, *suftaja* were issued "payable to bearer".

Fig. 4.1 Islamic finance main trade routes during Phase 2

instead of *Sukuk*[4] and money transfer (Al Doori 1995: 70). '*Istisna, as an Islamic finance principle, was innovated by the Hanafi School of jurisprudence*' (this quote is from an interview with a prominent Shariah scholar). However, the other three schools of jurisprudence, Shaf'i, Maliki and Hanbali and Imam Zufar from the Hanafi school, did not share the same view regarding the *Istisna'* contract. They see *Istisna'* as a debt for debt contract and a sale of the non-existent, which is not acceptable in Shariah, unless the *Istisna'* price is paid in advance.

4.2.3 Phase 3: Decline (Tenth–Thirteenth Century)

This phase started when the Abbasid Al Muttaqi Billah became caliph during which the *khilafa* weakened and lost control over many of its territories and regions. This is because, he was perceived as a weak ruler, in addition to on-going external and internal conflicts. Rulers of the Islamic state also moved away from their main role of protecting the interests of their people and the state into focusing on their private interests and how they can utilise their position to serve themselves (Al Qalqashandi 1963: 3/268). This decline was manifested in the division of the Islamic Empire into three states, the Abbasid *khilafa* in Baghdad, the state of Bani Omayyah (the Omayyad) in the West in Andalus (Spain) and the state of Al 'Abediyyen and the Fatimite in Africa in the tenth century (Ibn Khaldoun n.d: 2/752).

During this period the Islamic state was torn into small independent states, involved in many battles and the state's expenses increased substantially while the income decreased due to the political instability (Al Dhabi 1996: 1/425).

This instability in the fractioned Islamic state resulted in a decline in the economy and financial activities and trade in the Islamic state. Public money and the state revenue were mixed with the private money of the rulers who were corrupt. This is because; they were appointed only because they were related to the caliph rather than being qualified, strong, religious and honest rulers (Shalaq 1997: 277). Hence, the financial system and financial accounting of the Islamic state did not develop during this phase in comparison with Phase 2.

4.2.4 Phase 4: Partial Growth (Thirteenth–Sixteenth Century)

The Islamic state, in this phase, started to revive in some aspects and decline in others. This revival began in Greater Syria (*Bilad al Shaam*) from 1168 when

[4]**Sukùk:** (singular **sakk**): deposit certificate. A document or certificate, which evidences the undivided pro-rata ownership of underlying assets—the Sakk (singular of Sukuk) is freely tradable at par, premium or discount.

Salaah El-Deen Al Ayyoubi conquered Egypt. This lasted until the fall of the Ayyoubian state after the death of Salaah El-Deen in the thirteenth century due to the conflict with the Seljuq Turks.[5] This was the beginning of the Seljuq Turk's state in Syria and Egypt in 1250. During this phase, the Crusaders fleet of ships dominated the sea and all its trade and transport. The Tatar invasion also made the situation worse for the growth of the Islamic state and affected economic and financial development (Al Omar 2003: 110). This was concluded by the fall of Baghdad, the capital of the caliphate, which was destroyed by the Mongols (1220–1500), and the Euphrates, as historians tell us, were swamped with corpses. Even the lives of the Abbasid caliph and his delegates who hurried to receive the Mongol Chieftain Hulagu to surrender were not spared (Al Doori 1981: 103).

Trade and finance, on the other hand, flourished in Syria and Egypt during this time under the Mamlouk rule. This was due to the relative political and economic stability during which trade increased with the Italian cities, this period of economic growth lasted until 1382 (Al Doori 1981: 103). Trade finance practised at that time was somehow similar in concept to what Islamic banking does currently except, it was more aligned with Shariah because it was practised as a joint venture between skilled merchants, suppliers and investors rather than being based on debt (*Murabaha* (credit sale), an Islamic finance principle) as is widely practised currently by Islamic banks.

By the end of the thirteenth and the beginning of the fourteenth centuries, those who fought the Islamic world now assimilated into it. The four Mongol empires had converted to Islam and had become staunch Muslim supporters in the central Islamic land. These were the Il-Khans in the Tigris-Euphrates valley and the mountainous regions of Iran, the Chaghaytay in Syr-Oxus basin, the White Horde in the Irtysh region, and the Golden Horde around the river Volga (El-Ashker and Wilson 2006: 285). From these four, two powerful Islamic empires emerged: the Shi'ah Safawid[6] Empire, which became the foundation of what Iran is today, and

[5]The Seljuqs originated from the *Qynyk* branch of Oghuz Turks who in the ninth century lived on the periphery of the Muslim world, north of the Caspian and Aral seas in their Yabghu Khaganate of the Oghuz confederacy, in the Kazakh Steppe of Turkestan. In 985, the Seljuq clan split off from the bulk of the Tokuz-Oghuz. They set up camp on the west bank of the lower Syr Darya (Jaxartes), where they converted to Islam.

Later, in the tenth century the Seljuqs migrated from their ancestral homelands into mainland Persia, in the province of Khurasan, where they encountered the Ghaznavid Empire. Following the defeat of the Ghazavids to the Seljuq Turks at the battle of Nasa plains in 1035; Toghril, Chaghri and Yabghu received the insignias of governor, grants of land and were given the title of dehgan. At the battle of Dandanaqan they defeated a Ghaznavid army and following Tughrul's successful siege of Isfahan in 1050–1051, led to the establishment of an empire which would later be called the Great Seljuk Empire.

The Seljuqs mixed with the local population and adopted the Persian culture and language in the following decades. See: M. Ravandi, (2005), "*The Seljuq court at Konya and the Persianisation of Anatolian Cities*", in Mesogeios (Mediterranean Studies), vol. 25–26 (2005), pp. 157–169.

[6]The Safawid dynasty was one of the most significant ruling dynasties of Iran, and is often considered the beginning of modern Persian history. They ruled one of the greatest Persian empires after the Muslim conquest of Persia and established the 12 Schools of Shi'ah Islam as the official

the Sunni Moghul, or Mongol Empire in the Indian subcontinent which constitutes the present Pakistan and some parts of India. Moreover, to the west of the Mongols, came another, and long lasting, source of support to Islam, the Ottoman Turks[7] (El-Ashker and Wilson 2006: 285).

These three empires dominated the political scene in the Islamic world as depicted in Fig. 4.2 below: the Ottoman, the Safawid and the Mongol. Each had different socio-economic conditions, features of intellectual development and influence over the development of Islamic economics and finance (El-Ashker and Wilson 2006: 285).

Many political and economic aspects shaped this phase, such as wars (that exhausted the treasury of the Islamic state and imposed more taxes on people to finance those wars) among the Islamic states themselves. This was in order to acquire a bigger piece of the Islamic state territories for themselves and be more powerful, the Tatar and Mogul invasion, the Crusade wars and natural disasters that affected mainly Western Europe and the trade with the East (Issawi 1991: 45). Also influential was the discovery of new sea trade routes that changed trade and shifted the balance of power and the revenue generated from the use of the old routes controlled by the Islamic state. From the start of the eleventh century, the European ships dominated the Mediterranean Sea and its trade until the eighteenth century (Issawi 1991: 45).

The underdevelopment of the concept of institutions, which means here a system of socially produced regularities, impacted negatively on the financial development and innovation during this period as it limited the mobilisation and deployment of capital (Kuran 2011: 14). During these same centuries, however, there were significant changes in the West regarding the concept of institutions, corporate structures, society and governing laws that fostered innovation in finance.

---

religion of their empire, marking one of the most important turning points in Muslim history. The Safawid ruled from 1501 to 1722 (experiencing a brief restoration from 1729 to 1736) and at their height, they controlled all of modern Iran, Azerbaijan and Armenia, most of Iraq, Georgia, Afghanistan, and the Caucasus, as well as parts of Pakistan, Tajikistan, Turkmenistan and Turkey. Safawid Iran was one of the Islamic "gunpowder empires", along with its neighbours, the Ottoman and Mughal empires. See: Helen Chapin Metz, (1989), *Iran, a Country study*, University of Michigan, p. 313; Emory C. Bogle, (1989), *Islam: Origin and Belief*. University of Texas Press. 1989, p. 145; and, Stanford Jay Shaw. History of the Ottoman Empire. Cambridge University Press. 1977, p. 77.

[7]The Ottoman Turks (or Osmani Turks) were the Turkish-speaking population of the Ottoman Empire who formed the base of the state's military and ruling classes. Reliable information about the early history of Ottoman Turks is scarce, but they take their Turkish name, *Osman* (corrupted in some European languages as "Ottoman"), from the house of Osman I (reigned ca. 1299–1326), the founder of the dynasty that ruled the Ottoman Empire for 620 years. After the expansion from its home in Bithynia, the Ottoman principality began incorporating other Turkish-speaking Muslims and non-Turkish Christians, becoming the Ottoman Turks and ultimately the Turks of the present. The Ottoman Turks blocked all land routes to Europe by conquering the city of Constantinople, the capital city of the Byzantine Empire, and Europeans had to find other ways to trade with Eastern countries.

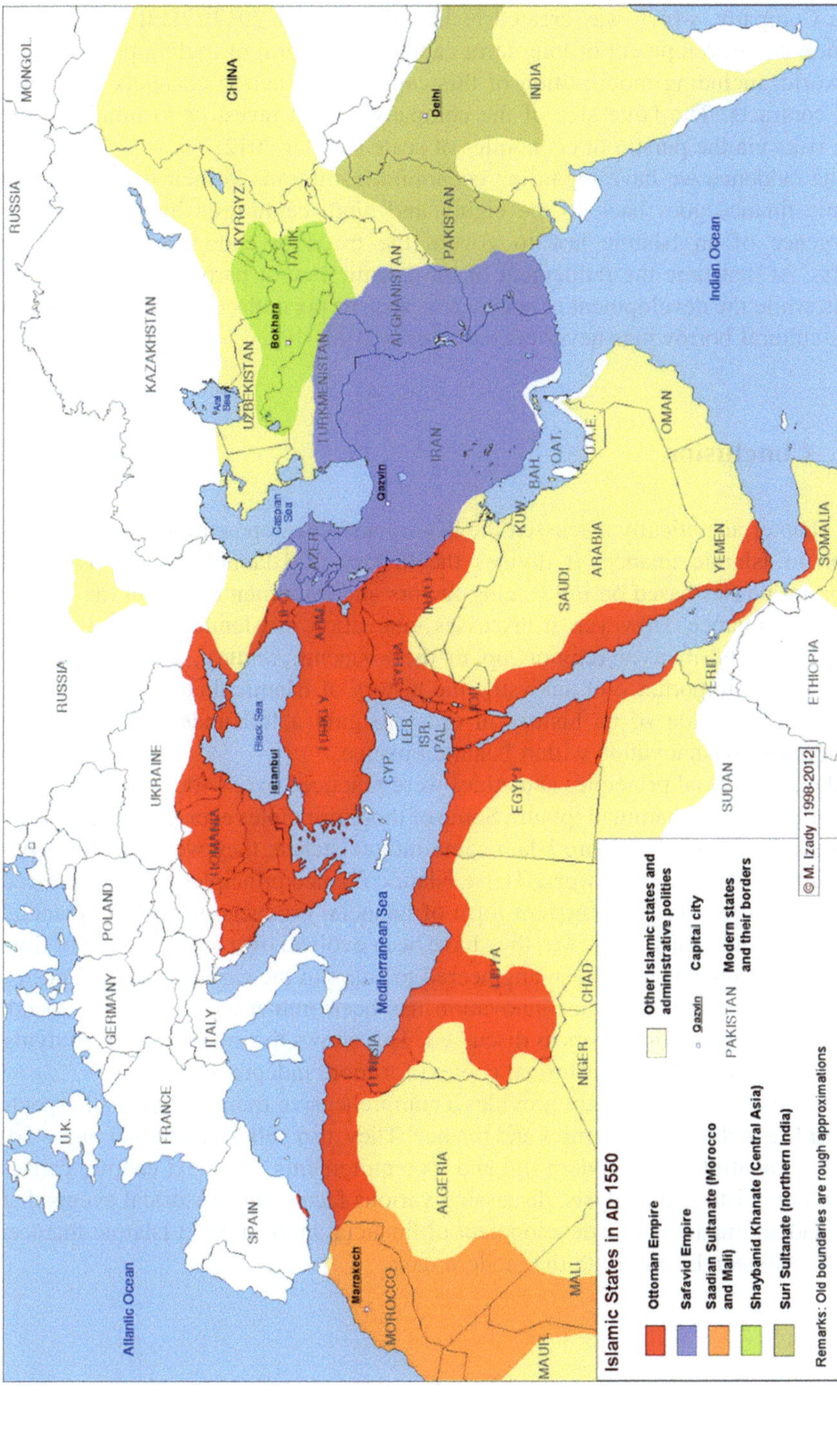

Fig. 4.2 Political aspects that influenced the development of Islamic finance (Katibi 1994)

In 1602, the invention of multinational corporation emerged with the Dutch East India Company, which was created in Holland (Shiller 2012: 7). It allowed the creation and development of long-term capital in the form of trading posts around the world, including mobilisation of this capital, distribution channels and long-term contracts. The large size of the company helped investors to minimise the huge risks via the pursuit of economies of scale (Shiller 2012: 7).

The evidence we have regarding economic institutions in their early forms in Islamic finance goes back to the eighth and ninth centuries which marked the emergence of an Islamic law to govern the trusts or endowment (known as waqfs). At that time the refinement of the Islamic law of partnerships also came about, while the development of some areas such as tax collection, innovations and cross-cultural borrowings never ceased (Kuran 2011: 10).

4.3 Conclusion

This chapter analytically discussed the history and development of financial innovation in Islamic finance. It divides the history of Islamic finance into eight important phases based on influencing factors and important events in the history of Islamic finance. However, it discusses innovation in Islamic finance from the inception of Islam as a religion up to the sixteenth century, Phase 4. It also discussed the importance of analysing the history of Islamic finance in its context and an examination of its history in order to gain a full understanding of the development of innovation within Islamic Finance.

Islamic financial principles and ethics were practiced over 1400 years ago at the time of Prophet Muhammad (pbuh). Some of those principles even existed and were practiced by the Arabs before Islam came into existence; they were then incorporated into an Islamic framework. Those Islamic finance principles were introduced as a new innovation in its modern form of financial products offered by financial institutions and banks. However, they have been evolved over a long period of time and new instruments have been engineered to adapt to the various financial needs. The development of financial innovation has been influenced by various social, political and economic factors as discussed. This shows the importance of studying Islamic finance within its historical context for more indepth insights.

Muslims believe that Islam provides a comprehensive framework for all aspects of their life including economics and finance. They also believe that this framework is also compatible with modern life and its requirements. The next chapter carries on with the historical analysis, discussing various factors and historical events that have had an impact on the development of financial innovation in Islamic finance, from the sixteenth century to the modern days.

Chapter 5
A Historical Analysis of Financial Innovation in Islamic Economics and Finance from the Sixteenth Century to Present

5.1 Introduction

The previous chapter discussed the phases of innovation in Islamic finance up to the sixteenth century; highlighting key issues and influencing historical, political and economic events during that time. The other phases of the historical analysis of financial innovation in Islamic finance (phase 5 onwards) from the sixteenth century to the present days are covered in this chapter. Each phase covers a critical period of the history of Islamic finance and its financial innovation in the context of economic, social, political, regional and global influencing factors.

This chapter starts with phase 5 that covers an important phase of innovation in Islamic finance as it reflects an era of stability and prosperity in the historical context of Islamic finance. This scene changes then in phase 6 due to important historical events and takes another turn in phase 7. These phases are discussed below.

5.2 Phase Five: Youthfulness (Sixteenth to Nineteenth Century)

As we have seen in the previous chapter, financial innovation in Islamic finance encountered various positive and negative historical events that have influenced its development up to the sixteenth century. This phase marks the beginning of the Ottoman Empire until the rule of Muhammad Al Qanouni The First (926–974 H, 1519–1566 C.E). The Ottoman state faced various political and economic changes that needed to be dealt with during the last quarter of the sixteenth century, such as the war with Safawid in Iran (1578–1639), the Jilali Revolution (1603–1610) in Anatolia and the revolution of Balkan states against the Ottomans (Haleem 1988: 141).

S. Alamad, *Financial Innovation and Engineering in Islamic Finance*,
Contributions to Management Science, DOI 10.1007/978-3-319-52947-9_5

This is in addition to, the need to strengthen their fleet of ships and cover the expenses of wars. The biggest economic challenge they faced was a weak financial system that was neglected and underdeveloped during that period and almost in deficit, because of the misuse of public funds and various wars. Furthermore, the low value of their undervalued currency which was made from silver made things worse (Haleem 1988: 141).

The Ottoman Turks grew in power in Anatolia and developed into a force that shaped the Islamic world for centuries to come. Established in 1299 by its founder Uthman, who reigned from 1299 to 1326, the Ottoman Turkish state, which began as a principality of march-warriors, was one of several states that appeared in Anatolia after the break-up of the Seljuq Sultanate. It lasted until 1922. Their predecessors the Seljuq Turks, are said to be devoted Muslims who had never been conquered by Muslims but by Islam itself (Lewis 1979). With regards to the Ottoman's financial policies, there was a noticeable increase in the national debt of the state from the nineteenth century onwards due to costs of wars and internal conflicts. This led to the Western intervention, which led eventually to colonisation, in order to protect the interest of the creditors, as happened in Egypt, Tunisia and Morocco (Issawi 1982: 62).

The Silk Road ceased serving as a shipping route for silk around 1453 with the Ottoman supremacy at Constantinople. Ottoman rulers at that time did not have good relations with Western countries because of the crusades, and were unhappy about the loss of Andalusia in the West. Thus, they expressed their displeasure by embargoing trade with the West. Things had eased a little around a century later, and Venice was able to cut an uneasy deal with the Ottomans, regaining for a time some of their economic clout as middlemen (Arbrey et al. 2008: 257).

The Ottoman state took a loan for the first time in 1894 from some European countries, mainly Britain, to fund the war of Al Qiram against the Armenian revolt backed by Russia, a financial necessity due to the weak financial policy of the state during the previous two centuries. Prior to this, the Ottoman state used to borrow from local banks or raising money by issuing financial papers or sukuk (Haleem 1988: 218–219). During the beginning of the nineteenth century, the state started a privatisation of land owned by the state; this enhanced the production of cotton, textile manufacturing and its export. Trade also increased with other nations, in particular during the time of Ayyoubi state in Syria and Egypt, moreover, trade with Europe also increased substantially during this period via Egyptian seaports ('Aashour n.d.: 141–143).

We could hardly witness any particular socio-economic work or cultural activity comparable to that of Muslim thinkers in the few preceding centuries. The work of Ibn Khaldun, (1332–1404) and to a far lesser degree that of al Maqrizi after him (1364–1441), seemed to have stamped a seal on the last of the great socio-economic works of Muslim thinkers (Hitti 1963). The Ottoman Empire, it seems, had left very little legacy of a specifically socio-economic nature. This is not to say that there were not notable achievements by the writers of the period, but these mainly involved bibliographical works, biographies, compilation and commentary works (Hitti 1963).

The Ottoman Islamic state focused during this phase on the development of the finance and manufacturing industries such as textiles, cotton and some equipment in some countries in particular, Turkey, Syria and Egypt. As a result of this policy, Bank of Egypt was established in 1920 by Tala'at Pasha Harb, the National Bank of Egypt, at that time, was British-owned, and all the other banks in Egypt were owned fully by foreigners (Issawi 1982: 20). Harb established Bank of Egypt and its companies on the basis that all its dealings were in Arabic, only Egyptians operated the bank, and the bank restricted share ownership to Egyptian citizens. Bank Iesh[1] in Turkey was established in 1924 as well. The objective of establishing both banks was to manage economic activities such as Treasury operations, money and credit transactions and trade in gold and foreign currencies (Issawi 1982: 20).

The first central bank to be established in the West was the Bank of England, founded by William Paterson in 1694. The idea of becoming a systemic regulator, that would keep financial crises under control, was not considered when the bank was founded (Shiller 2012: 7). Its role as the lender of last resort was invented and developed over the following centuries as it encountered repeated crises.

The concept of the large national corporation was enhanced by the invention of the New York State corporate law of 1811 which set the right of anyone to set up a company and the limited liability structure (Shiller 2012: 8). Therefore, it is argued

[1]The study did not find any information about Bank Iesh, which implies that the bank did not survive. In the Ottoman Empire, economic activities such as Treasury operations, money and credit transactions and trade in gold and foreign currencies were executed by various establishments such as the Treasury, the Mint, jewellers, moneylenders, foundations and guilds. In this organizational structure that prevailed until the second half of 19th century, the Ottoman Empire minted gold coins on behalf of the Sultan. The Ottoman Empire put cash banknotes (*Kaime-i nakdiye-i mutebere*) into circulation in 1840. During the Crimean War, in 1854, the Ottoman Empire, which borrowed from other nations for the first time in history, needed a state bank to assume an intermediary function in the repayment of external debts. As a result, the "Ottoman Bank (Bank-ı Osmanî)", headquartered in London, was established with English capital in 1856. The fundamental powers of the Bank were limited to lending in small amounts, making advance payments to the Government and discounting some Treasury bills. In 1863, the Ottoman Bank was dissolved and restructured as an English-French partnership under the name "Bank-Osmani Şahane (Imperial Ottoman Bank)" and became a state bank. The Imperial Ottoman Bank was granted the sole privilege of issuing banknotes for a period of thirty years. The Bank, acting as Treasurer of the State, was assigned to collect State revenues, make payments on behalf of the Treasury and discount Treasury bills, as well as making interest and principal payments pertaining to domestic and foreign debts. The capital of the Imperial Ottoman Bank retained by other nations triggered reactions in time and these reactions laid the foundation for establishing a national central bank. Efforts towards establishing a central bank with domestic capital culminated in the establishment of the "Ottoman National Credit Bank (Osmanlı İtibar-ı Millî Bankası)" on 11 March 1917. However, the defeat of the Ottoman Empire in the First World War prevented the bank from becoming a national bank, which would have assumed central bank functions. A law was enacted by the Grand National Assembly of Turkey on 11 June 1930, and published in the Official Gazette of 30 June 1930 under the name "The Law on the Central Bank of the Republic of Turkey No. 1715". Following the centralization of duties carried out by various institutions and organizations, the Central Bank started to function on 3 October 1931. Source: Central Bank of Turkey, Website, http://www.tcmb.gov.tr/yeni/eng/, Accessed on 16th June 2013.

that the lack of private organisational structure in the Islamic economic system alongside its dependency on the state as the main economic institution during Ottoman rule hindered its financial development (Kuran 2011: 18).

The limited liability structure in the Islamic Law was addressed in phase 1 and 2 i.e. prior to the tenth century in the partnership (*musharaka*) contract and its governing rules long time before the New York State corporate law. Each partner in the business venture is considered to be a trustee in managing other partner(s) share, and will not be liable in the normal course of managing the business unless proven to breach the terms of this trust. The organisational structure in that sense was based, in terms of business activities undertaken, on a profit sharing or sale and trading contracts with other parties that comply with Shariah. This is what makes it different from the Western limited liability in 1811 that mainly revolves around interest-based lending/borrowing dealings which was a relief as a company structure to limit the liability of any obligations payable to third parties and suppliers.

Commercial contracts registered in the Ottoman courts in the seventeenth century were in form identical to those used in the region around the year 1000. The other reason for less advanced financial capabilities during the nineteenth century is underdevelopment of the credit markets in contrast to those of Western Europe. The incompatible organisational structure, including the absence of banks and stock markets, limited the supply and flow of domestic capital to Middle Eastern states (Kuran 2011: 18).

5.3 Phase Six: The Decline of the Ottoman State and Subservience to the West (from the Beginning of the Nineteenth Century to 1970)

This phase started towards the end of the nineteenth century when the Ottoman state began to decline and became divided into smaller states. This period was marked as the phase of economic decline and political instability, there was not any development in the economic and financial structure of the Islamic state during this phase (Al Omar 2003: 99).

After a few centuries of military success, the Ottoman Empire began to undergo some decay. This could be related to several factors: economic decline resulting from the decentralization of government to province rulers who later exploited the weakening of the government, the discovery of the Cape of Good Hope its impact upon the Western commercial and political penetration (El-Ashker and Wilson 2006: 297).

The Islamic state was in a complete mess and corruption was widely spread, trade with different regions of the Islamic state decreased hugely, and financial debt of the state substantially increased, particularly, in Egypt and Turkey (Al Omar 2003: 99). This was the back door for the intervention of different Western countries trying to have a slice of the dying Islamic state. The Islamic state, then, gradually became weaker and weaker and was divided into small colonies ruled by the British, French, Italian and other Western countries ('Aashour n.d.: 141–143). During this colonial period, the conventional interest-based financial and banking system became dominant in the colonised Islamic states and that was the beginning of the shift towards the use of the conventional financial system in the declining Islamic state (Al Omar 2003: 99).

The economic decay in the Ottoman Empire may be related to two main influencing factors: the first is the maladministration of the Turkish provinces which was evidenced mainly in Syria and Egypt with an average term of the Turkish viceroys in office of 2 years or less (Hitti 1963). The reason for that was to ensure that viceroys do not stay too long in office to gain power and then break away from the central government in Istanbul. The second factor is the shift of trade route from land to sea after the discovery of the Cape of Good Hope. This diverted part of the European trades that passed through land routes in the north and Red Sea in the south for centuries to other routes outside the Islamic world (El-Ashker and Wilson 2006: 297).

The disappearance of the Silk Road following the end of the Mongols' reign was one of the main factors that stimulated the Europeans to reach the prosperous Chinese empire through another route, mainly by sea. Huge profits were to be obtained by anyone who is able to achieve a direct trade route with Asia. This was the main driving motive for the Portuguese exploration voyages of the Indian Ocean, including the sea of China. This resulted in the arrival in 1513 of the first European trading ship to the coasts of China (Arbrey et al. 2008: 257).

This reduced the impact of the Islamic lands as a commercial centre and as main routes for world trade, which used to generate income and commercial interaction. The new trade routes were less costly for European traders as they were shorter and gave them an advantage in the hostilities with the Islamic state, as their goods will not have to pass through Islamic territory, reducing the need for diplomacy from the west.

The Muslims' spice trade, for example, was severely damaged by European competition, which had the opportunity to channel these valuable products from the very source of production without having to pass through the Islamic world (Raymond 1981). This had led to undesirable economic effect on the Islamic world. It was three and half centuries later that the route of the Cape of Good Hope was to face severe competition when the Suez Canal was opened in 1869 as shown in Figs. 5.1 and 5.2 below. Only then, did the Red Sea, which was once the centre of trade, come back to life (Raymond 1981).

Increasing financial transactions with foreigners, in the mid-nineteenth century, was one the main reasons for attitudinal transformation as shown above in Figs. 5.1 and 5.2. This pushed the adoption of new business practices for better productivity and profitability, such as stock markets, municipalities and laws supportive of large companies capable of outliving their founders (Kuran 2011: 11).

The urge for financial development in order to foster economic dealings with foreigners and Western Europe facilitated the establishment of the commercial courts in the mid-nineteenth century. These courts adjudicated legal cases

Fig. 5.1 Planning the Suez Canal sea routes (Katibi 1994)

according to the French commercial code in Egypt, Syria, Turkey and elsewhere in the region. Nevertheless, Islamic courts continued to handle commercial cases and disputes, but its share was declining gradually (Kuran 2011: 12).

This adaptation of Western financial laws escalated in the following years in an attempt to catch up with the Western economic system. However, this uncalculated approach, created challenges later on for the compatibility between a new innovation known as Islamic banking with applicable financial laws and regulations that had become dominant.

5.4 Phase Seven: Islamic Finance Revivalism (1950s–1960s)

Having discussed the different phases of Islamic economics and finance development, its growth and decline and factors that influenced its development, it is now the time to analyse its modern revival and the emergence of its great innovation of Islamic banking in modern history.

Following the economic development and the political changes that we analysed in the previous six phases of the history of Islamic finance, most Gulf countries, in

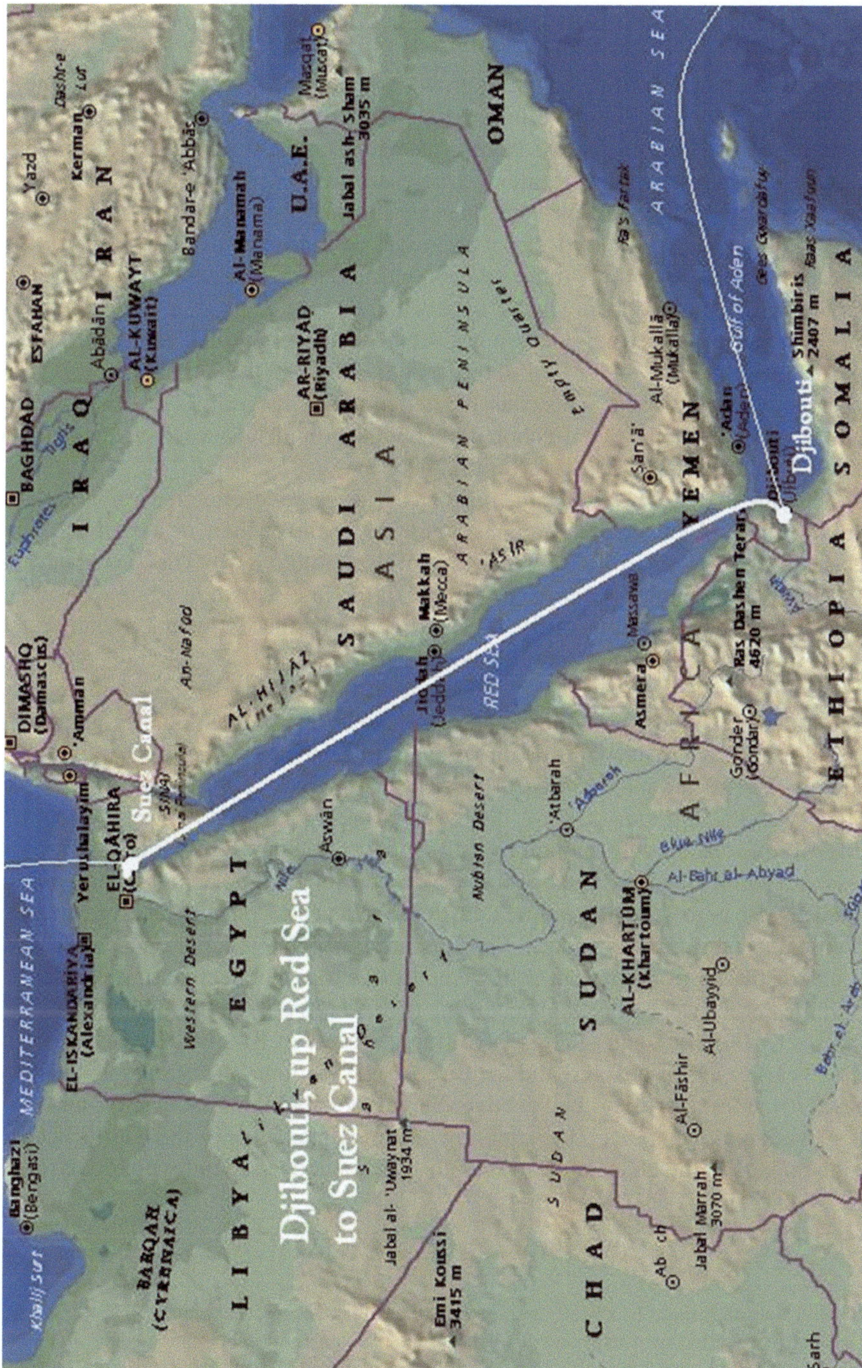

Fig. 5.2 The Suez Canal sea routes and shift it made in the trading routs (Katibi 1994)

this phase, in the 1950s and 1960s had their first introduction to the modern banking system. The focus on the Gulf countries is because Islamic banking emerged successfully there for the first time.

This introduction according to Smith proved to be problematic. Throughout the Gulf countries, mainly in Saudi Arabia, religiously observant individuals chose to leave their money in non-interest bearing accounts or they avoided the formal banking system altogether. The challenge increased to reconcile the Gulf financial system sectors and norms of Western finance with the prevailing belief amongst Gulf people that dealing in any form of interest is forbidden in Islam (2006: 1).

'These religious constraints imposed economic costs, as the gap between local norms and global financial practices impeded free capital flows by preventing global financial markets from accessing a segment of Gulf capital and Gulf citizens'. A solution to this problem was introduced in 1970s[2] in the form of a new type of financial intermediation. This was created through the efforts of observant Muslim activists, Islamic legal scholars, economists and businessmen to apply Islamic law to the economic realm (Smith 2006: 2).

Throughout the history of Islam, religious leaders have emerged, invariably identifying the problems of Muslims as being the result of their desertion of the correct path of their religion (El-Ashker and Wilson 2006: 315). This has always been the case throughout history from the time of the first schism in Islam over the caliphate, *Fitnah*, to the time of the crushing defeat of the Egyptian, Syrian and Jordanian armies by the Israelis in the 1967 six-day war. Calls for religious reform did not go unopposed. The call for secularization was equally strong, from some modern movements that were influenced somehow by liberal ideologies, though it was a call for a move in the opposite direction in order to move away from religious constraints (El-Ashker and Wilson 2006: 315).

If this was the full story, as we believe it to be, of Islamic finance it would definitely prove challenging enough for current economic theories. Smith (2006: 5) argues that Islamic finance cannot be fully captured by economic or cultural studies. It should be also perceived as a political institution that seeks power and presence in the political sphere through finance. She further argues that Islamic finance represents one of the more prominent achievements of broad intellectual and political programme known as Islamisation according to Stenberg (1996) and Euben (2002).

Smith's (2006) argument ignores the different phases of Islamic finance that we discussed earlier in this chapter, and focuses only on the founding of Islamic banks in the 1970s from a political perspective. She argues that the Islamisation movement gained political power by adopting Islamic finance, this then influenced decision makers in the Gulf States to ride this wave and keep it under their control.

---

[2]We should note that there had been attempts in establishing Islamic banking in the 1960s in Pakistan and the well-known experiment in the founding of a rural development bank in Mit Ghamr Savings Bank in Upper Egypt in 1963, however, the first commercial Islamic banks appeared in the 1970s in the Gulf.

It is not fair and accurate for Islamic finance to be studied and explained out of context and in isolation of its history and development.

Some writers (see Kerr 1971 and Smith 2006) attribute the founding of Islamic banks to a political agenda pursued by the Muslim Brotherhood which was founded in Egypt in the 1920s as an anti-colonial, pan-Islamic political movement.

Kerr argues that during the Arab Cold War of the 1950s and 1960s which pitted Arab nationalists against conservative monarchies, many Islamic activists from the Muslim Brotherhood found refuge in the Arab Gulf. Members of the Muslims Brotherhood from Egypt and other countries assumed professional positions in the public sector and were mainly prevalent in the rapidly expanding educational system (1971: 25–45). From that position, they were able to share their views on Islam and public life to persuade many Gulf people of their way of thinking. Overtime, the Gulf witnessed the formation of Islamic social reform that was affiliated to varying degrees with the Muslim Brotherhood. These groups and affiliations were later instrumental in bringing Islamic banking to the Gulf region (Kerr 1971: 25–45).

The direct role of Islamic political movements in Islamic finance is a subject of debate. This central and formal role of the political movements and the attribution of it to the Muslim Brotherhood is argued largely and disputed by some writes like Kahf (2004).

This is because, Islam is the guide and Islamic law is the framework that governs all aspects of life for Muslims including economics and finance. This has been the case during the history of Islamic finance which we discussed in its different phases. Therefore, Islamic finance cannot be viewed in isolation of the society and its history, or be interpreted as being a political motive; it should be studied in its, first and foremost, religious context, then social, historical and cultural contexts. This is in order to understand its aspirations and the recent innovation of the phenomenon of Islamic banking. It is hard to believe that members of the Muslim Brotherhood had that large an impact in changing the course of the whole of the Gulf region, as if people of the Gulf were completely ignorant about their religion and the prohibition of interest. This argument does not, however, dismiss completely the role of the specific Islamic movements, such as the partial role played by the Muslim Brotherhood in that regard.

5.5 Phase Eight: Interest-Free Islamic Banking (1970s–Present)

Muslims became more convinced than ever that their religion could still provide practical solutions to their problems: spiritually, politically and economically. In the wave of Islamic revivalism that characterized the mid to the late twentieth century, two main developments occurred as far as economics was concerned: the emergence of an extensive body of literature on Islamic economics and the establishment of Islamic banks (El-Ashker and Wilson 2006: 327).

5.5.1 Emergence of Islamic Banking

It has been argued in the literature whether the restrictions in Islamic finance on some financial activities, such as derivatives, options and future contracts would enable Islamic finance to provide a wide spectrum of financial instruments that sufficiently serve the needs of a developed, or even at least developing, economy without compromising its principles. Visser (2009: 140) suggests that a country considering the adaptation of Islamic finance, across-the-board, and the operation of the economy exclusively according to its principles, might be condemned to permanent low growth rates.

Visser (2009: 5), controversially, attributes the origins of Islamic finance as known and applied to Abu Al A'laa Al Mawdudi in 1941, which most of the Arab writers would strongly disagree with. Smith (2006) has addressed this issue by conducting a case study on three Gulf States tracing the origins of Islamic finance and the pioneering Arabs behind its emergence. Al Qaradaghi (2010) also disagrees with Visser's claim as he discusses in his work this argument by stating that the beginning of Islamic economics in the modern days is attributed to the pioneering Arabs in setting up Islamic banks, its theories, system and its relationship with the conventional economic system.

Visser (2009) argues that the efforts by Muslims to establish a well-recognised Islamic economics system have been a frustrating experience with little success even across other religions. He asserts that Islamic finance is a mere facet of important Islamic teachings, with implications for finance. It is something that he shares with Ramadan (2009) who argues that there is nothing called Islamic economics or Islamic finance as an actual system rather; it is a set of ethics that govern the conduct of business transactions.

Smith's (2006) study has developed an analytical framework to explain the emergence of Islamic banking. She argues that her approach in conducting the study cannot be fully understood without recognising Islamic finance as a constructivist project. Then she builds on this argument by studying Islamic banks, their origins and development in the Gulf States, their negotiation with the global conventional finance and their relationship to political Islam. The author employs multi case studies method in collecting her data, the three Gulf Countries included as case studies are Saudi Arabia, Bahrain and Kuwait.

She defines Strategic Constructivism as the act of making an institution work towards alternative political objectives via symbolic action. Conceptually, the study tries to introduce a framework for incorporating symbolic power into the study of institutions with the aim to generate a political theory of institutional change.

Smith (2006) implies that the emergence of Islamic banking enabled the Islamists to put capital in this industry and use it with a hidden agenda for political gains. The study ignores the fact that the Islamic finance principles and techniques existed over 1400 years ago and developed over time to accommodate different commercial needs (El-Gamal 2006 and Visser 2009). The study focuses on the post-colonial period of the history of the Gulf States, it was very normal, after having gained their independence, to develop their financial system in a way that complies with Shariah and is compatible with the existing conventional finance and banking system. However, the author believes that this development was for political reasons with ulterior motives.

This shows that the study was heavily subjective rather than objective as it ignored some facts in the development of the Islamic banking, as mentioned above, which would argue against the author's theory. This view would imply that this argument permeate Western studies of Islamic finance. A counter argument would state that there is, generally, a strong link between politics and financial policies. Moreover, countries have the right to determine their own political ideologies and destinies without needing the approval from their colonial rulers, hence, to suggest otherwise it would imply a colonial attitude.

Hence, Smith (2006) in her study addresses the political motive in the development of Islamic banking and the relationship between petro-dollar industry in the Gulf States and the emergence of Islamic banking.

Despite the abundant theoretical work on Islamic banking up to the end of the twentieth century, empirical work on the operation of Islamic banks seemed to be very limited. Some case studies have been conducted in Bangladesh, Egypt, Malaysia, Pakistan and Sudan, but the number of studies is still small (Ariff 1988).

What is new about the writing on interest-free Islamic economics in the twentieth century, particularly in the second half of the century, is that Islamic economists treated the subject in relation to major contemporary financial issues: (a) the operation of banks and financial institutions, and (b) monetary and fiscal policy. The objective was very clear: on the one hand it was to address the question of modernity once more with a view to proving that Islam is still relevant to contemporary life, but indeed it required innovation in financial instruments and banking systems in order to ensure that banks can be successfully run on an interest-free Islamic basis (El-Ashker and Wilson 2006: 367).

Ramadan (2009) discusses three fundamental propositions that the modalities of the reform process should be reconsidered by all Muslims based on the changing world as we know it today. He distinguishes between 'adaptation reform' and 'transformation reform'. His third proposition is that it is not sufficient to rely only on scriptural sources when examining the relationship between human knowledge and applied ethics. He suggests that text and context scholars must work together to achieve the higher objective in combining human knowledge and applied ethics.

Ramadan (2009) argues that there is no 'Islamic economy' and if we look into it differently, we find a set of principles for an ethical framework. These ethics are a general philosophy of the economy's aims, but there is nothing called an 'Islamic economy', it is just mere ethics that govern business transactions. However, the author completely dismisses a whole section in the Islamic classical books of jurisprudence (*fiqh*) called Islamic commercial law (*fiqh al-mu'amalaat*). This section outlines all Islamic contracts, agreements and principles that can be used in structuring financial and business activities. Ethics, as part of Shariah, articulate how business can be conducted in terms of manners when Muslims undertake different activities and interact with each other and with non-Muslims.

There is a clear difference between the principles and contracts such as *Ijara* (lease), *Musharakah* (partnership), which form part of the Islamic economics system and ethics, such as the seller is obliged to disclose all hidden defects in the commodity being sold, not to cheat and not to overstate the benefits of the product being sold. There are other elements, such as *Zakat* (the poor due), taxes, international business principles and the rules that govern the state financial system in deploying the state's income and taxes.

All the above and more form the Islamic economy, the Islamic finance and banking system is part of this economy. The author correctly asserts that Muslims should reform the instruments of deducting the legal rulings to address contemporary issues as required. However, it could be argued that his dismissal of the fact that an 'Islamic economy' exists and it is just a mere series of ethics is not supported by Islamic Scriptures.

Tripp quoted the argument by Abd al-Rahman Yusri (Director of the Higher Institute of Islamic Economics in Egypt) who argues that an Islamic economy can be established by inculcating Islamic values into a successful programme of economic development. He cites the fundamental respect within Shariah for capital and its productive use in a market designated as free and competitive, but nevertheless under the moral guidance and supervision of the institution of the *hisbah*: 'all wealth belongs to God and must be spent on whatever can bring a profit for Islamic society'.

Despite the valuable work on Islamic banking up to the last quarter of the twentieth century, the literature had two particular limitations: first, writers based their analysis on the premise that *riba* (interest) would be absent from the economy, and second, they did not discuss, or at least not thoroughly, issues concerning monetary and fiscal policy. This was to come a decade or so later within the writing on an interest-free economy and the Islamic banking system, that continued to the end of the century (El-Ashker and Wilson 2006: 368). Following the development we discussed in phase 7 regarding the emergence of Islamic banking, further Islamic banks and corporations were established in the Islamic world in the 1970s and 1980s onwards.

In chronological order these were the Dubai Islamic Bank in 1975, Kuwait Finance House in 1977, al-Rajhi Co. for Currency Exchange and Commerce in Saudi Arabia in 1978, Jordan Islamic Bank for Finance and Investment in 1978, Bahrain Islamic Bank in 1979, the Iran Islamic Bank in 1979, the Islamic Exchange and Investment Corporation in Qatar in 1979, the International Bank for Investment and Development in Egypt in 1980, International Islamic Bank in Bangladesh in 1983, Tadamon Islamic Bank in the Sudan in 1983, Bank Islam Malaysia in 1983, Beit Ettamouil Saudi Tounsi in 1984, and West Sudan Islamic Bank in the Sudan in 1984. A group of Faisal Islamic Banks, named after the late King Faisal of Saudi Arabia, emerged in 1970s and 1980s: in Egypt in 1977, in the Sudan in 1977, and in Turkey in 1985. The al-Barakah group emerged in the early 1980s: al-Barakah Bank in Sudan in 1982, al-Barakah Investment and Development Co., in Saudi Arabia in 1982, al-Barakah Islamic Investment Bank in Bahrain in 1984, and al-Barakah Turkish Finance House in 1984 (El-Ashker 1987).

5.5.2 An Empirical Account on Islamic Banking in the West

Modern Islamic banking, a system of banking compliant with Sharia, has been developing in the Islamic world for a number of decades. However, it has been the last 15 years or so that has seen it emerge as a noteworthy alternative to conventional banking. Over this period, there has been significant development in the range of and innovation in Islamic finance products, in banking as well as with Islamic mutual insurance, investment funds and syndicated finance. Together with greater religious leader and consumer understanding of Islamic finance, Islamic banking is now an established presence in many Islamic and non-Islamic markets. Over that period, there has been strong growth in both number of providers and Sharia-compliant assets (SCA), with the latter reaching the $700bn mark at end of 2008.

From a global perspective, this has shifted Islamic finance from being a niche market to one that is attracting attention across the world due to its strong expansion and, with a potential global customer base of around 1.5 billion Muslims, one that still has very significant potential for continued growth. This has not gone unnoticed outside the Islamic world, and with much of this growth centered in the oil-producing and capital-rich Middle East region, a number of Western banks have started to look at the Islamic world as a potential source of funds and revenue opportunity.

5.5.2.1 Islamic Banking in Western Europe

The ascent of Islamic finance remains nascent in Western Europe, despite a sizeable Muslim population. Islamic finance remains a niche sector, serviced by only a few providers, particularly on the retail Islamic banking side. However, as the maturity of Islamic finance as an alternative banking offering has increased over the 15 years, many Western governments are now starting to take a more actively favorable view towards Islamic banking, seeing it as a means to more effectively service a significant minority community group. This is likely to drive a new wave of interest by incumbent domestic banks and entrants from Islamic markets into Western Europe. However, government support alone is unlikely to produce a step-change in the market and to assess whether this will drive Islamic banking from a nascent to emerging position the following areas needed to be considered:

- Development and structure of Islamic banking;
- Market potential and the extent of both latent and possible demand for Islamic finance across Europe;
- Regulatory, legal and tax barriers to Islamic banking and likely developments;
- Competitive dynamics and funding of future Islamic banking expansion;
- Impact of financial crisis and economic downturn on market development.

A corollary of the variations in Sharia interpretation is that Islamic institutions compete not only on the financial attractiveness of a particular product, but also with respect to their Islamic credentials. Thus, within certain boundaries, there is a trade-off banks can select between Sharia strictness and structure/product innovation that banks can choose depending on country market, target customer base and competitive conditions. The main instance of this in practice is in organization structure/delivery model for provision of Islamic products. There are three main structures for this:

- Islamic window—this term is used to describe conventional banking institutions that offer Islamic products through their main distribution network (e.g. branches provide both conventional and Islamic banking products). Sharia restrictions around co-mingling of funds apply; thus funds, accounts and reporting needs to be maintained separately. This effectively means the Islamic window operates as a separate entity, but leverages the same infrastructure. Although the practical implications of this (e.g. separate teller windows, business processing functions) do vary depending on Sharia interpretation. Given that processes and operations are shared (e.g. treasury and liquidity management is typically managed by parent company), Islamic windows are typically situated at the lower end of the Sharia compliance credibility scale;
- Islamic subsidiary—here a conventional institution operates a separate subsidiary, so that the distribution and operational infrastructure is completely separate from the conventional bank. The Islamic product range will generally be broader than bank operating through an Islamic window. Typically only Islamic products are provided; although client relationships and risk may be managed across both conventional and Islamic side (e.g. corporate client may have relationship with conventional bank, but obtain Islamic products from the Islamic subsidiary). Significantly, capital funding (at least initially) is provided by the parent company, which would be regarded by some as not fully Islamic compliant, although steps can be taken (e.g. charitable donations) to purify the original funds;
- Full Islamic bank (pure or converted)—this would be a solely Islamic banking institution that operates as a standalone entity. This would offer just Islamic products and typically having a full range of products compared to an Islamic window. A pure Islamic bank would be capital funded and set up from Sharia-compliant funds, whereas a converted Islamic bank would be one that converted from a conventional bank operation into an Islamic bank. With a full Islamic bank all transactions within the bank need to be Sharia compliance; this would extend to treasury and risk management operations, with liquidity and risk management tending to look quite different for Islamic versus conventional banks.

A cursory view on Islamic banking in Western Europe would identify a number of primary markets. France has most significant Muslim population presence, both in terms of absolute population and also population density, housing close to half of Western Europe's Muslim population. In terms of absolute population size Germany, the UK, Italy and the Benelux region are the other significant markets from a potential Islamic banking perspective. Other countries, such as Denmark, Switzerland and Sweden do have comparatively high Muslim population densities, but due to the size of their respective population bases contain a relatively small potential Muslim customer base.[3]

It should be noted that due to methodology differences and decennial timeframe for most census statistics, exact Muslim population figures are hard to verify. Perhaps more significantly, migration movements (particularly illegal), as well as temporary travel movements, mean official figures understate the actual Muslim population in many countries.

Given greater size of Islamic populations in France and Germany, it may seem somewhat surprising that the UK is currently the most developed market in respect of the provision of Islamic banking. While this is partly driven by earlier government/regulatory backing, this is largely reflective of the background of the Muslim population itself, which drives the latent demand for Islamic banking.

As discussed, despite a potential attractive customer market to be developed in Western Europe, Islamic banking remains, to some extent, nascent. Based on Sharia-compliant assets (SCA), the UK does appear significant from a global perspective. However, this is based largely on HSBC Amanah, the main Islamic subsidiary of HSBC Holdings (headquartered in UK); while a top-ten global Islamic bank (based on SCA) its Islamic asset base is largely derived from outside the UK. It is important to note that HSBC Amanah operations have been phased out in the last 3 years after a strategic review according to the bank.

Additionally, much of the development of the UK has been based on the City seeking to establish itself as a leading Islamic center on the corporate & investment banking side. However, the main focus has been to use its financial expertise to service the Islamic world (particularly GCC states) rather than indigenous Muslim population. Thus, at best, on the retail banking side the Islamic sector could be described as niche within the UK, and dormant would apply to rest of Western Europe up to 2012. This started to change in 2015 and 2016 by the emergence new Islamic bank in Germany, such as KFH Germany and assest management and investment funds in Luxemburg.

On the retail banking side, the UK has led the Western European market in providing a legal and regulatory provision for Islamic banking. Retail Shariah compliant financial products did appear in the UK as far back as the 1990s (mainly around home finance products, e.g. Ahli United Bank in 1997), however, these were general uncompetitive in relation to conventional products and outside FSA banking regulatory framework.

Consequently, little traction was obtained in the market. The market mode changed in mid-2003, with HSBC Amanah expanding its offering into the UK with home finance and a Shariah compliant current account through an Islamic window (i.e. HSBC UK distribution network), followed at the end of 2003 with LloydsTSB moving into the market (also through an Islamic window) with a focus

[3]Datamonitor, market opportunity report, 2009.

on Shariah compliant current accounts (direct) and home finance, via an introduction service relationship with Alburaq, a joint venture between Arab Banking Corporation International (ABC) and Bristol & West (Bank of Ireland). With two of the top UK high street banks pushing Islamic products through their nationwide branch networks, Islamic banking entered the mainstream market. Then 2004 saw the launch of the first retail Islamic standalone bank in Europe, the Islamic Bank of Britain (IBB), which offered a range of Islamic savings and financing products.

Since then a number of other standalone Islamic banks have entered the UK market, including the European Islamic Investment Bank in 2006 (currently Rasmala), the Bank of London and the Middle East, European Finance House (currently QIB UK) and Gatehouse Bank, although IBB remains the only standalone retail bank. There have also been a few other institutions offering Sharia–compliant products (e.g. Child Trust Funds) such as West Bromwich Building Society, based on Children's Mutual's Islamic investment fund (also available through LloydsTSB) and Principle Insurance launched a Sharia based insurance offering (Salaam Halal) at end of 2008, based on *Takaful*.

5.5.2.2 Islamic Banking in the United States of America

Abdul-Rahman (2010) started a financial adventure with group of friends to provide interest-free financial products and services in the US. The project started with a modest beginning and kept growing to become the current American Finance House LARIBA.

It is interesting to find a book about Islamic finance written by a person from a chemical engineering background. However, the author also has a relative experience of 22 years in the field of Islamic financial services as one of LARIBA's founders. Contrary to what the book's title would imply, the book does not offer a contribution about the art of structuring and developing the tools and techniques of Islamic finance. Rather, the author utilises his book to offer us an insight of the Islamic banking and finance in the US through his own experience which is an interesting one.

The author argues that Islamic finance and banking is a 'community-based banking' model. This might be true in the context of the US, but that would not be the case with respect to the Gulf Region, Malaysia and other Islamic countries where the Islamic banking system is very dominant. This approach limits the Islamic finance and banking system to being viewed as a community-based banking rather a competitive financial approach. The author discusses in details the issue of interest (*riba*) and lending from cross-religious perspective based on the Judeo-Christian-Islamic values in light of the laws of America. Abdul-Rahman (2010) goes on explaining the steps to establish interest-free banking in the USA based on the LARIBA model highlighting different legal and financial challenges.

The author in his conclusion and vision for the future of interest-free banking suggests that, this model should only employ well trained bankers who believe sincerely in this model. He also recommends, based on his experience with Bank of

Whittier as an extended branch of LARIBA, to avoid the branch model of banking because it is costly without real benefit. Instead he believes that using internet and modern communication channels is the solution for the fixed cost approach of branches.

5.5.3 Evolution of Islamic Banking in South East Asia, Pakistan and Iran

As South East Asia, and in particular Malaysia, is currently a financial centre for Islamic finance, it is important to provide an insight on the evolution of Islamic banking there.

5.5.3.1 Malaysia

Malaysia, and other South East Asian countries, had its first introduction to Islam via Arab and traders in the thirteenth century, dealing with Muslim traders and experiencing their honest dealings has attracted the Malaysians to know more about the religion of Muslims. This contributed towards bringing to an end the age of Hinduism and Buddhism there. Islam arrived in the region gradually, and then became the religion of the elite before it spread to the rest of the Malaysian population (Devahuti 1965: 3).

Malaysia is believed to have a liberal approach towards the application of Shariah into banking. The reason for that, according to Wilson is due to the predominance of the Shafi'i school of jurisprudence in Malaysia as well as in Indonesia. This school is regarded as being the most liberal of the other three main schools of jurisprudence including matters of finance. This, therefore, explains the different approach to Islamic finance in the Gulf Countries where the Hanbali school is followed. This contrast arises as the Hanbali school is regarded as the strictest because it limits the scope of judicial interpretation of the Qur'an and Hadith (2012: 31).

The earliest form of Islamic banking in Malaysia can be traced back to September 1963 when Perbadanan Wang Simpanan Bakal-Bakal Haji (PWSBH) was established as an institution for Muslims to save for the cost of doing hajj (pilgrimage to Mecca). In 1969, PWSBH merged with Pejabat Urusan Haji to form Lembaga Urusan dan Tabung Haji (known as Lembaga Tabung Haji), (Bank Negara Malaysia 2005). This was the beginning of introducing religious based savings product in Malaysia for doing a religious duty and the first introduction to the concept of Islamic banking.

Hence, the first Islamic bank, Bank Islam Malaysia Berhad, was set up under the Islamic Banking Act 1983. On 4th March 1993, Bank Negara Malaysia (BNM), the Central Bank of Malaysia, introduced a scheme known as 'interest-free banking scheme'. Under this scheme, commercial conventional banks and finance companies were also allowed Islamic banking products and services. These institutions were required to ensure complete separation of their Islamic banking operations from the conventional side (Adam and Thomas 2004: 48).

The National Sharia Advisory Council in Malaysia was established by Bank Negara Malaysia (BNM) to advise on all aspects of Sharia and its application in Islamic banking. This enabled the existence of a dual banking system conventional banking and stand-alone Islamic banking system. There are currently in Malaysia ten fully-fledged Islamic banks (Bank Negara Malaysia 2005).

5.5.3.2 Indonesia

As the world's largest population of Muslims, Indonesia entered the realm of Islamic banking fairly late in comparison with other Muslim majority countries. This is probably due to Suharto's policies at that time. The development of Islamic banking in Indonesia started before any legal or regulatory structure exists. There have been many non-banking financial institutions such as Bait Maal Wat Tamwil (Islamic Savings and Loan Cooperatives) offering Islamic finance to the rural sector. The government allowed the operation of Islamic banking in the Act No. 7 of 1992 under the Government Decree No. 72 of 1992, in order to meet the demand for Islamic banking financial products (Haron 1995).

Bank Muamalat was the first Islamic bank established in Indonesia and commenced its operation in 1992. In 1998, the Act No. 10 that amended the Act No. 7 of 1992 concerning banking regulations came into force to provide a stronger legal ground for the existence of Islamic banking system. Bank Indonesia (the central bank) took a major step in September 2002 for the development of Islamic banking when it issued a blueprint for Islamic banking and set the regulation of 4/1/2002 in relation to the establishment and operations of commercial banks and bank offices based on the principles of Sharia (Khir et al. 2008: 198).

Later on, in January 2006 Bank Indonesia allowed conventional banks to have branches with Sharia compliant units and offer Sharia compliant financial products and services, setting up a dual banking system like Malaysia (Adam and Thomas 2004: 49). As of December 2005, there were three Islamic general banks, 19 Islamic commercial bank business units and 92 small banks limited to financing and lending in certain areas (Khir et al. 2008: 199).

5.5.3.3 Thailand

Although Thailand is predominantly a Buddhist country, A Muslim population is concentrated in certain provinces such as Yala, Pattani, Songkhla, Satun and Narathiwas. Nonetheless, while only 4 per cent of the country is Muslims, they are wealthy and influential. Islamic banking can be traced there back to 1987 when the Pattani Islamic Savings Cooperative was established. The objective was then to create a separate Islamic fund for the benefit of the poor of the Muslim community (Adam and Thomas 2004: 50).

Thereafter, four similar Islamic institutions were established, Ibnu Affan Savings Co-operative, As-Siddiq Savings Co-operative, Saqaffah Islam Savings Co-operative and Al-Islamiah Savings Co-operative. The idea of establishing the first stand-alone Islamic bank in Thailand was initiated in 1994 when the Thai government signed the Indonesia-Malaysia-Thailand Growth Triangle Project (IMT-GT Project) with a view to promote banking services with focus on the needs of Muslim consumers, in particular those in the four southern provinces (Bank Negara Malaysia 2005).

Islamic banking was first provided by a commercial bank in late 1997, but closed down as a result of the financial crisis. The next major step was establishing a full-fledged Islamic branch by state-owned Krung Thai Bank in 2002. Krung Thai Sharia Services is now under the Islamic Bank of Thailand (a major player in the Thai financial system) which was set up in 2002, to meet the demands of Sharia compliant financial products, under the Islamic Bank of Thailand Act B.E 2545 (Khir et al. 2008: 200).

5.5.3.4 Brunei

A dual banking system is also adopted in Brunei whereby Islamic banks operate in parallel to conventional banks. Islamic banking started in 1991 with the establishment of Perbadanan Tabung Amanah Islam Brunei (TAIB) by a constitution of Brunei Darussalam (Order under section 83[3]) Emergency Order, 1991. TAIB is government owned with the objective of offering Islamic financial services and raises the socio-economic status of the population (Haron 1995).

Islamic Bank of Brunei (IBB) was the second fully Islamic bank established in 1993; it replaced the International Bank of Brunei. Banks in Brunei are regulated under the Banking and Finance Companies Act through the Ministry of Finance. There is not a central bank in Brunei. To further strengthen Islamic banking in Brunei, two Islamic banks have merged to become Brunei's largest Islamic bank, the Islamic Bank of Brunei Ltd and Brunei Islamic Development Bank Ltd (Khir et al. 2008: 201).

5.5.3.5 Pakistan

The process of converting the financial system in Pakistan to be an Islamic system was initiated in 1979. Pakistan took a gradual transition approach to an interest-free banking system. All steps were taken into consideration to ensure that, as a result of new banking rules and regulations, disruption to the existing financial system is kept to the minimum (Anwar 1992). This gradual approach was adopted in order to establish new laws, institutions, concepts and practices on sound intellectual ground, develop a wide agreement and broad acceptance of the new measures and ensure flexibility to accommodate differences on minor issues in the Islamic commercial law (Khan 1984).

Then, the specialised institutions in the public sector reoriented their financial activities to be operated on a non-interest bearing basis of profit and loss sharing (PLS). All commercial domestic banks were allowed to accept deposits on the basis of PLS on 1st January 1981. Hence, over the next 3 years measures were taken to develop new financial instruments in which PLS deposits could be invested (Iqbal and Mirakhor 1987: 4).

The Pakistani model aimed to ensure that the new instruments of financing did not upset the basic function and structure of the existing conventional banking system. This and the gradual transition made it easier for the Pakistani banks to adapt the new system (Ariff 1988). This gradual transition also included the government and its agencies, export bills, investment in shares, purchase of participation term certificates, provision of loans to the credit specialised institutions, partnership lending and hire purchase (Iqbal and Mirakhor 1987: 4). However, this progress has slowed down due to the actions of successive governments that held power thereafter.

5.5.3.6 Iran

Following the Islamic revolution in Iran in 1979 and the overthrow of the Shah, Iran initiated its conversion into an Islamic banking system in August 1983 with a transition period planned over 3 years (Ariff 1988). Banks were allowed to accept current and savings deposits without having to pay any return, but the government permits banks to offer incentives instead such as variable prizes or bonuses in cash or kind to account holders. Term deposits earn a rate of return based on the profit generated and the maturity of the deposit (Ariff 1988).

People were hesitant in the beginning to make investment deposits, but with time the number of term investment deposits substantially increased. The number of deposits increased by 6.3 times in 1991, in contrast with 1985. Iran established and strengthened collaboration and coordination of the credit policies of banks with the economic policies of the government in various spheres (Anwar 1992).

5.5.4 Various Approaches to Shariah Governance

The examination of the current approach to Islamic finance shows that there are various practices and structures to Shariah governance, according to different jurisdictions. Some regions have chosen a more hands-on regulator approach with regards to regulation, while others have adopted a less interventionist approach.

For the purpose of this section, and to briefly illustrate further the reasons behind the aforementioned diversification of approaches towards Shariah governance, we will use three categories of approaches and illustrate their use in different jurisdictions. The approaches are proactive, reactive and a mesh of both reactive and proactive tactics.

5.5.4.1 Proactive Approach to Shariah Governance

This approach is adopted by the regulatory authority in Malaysia, following the introduction of Islamic finance and banking to the country, the Malaysian regulator took a proactive approach in regulating this industry. The sole objective was, according to Hasan (2010), to streamline Shariah governance on a regulatory based methodology and to issue a comprehensive regulatory Shariah governance framework for Islamic financial institutions. Several laws and amendments were approved by parliament, from the Islamic Banking Act (1983), to the Central Bank of Malaysia Act (2009), which stated that the National Shariah Advisory Council is the only authority for Islamic finance. This was then complemented by the issuance of the Registration of Shariah Advisers Guidelines (2009) by the Securities Commission of Malaysia (Hasan 2010).

5.5.4.2 Reactive Approach to Shariah Governance

This approach is evident in non-Muslim jurisdictions such as the UK and to some extent Turkey. There is not any specific legal or regulatory legislation to cover Shariah governance in Islamic financial institutions. This is due to the secular legal nature of such jurisdictions and the refraining of regulating the Shariah governance by any regulatory authority or central bank (FSA 2007).

5.5.4.3 A Hybrid Approach of Proactive and Reactive Approaches to Shariah Governance

This approach is adopted by the GCC countries, excluding Saudi Arabia and until recently, Oman. Unlike the proactive and reactive approaches, this approach uses a minimal intervention of the financial regulatory authorities in the Shariah governance of Islamic banks. The regulatory authorities require Islamic financial institutions to have proper Shariah governance in place, without however, specifying or imposing any details. Thus, the regulations around Shariah governance do not come from regulatory bodies or parliament, as is the case in Malaysia (Hasan 2010).

There are also no restrictions regarding multiple appointments of Shariah scholars on the Committees of various Islamic banks at the same time. This approach advocates that it is better for the market to develop its own Shariah governance system, without greater intervention by the regulatory authorities. Some countries like UAE, Qatar and Bahrain favour the adherence to the Accounting and Auditing Organisation for Islamic Financial Institutions (AAOIFI) Sharia Standards (Wilson 2012), This is because the AAOIFI Shariah standards have a strong scholarly basis and are highly regarded throughout the industry, thus these standards can act as substitute for governmental regulation.

Saudi Arabia, on the other hand, is taking a more passive stance, as there is no national Shariah advisory body or any other regulatory authority regarding Islamic financial institutions within Saudi Arabia. The existing Shariah governance system is a result of self-initiative by individual Islamic banks, rather than any regulatory requirements (Wilson 2009).

Pakistan, however, follows a more interventionist approach, which allows third party institutions to assess and decide on issues pertaining to Shariah and Islamic finance. Although there is a national Shariah board on the level of the State Bank of Pakistan, the Shariah Federal Court is still the highest authority regarding matters of Islamic finance (Hasan 2010). Countries such as Bahrain, Sudan, Qatar, Jordan and UAE made AAOIFI standards obligatory and this is imposed by the central banks of the respective countries. Others such as Saudi, Kuwait, Lebanon, Malaysia and Indonesia have used the AAOIFI as voluntary guidelines.

5.6 Conclusion

The historical analysis, in this chapter, shows that the more powerful economy usually prevails over others and dictates the rules of economic and financial engagement in relation to structure and practices. This was obvious during certain phases of the Islamic finance history, when the state was politically and economically stable and strong.

However, this factor changed later in recent history, with the domination of interest-based capitalism on the financial system worldwide enforcing its rules on the financial sphere. Hence, Islamic finance has had to make some concessions and compromises in its modern history to create its own space in the new global economic order.

The discussion concludes that Islamic banking as a new phenomenon and innovation is here to stay and it is not a temporary phase. Yet, it needs to grow and develop more to be considered a truly viable alternative to interest-based banking system. This will require designing more beneficial financial innovations that are based on solid Islamic rules and rooted in its core Islamic principles. What will also be required is the building and developing of a clear theoretical framework of financial innovation from an Islamic perspective, which will be dealt with in the following chapters.

The main reasons for the decline in the Islamic economic and financial structure during the different eight phases (covered in this chapter and Chap. 4) of the history of the Islamic finance, which were discussed above, are summarised below:

1. Natural disasters.
2. Poor governance of the public finances due to mismanagement, corruption and internal conflicts.
3. Lack of development in the financial system and the formation of a new, competing modern economic and financial system. This was a significant factor in the decline of the Ottoman Empire.

Table 5.1 Main negative influencing factors for Islamic financial innovation

Negative factors	Root cause
State structure with a low capability for innovation and experimentation	The lack of focus and attention given to the private sector and institutional structure
Political policies and planning	Authoritarian ruling, high corruption and lack of trust in organizations
Reaction to economic failure	Social problems and political insecurities, also a loss of economic standing created fertile soil for the spread of economically protectionist ideologies, such as Turkish statism and Arab socialism (Kuran 2011: 294)

4. Focusing on the collection of taxes and ignoring economic development, this was particularly the case when the Islamic state was involved in various wars and trying to fund them via different means including taxes.
5. Irresponsible financial management and unfair taxes. This occurred mainly during the fragmentation of the Islamic state, when rulers of different regions started to break away from the empire. Rulers were focused on their own personal interests and the rapid acquisition of personal wealth due to their short appointment in office.
6. Increased military control and expenses.
7. External threats and foreign intervention.
8. Political instability and divisions in the Islamic state and the society.
9. Decline in the standard of living that provoked public unrest and revolutions.

In addition to the above factors, the absence of an advanced private organisational commercial system has negatively impacted the Islamic financial system and its scope of innovation. The centralisation of the financial system in the institutions of the state, which were less flexible and responsive to economic and social changes did not improve matters. The most influential negative factors to the underdevelopment of Islamic finance are summarised in Table 5.1 below.

The main financial innovations that were discussed in this chapter and the previous chapter throughout the eight phases of the history of Islamic finance are summarised in the Table 5.2 below.

Hence, there are many lessons to be learned from the history of Islamic finance, as shown in Table 5.2 above that should be considered today. It is vital that Islamic banks do not divert from the path of offering a new financial model that is fair, transparent, based on profit and risk sharing, a system that promotes social justice and welfare.

This was the main objective that marked Phase 7 and 8, Islamic finance revivalism in the modern history of Islamic finance. Any deviation from this path could lead Islamic finance and banking to lose its main features as a moral and ethical financial model. The next chapter (Chap. 6) focuses on the traditional innovation theory and discusses its approach and schools, highlighting innovation bias and the role of financial innovation in triggering financial crises.

Table 5.2 Summary of the eight phases and development of financial innovations

Historical phase	Financial innovation	Historical factors
Phase one: 622–661 Region: The Arabian Peninsula and Iraq.	• The concept of social and economic justice in the Islamic society is backed by religious obligations rather than a legal system, this was established by the bond of brotherhood between the people of Makkah and Madina. • The development of the profit sharing contract within the Islamic context. • Currency Exchange. • Credit Sale and Mortgage. • Murabaha Sale. • Forward Sale. • Transference of a debt from one person to another (Al-Hawaala). • Business by proxy (Wakala). • Partnership.	• The modern concept of social justice, in contrast, emerged in the West out of the early industrialisation movement in France and Britain in the 1840s, which is believed to be in phase 5 of the phases of Islamic finance history. However, it is mentioned here for comparison purposes only.
Phase two: seventh to tenth century Region: The Arabian Peninsula, Iraq, Syria, Egypt, North Africa, Spain (Andalus) and Persia.	• Establishment of the state treasury. • The foundation of the land tax system. • The invention of economic institutions in its early form in Islamic finance was founded in the eighth and ninth with the emergence of an Islamic law to govern the trusts or endowment (known as *waqfs*). • The principle of *Istisna'* was founded. • The contract of *Suftajah* was developed.	• As the Islamic state grew and expanded, a treasury system was needed to be developed to organize the state finances. This system was influenced by the already established treasury system in more mature nations such as the Roman and Persian empires.
Phase three: tenth to thirteenth century Region: The Arabian Peninsula, Iraq, Syria, Egypt, North Africa, Spain (Andalus) and Persia.	• Reform of the tax system. • The refinement of the Islamic law of partnerships. • The development of some areas such as tax collection, innovations and cross-cultural borrowings never ceased	• In 1602, the invention of multinational corporation emerged in the West with the Dutch East India Company.
Phase four: thirteenth to sixteenth century Region: The Arabian Peninsula, Iraq, Syria, Egypt, North Africa, Spain (Andalus) and Persia.	• Trade finance was emerged as a joint venture between traders, suppliers and investors in unstructured way.	• The first central bank to be established in the West was the Bank of England, founded by William Paterson in 1694.

(continued)

Table 5.2 (continued)

Historical phase	Financial innovation	Historical factors
Phase five: sixteenth to nineteenth century Region: The Arabian Peninsula, Iraq, Syria, Egypt, North Africa, Spain (Andalus), Persia Mongolia and Turkey.	• The reform of the export sector and financial tools such as credit sale and credit finance. • The establishment of first national banks in Egypt and Turkey.	• The large national corporation was enhanced by the invention of the New York State corporate law of 1811 which set the right of anyone to set up a company. • The limited liability structure was developed.
Phase six: nineteenth century to 1970 Region: The Arabian Peninsula, Iraq, Syria, Egypt, North Africa, Spain (Andalus), Persia Mongolia, Turkey and Balkans.	• New business practices such as stock markets, municipalities and laws supportive of large companies capable of outliving their founders were established. • Financial development in order to foster economic dealings with foreigners and Western Europe facilitated the establishment of the commercial courts	• Increased trades and business with foreigners stimulated this development in the financial system.
Phase seven: 1950s to 1960s Region: The Arabian Peninsula, Iraq, Syria, Egypt, North Africa, Spain (Andalus), Persia Mongolia, Turkey, South East Asia, Pakistan and Iran.	• Islamic revivalism and financial and economic reform in the Islamic thought. • Deployment of surplus liquidity from selling oil.	• Financial intermediation with Arab countries.
Phase eight: 1970s to present	• The emergence of Islamic banking. • The amendments of laws and regulations to accommodate the requirements of Islamic banking. • The diminishing *musharakah* financial instrument as a type of the partnership contract was engineered.	• The role of the Bank of England as the lender of last resort was invented and developed as it encountered repeated financial crises.

Chapter 6
Traditional Theory of Financial Innovation

6.1 Introduction

The previous chapters (Chaps. 4 and 5) provided an analysis of the history of financial innovation in Islamic finance from its inception as a concept over 1400 years ago. It also discussed the main influencing factors and elements that played a critical role in its development until the modern day.

Innovation today is the most important item of the strategic agenda of firms and financial institutions. It is not only seen as the key driver of the corporate success, but as a critical requirement for organisational survivor (Sveiby et al. 2012: 3). Innovation is believed to be one of the key ingredients for economic growth in a society; this growth leads to generating national wealth and prosperity. Therefore, innovation is often perceived as the ultimate solution to existing economic problems in society. This belief does not necessitate, by default, the desired outcome for growth, as described by Adam Smith (1976), if it does not meet and undertake the required steps and economic factors to achieve national wealth.

Hence, there are constant tireless efforts to innovate, particularly in the West. This is usually driven, by the incentive of competition in the market, profit making, hedging risks, achieving personal satisfaction and finding ways around applicable regulations and taxation. It is worth noting that innovation is one of the most widely mentioned concepts in social sciences however, unintended and uncalculated risks and consequences are rarely studied (Sveiby et al. 2012: 1).

In fact, according to Tzeng (2009) the current catch phrases such as 'creative response' and 'creative destruction' can be traced back to Schumpeter's Theory of Economic Development (1934) and Capitalism, Socialism and Democracy (1942). Drucker[1] (1986: 104) stated that both Schumpeter and Keynes are the 'two greatest

[1]**Peter Ferdinand Drucker** (November 19, 1909–November 11, 2005) was an Austrian-born American management consultant, educator, and author, whose writings contributed to the philosophical and practical foundations of the modern business corporation. He was also a leader

S. Alamad, *Financial Innovation and Engineering in Islamic Finance*,
Contributions to Management Science, DOI 10.1007/978-3-319-52947-9_6

economists of the last century’. However, Drucker feels that it is Schumpeter who would shape the thinking on economic theory and economic policy for the coming 50 years. This is because of his view of the role of innovation as the key generator of economic growth.

This chapter aims to analyse financial product innovation and its consequences that are often ignored by highlighting three Schumpeterian schools of innovation. In order to do so, we will approach this goal by focusing first on the role played by financial innovation in creating financial crises. This will provide a theoretical understanding of what would have caused the current (i.e. 2008) and previous financial crises and their effects. Most of the analyses conducted have focused on the nature of financial innovations with exploring and contrasting the current financial system with the Islamic financial system, and extracting some lessons to be learned.

This chapter further explains what would happen following a financial crisis, and brings to light that the resilience of the banking system is a crucial element for a strong financial system. It also argues that there is an innovation bias across academic research and that financial market is under regulated, and that more robust regulations are required. It also aims to critically discuss financial innovation, its theory, schools, and impact on society through uncalculated risks.

6.2 Analysis of the Role Played by Financial Innovation in Creating Financial Crises

Academic research has explored the main causes of financial crises in recent decades, see e.g. Persons and Warther (1997); Bhattacharyya and Nada (2000); and Finnerty (1992). However, this research tackled the issue of financial crises from different perspectives, some of these are: separating banking functionality, i.e. investment and retail. Others looked into it from a financial innovation perspective, for example, competition in the financial market and complexity of this innovation.

Some academic research argues that there is a major flaw with the current financial system in the new capitalist era. This financial system is under regulated

in the development of management education, and he invented the concept known as management by objectives (see: Drucker, Peter F. “Reflections of a Social Ecologist,” *Society*, May/June 1992). Among Peter Drucker’s early influences was the Austrian economist Joseph Schumpeter, a friend of his father’s, who impressed upon Drucker the importance of innovation and entrepreneurship. Drucker was also influenced, in a much different way, by John Maynard Keynes, whom he heard lecture in 1934 in Cambridge. “I suddenly realized that Keynes and all the brilliant economic students in the room were interested in the behaviour of commodities,” Drucker wrote, “while I was interested in the behaviour of people”. See, Beatty, Jack. *The World According to Peter Drucker*, 1998, p. 163; Drucker, Peter F. *The Ecological Vision: Reflections on the Human Condition*, 1993, p. 75; and Drucker, Peter F., *The Ecological Vision*, 1993, pp. 75–76.

and requires a fundamental reform (see Kaminsky and Reinhart 1999, 2000). In contrast, there are some emerging financial systems such as the Islamic finance and banking system which has survived the recent financial crisis with minimum effects due to its inbuilt characteristics.

Plosser (2009), neatly states that financial innovations such as subprime mortgages and the sophisticated financial securities triggered the 2008 financial crisis, the negative impact of which, is still being felt. This chapter relies on this theory in proving that some financial innovations are believed to be harmful to the economy and society, unjust and that there are some lessons to be learned by studying the theory of innovation in the Islamic financial system as a potential ethical alternative to existing practices in the current financial system.

6.3 Fundamental Elements Influencing the Financial Market

Financial markets are normally afflicted with either a boom or bust syndrome, which often results as a manifestation of irrational excess (Persons and Warther 1997). According to Boyer (2007), a discrepancy in the financial system is not derived from typical information asymmetry or minor imperfections in the financial market, but rather it is believed to be the direct result of the fact that financial markets are much different from other markets. They are driven by future predictions and sophisticated financial innovation, which make financial markets inherently volatile.

A great deal of new and sophisticated financial innovations has been developed in recent years. It is argued that this profusion of new financial engineering has been attributed to different causes, such as volatile interest rates, floating exchange rates, regulatory policy and taxes (that flourished off-shore financial structures) (Finnerty 1992). Bhattacharyya and Nada (2000) added that investment banks have played a vital role in the development and presentation of these innovative products.

6.4 The Resilience of the Banking System: A Key Factor in the On-Going Financial Crises

Boyer (2007) argues that the banking system could be both a cause of financial crises and a solution to cases when the reversal of a speculative boom causes a run towards liquidity by financial firms and institutions. It is known that the degree of fragility or resilience of the financial and banking systems is a crucial element in the unfolding financial crises.

Boyer (2007) further explains that a cumulative depression can be triggered by a persisting and strong liquidity constraint (e.g. the Great Depression of 1929–1932).

On the other hand, an economic rebound could be organised through an adequate supply of liquidity (e.g. the 1987 stock market crash in the US). The run towards liquidity, when financial crises break out, would put banks once again at a process that might lead to a recession and then a recovery or to a depression.

The era of financial liberalisation dictates that the centrality of the banking system is a pivotal element to the economy. A change in the strategy of banks towards various and generally more risky creditors has been induced since the shift from banking intermediation to direct finance. Following the shift of many large firms towards the stock market, banks moved into new opportunities represented by sophisticated financial innovations oriented towards small and medium size businesses, households and foreign firms in order to compensate for this shift (Kaminsky and Reinhart 1999, 2000).

As a result of rather low real short-term interest rates, the emergence of bubbles has been favoured by the high liquidity. Hence, it was no surprise, since then, that the number of financial crises caused by banks has gone up since the early 1980s, which also implies that there is clearly a major flaw in the way banking operates and a link between banking crises and a deregulated financial system (Kaminsky and Reinhart 1999, 2000).

6.5 The Race by Financial Institutions to Develop Sophisticated Financial Products

Bhattacharyya and Nada (2000) clearly recognise that the motive to develop financial innovation is diluted unless competitors can be prevented from mimicking this innovation. Such problems may be very particular to financial innovation. There would be a substantial cost involved in innovating and developing financial products, legal expenses and marketing. Tufano (1989) further added that financial products cannot be hidden and all details of a newly developed product or security become public knowledge once it is launched on the market. Hence, the 'first mover' advantage in the market would be limited before rival banks copy the product and take away any monopoly profits.

Miera and Repullo (2010) have concluded that increased competition affects the risk of bank failure in which (1) banks invest in business loans; (2) the default of these loans is endogenously chosen by the entrepreneur; and (3) loan defaults are imperfectly correlated. The risk-shifting effect as identified by Boyed and De Nicolo (2005) emerges from number (1) and (2) above which works as follows: more competition leads to lower loan rates, which results in lower probabilities of default, and hence safer banks. The margin effect resulted from number (3) above reveals that more competition leads to lower loan rates, and as a consequence less revenue from performing loans, which provide a buffer against loan default, and hence, this results in riskier banks.

This means as banks take on more risk for sake of maximising profit, they will need to shift this risk in various ways, most notably financial innovation. Those innovation act as a shield for irresponsible banking practices for shifting, legal, market, rate of return, tax, credit and regulatory risks. This raises the question of who the actual beneficiaries of financial innovation are! Definitely, not me or you as consumers and clients of banks, and most certainly not the society. This was evident by the financial crisis of 2008 and it was clear who suffered most from its consequences, the average people in society. Does that mean financial innovation is bad as a fact? We are not suggesting that at all, the aim of this chapter is to critically analyse the process of innovation, its unintended consequences and innovation bias as we will see in the following sections.

The structure of the banking industry impacts the interbank competition as well as the price offered by commercial bank credit. This shows a link between banking sector structure and the quality cut-off that delineates bank borrowers from capital market borrowers. Furthermore, the complexity of the financial market is a pivotal determinant of the effect of a financial innovation (Boot and Thakor 1997).

6.6 The Root Cause of Financial Crises

Plosser (2009) argues that a critical role in promoting economic growth has been played by financial innovation. This innovation has been sparked, to a major extent, by developments in finance theory and financial econometrics. It is worth contemplating some critical questions raised about the nature and structure of financial innovation in maintaining financial stability in the current turmoil.

Following a financial analysis of the effects of financial crises, it was observed that the impact on innovation differs according to the underlying informational structure of the financial market, which the new asset is introduced into. This could be addressed by reallocating the portfolio of the risky asset. Boyd and Smith (1996) describe financial innovation as a cyclical process, which is influenced by the development of real sector, and also, influences the development of that sector.

As a solution to this problem, Wilson (2010) argues that the principles of good practice, fairness and justice in Islamic financial transactions can put Islamic finance on the path towards greater penetration in the global financial market, particularly if an emphasis is placed on these values.

If these values of Islamic finance were taken into consideration as general guidelines, subprime mortgages and the securitisation of these mortgages, would not, possibly, have been able to cause such severe damage to the financial system. This is because as Plosser (2009) puts it, such financial innovation and products were presented in a very complex product structure.

It is worth noting that the financial crisis of 2008 has not resulted in a real structural reform or changes in the design of the global financial system. Policy-makers and regulators are more focused on conducting a quick and short term repair

Table 6.1 A summary of the main root causes of financial crises in the literature

	Contributing factors to financial innovation in the literature	Academic literature
1.	Combining banking functionalities, investment and retail	Persons and Warther (1997)
2.	Competition in the financial market and complexity and miss-pricing of financial innovation products, CDOs	Bhattacharyya and Nada (2000) and Finnerty (1992)
3.	Under-regulated financial system	Kaminsky and Reinhart (1999, 2000)
4.	Subprime mortgages, miss-pricing of risk and the sophisticated financial securities, risk-inducing remuneration packages,	Plosser (2009) and Foster (2010)
5.	Future predictions and speculations in the financial market which make it volatile and risky	Boyer (2007)
6.	Profusion of new financial engineering lead to volatile interest rates, floating exchange rates, regulatory policy and taxes	Finnerty (1992)
7.	Persisting and strong liquidity constraint (e.g. the Great Depression of 1929–1932) can trigger a cumulative depression in the financial market	Boyer (2007)
8.	Greed and increased competition which affect failure of the banking system and poor risk control by banks	Miera and Repullo (2010)
9.	We would add to the above as a conclusion, the strong link between the banking system and inter-banking dealings on one hand and the financial market on the other. These strong linkages, in particular, among market-maker banks, play a domino effect in the financial market if one or two of those banks fail.	The researcher's view

of the current system rather than fundamentally changing it (Baccaro 2010, and Traxler 2008). Table 6.1 below provides a summary of the main root causes of financial crises in the literature.

Table 6.1 above provides a summary of various factors in the literature that were identified as a possible trigger of financial crises. These factors acted as a driver for developing and launching various financial innovations to satisfy such factors.

6.7 What Is Financial Innovation?

Having discussed different aspects of financial innovation and its consequences, let us have a closer look on it. Financial innovation is the creation of new financial instruments, technologies, institutions and markets. As in other technologies, innovation in finance includes research and development functions as well as the demonstration, diffusion and adoption of these new products or services (Merton 1992).

In finance, particularly, innovation involves adapting and improvising on existing products and concepts. Advances emerge initially as either products, such as derivatives, high-yield corporate bonds and mortgage-backed securities or processes such as, prices mechanism, trading platforms and means and methods for distributing securities (Allen et al. 2012: 10).

6.7.1 Financial Innovation in History

An analytical review of the recent history of financial innovation and its phases shows us that, the invention of financial theory has taken place over centuries and in parallel with many inventions in mathematics and economic theory. The first beginnings of the mathematical theory of probability in the seventeenth century led to the first insurance companies in that same century, which based their operations on sound statistical risk analysis (Shiller 2012: 7). The mathematical thinking that led to the Laplace[2] transform in the mathematics of the eighteenth century also led to the concept of present value of a flow of income, and as a consequence to modern investment theory. Also, advances in the theory of stochastic processes in the nineteenth century led to the concepts of statistical innovations and of the random walk, and thus, to the twentieth-century concept of efficient markets. Furthermore, advances in theoretical physics in the twentieth century led to the mathematics of the Black-Scholes[3] option pricing theory (Shiller 2012: 7).

[2]The Laplace transform is a widely used integral transform with many applications in physics and engineering. Denoted $\mathcal{L}\{f\}$ (or alternatively $\mathcal{L}_t\{f(t)\}$), it is a linear operator of a function $f(t)$ with a real argument t ($t \geq 0$) that transforms $f(t)$ to a function $F(s)$ with complex argument s. This transformation is objective for the majority of practical uses; the most-common pairs of $f(t)$ and $F(s)$ are often given in tables for easy reference. The Laplace transform has the useful property that many relationships and operations over the original $f(t)$ correspond to simpler relationships and operations over its image $F(s)$. It is named after Pierre-Simon Laplace, who introduced the transform in his work on probability theory. See, Korn, G. A.; Korn, T. M. (1967), *Mathematical Handbook for Scientists and Engineers* (2nd ed.), McGraw-Hill Companies.

[3]Following early work by Louis Bachelier and later work by Edward O. Thorp, Fischer Black and Myron Scholes made a major breakthrough by deriving a differential equation that must be satisfied by the price of any derivative dependent on a non-dividend-paying stock. By employing the technique of constructing a risk neutral portfolio that replicates the returns of holding an option, Black and Scholes produced a closed-form solution for a European option's theoretical price. At the same time, the model generates hedge parameters necessary for effective risk management of option holdings. While the ideas behind the Black–Scholes model were groundbreaking and eventually led to Scholes and Merton receiving the Swedish Central Bank's associated Prize for Achievement in Economics (a.k.a., the Nobel Prize in Economics), the application of the model in actual options trading is clumsy because of the assumptions of continuous (or no) dividend payment, constant volatility, and a constant interest rate. Nevertheless, the Black–Scholes model is still one of the most important methods and foundations for the existing financial market in which the result is within the reasonable range. See, Black, Fischer and Myron S. Scholes, (1973), "The Pricing of Options and Corporate Liabilities," *Journal of Political Economy*, 81 (3), 637–654.

6.7.2 *What Drives Financial Innovation?*

Innovation in the financial sector, as in other industries, primarily arises as a response to the needs of users of financial products. These basic financial needs, such as the safe transfer of funds, the financing of private and public venture, the facilitation of savings and investments and the reallocation of risks, led not only to the creation of money as an abstract means to store and transfer value, but also the introduction of banks (Ackermann 2012: 223).

Shiller (1993) has argued that financial innovation can and should be deployed to manage society's largest economic risks. By this argument, he advanced many proposals on how financial instruments can be deployed to manage and help reduce fluctuations in people's lifetime income and wealth. Shiller (1993) also addresses one of the most powerful drivers of financial innovation, the desire to reduce income volatility and insure against the occurrence of adverse events. It is argued by Levin et al. (1987: 785) that most if not all, financial innovations were potentially useful for hedging purposes, as a driver of financial innovation. However, it also provided speculative opportunities, which led to the misuse and abuse of such financial innovation products.

One of the main challenges that remain is the interdependencies between financial institutions across markets and countries generated through the advances in financial instruments. This raises a question of how one can assess whether a new financial instrument is disproportionately risky or not (Ackermann 2012: 224). In this case, theoretical underpinnings become essential in the absence of adequate field tests. In principle, financial innovation could be tested in a model-based world derived on the basis of economic theory. However, it can be argued at the same time that financial instruments that do not work in theory should not work in practice either. Having said that, not everything, on the other hand, that works in theory does so in practice (Ackermann 2012: 224).

Therefore, many financial products that could be considered harmless if judged on an individual basis, or from private individualistic interest, may turn harmful and dangerous in an environment marked by a toxic combination of market developments. In most cases, a useful theory is built only after the fact to explain what was previously observed in the market or financial system. Hence, the recent financial crisis of 2008 provides a case in point (Ackermann 2012: 224).

6.8 Undesirable Consequences of Innovation

It is not surprising that the undesired risks and consequences of innovation are rarely researched as the typical assumption is that innovation is always good. This assumption remains unquestioned and widely accepted (Sveiby et al. 2012: 1). This is confirmed by Rogers (1983) in his literature review of innovation over 25 years ago, where he concluded that only 0.2% of research related to innovation addressed consequences of innovation.

To follow up on Rogers's (1983) findings, Sveiby et al. (2012: 1) conducted a literature review of all papers in the EBSCO database on innovation that study the undesirable consequences of innovation. The study found only 26 papers on 'unintended or undesirable consequences of innovation'; 1 per 1000, a proportion that has not changed since the 1960s. Sveiby et al. (2012: 1) concludes that this is still the case today on all areas in the scientific field of innovation in general and financial innovation in particular, where the study of negative impact and consequences seems to be marginalised.

Sveiby et al.'s (2012: 62) subsequent theoretical framework has been inspired by contributions from four theories. These theories are economic theory, communication theory (diffusion of innovation), Merton's sociological theory and stakeholder theory. Unintended consequences have been a cornerstone factor in economic theory since Adam Smith's work in the eighteenth century.

According to Smith (1789) prosperity for society as a whole is generated by individuals, who are led by an invisible hand to promote an end, which was no part of his intention.[4] In economics, diffusion theory is regarded as the third step in the Schumpeterian 'trilogy', after invention and product development. This is when the new product and process spread across the market and many different impacts emerge and become known (Stoneman 1995: 2–4).

The innovator's agents are considered as driving powers, with the intention of spreading or increasing the usage of the innovation among adopters. Hence economic theory defines diffusion from the innovator's perspective (Stoneman 1995: 4). This theory emphasises, in particular, on the economic impact on the industry and corporations, however, unintended or undesirable consequences are not part of the theme of this theory (Lissoni and Metcalfe 1993).

The sociological diffusion theory of innovation, however, recognises unintended and indirect consequences on groups of individuals. Hence, it defines innovation from an adopter's perspective, in terms of seeing diffusion as the process of communicating an innovation via certain channels (Rogers 1976).

Schumpeter (1939: 86) sees innovation together with all its effects and the response to them by the economic system as a key generator of growth in the economy. Innovation is the most distinguished element in the economic history of capitalism and is mainly responsible for what we, at first sight, attribute to other factors, such as industrial processes. In the Schumpeterian economic theory, the effects of innovation are disruption in the economy, which eventually becomes the cause of both the growth of new industries and firms and the demise of old ones. Therefore, for some the direct and indirect consequences will be desirable, and

[4]In economics, the 'invisible hand of the market' is a metaphor conceived by Adam Smith to describe the self-regulating behaviour of the marketplace. This phrase has come to capture his important claim that individuals' efforts to maximise their own gains in a free market benefits society, even if the ambitious have no benevolent intentions.

others will suffer, such cycles, as Sveiby et al. (2012: 62) put it, are an integral part of the capitalist economic system. Schumpeter's (1939: 87) theory has been widely criticised and his view of the role of innovation as the key generator of economic growth has been reduced in later economic theory. However, his definition of innovation as 'the setting up of new production function', in which he has distinguished between products and process innovation, still in principle the basis of later definitions.

6.9 Pro-Innovation Bias

It is clear from the academic research about innovation, that innovation is based on a predominant assumption, which dictates that 'innovation is good' regardless of its consequences. This is also known as the pro-innovation bias that would raise an alarm (Abrahamson 1991; Rogers 1983; Kimberly 1981).

This bias reduces the ability of decision makers and change agents to predict undesirable and unintended consequences. In order to understand how the pro-innovation bias is constantly reinforced, we should understand how innovation is socially constructed on different levels of participants in the society (Sveiby et al. 2012: 2).

The pro-innovation bias is the implication in diffusion research that an innovation should be diffused and adopted by all members of a social system, that it should be diffused rapidly and be neither reinvented nor rejected. Rarely, a pro-innovation bias is stated straightforwardly in academic research. Rather, the bias is assumed and implied, therefore, this lack of recognition of the pro-innovation bias makes it difficult and potentially dangerous from an intellectual perspective (Rogers 2010: 100–107; and Leeuwis 2013).

It is also important to consider what assumptions innovation is built on and what are the consequences of these assumptions. Moreover, how innovation is discussed by various players, such as academic researchers and how the research about innovation is conducted, by policy makers, funding bodies and other authorities is also an important area to examine (Sveiby et al. 2012: 2).

Rogers (1983) concludes that one of the main reasons for this bias in innovation research is historical. This is because innovations have had such positive outcomes on economic growth in the United Sates post World War II that any other outcomes would have been considered marginal, and thus received little attention. Hence, this bias still with us today and is reflected in innovation research.

Pro-innovation bias, however, can be overcome by taking the following points into account when examining an innovation or class of innovation:

1. Investigate the diffusion of innovation while the process is underway to ensure collection of reliable data.

2. Be thoughtful when selecting an area of study, comparative analysis of both successful and unsuccessful cases of innovation diffusion would be useful, because such a wide range of innovation helps overcome pro-innovation bias.
3. Understanding individuals' perception of innovation and their situation given that personal conception could lead to rejection, discontinuous or reinvention of the innovation in question.
4. Diffusion of innovation should be studied in a broader context (Tuan 2010: 268 and Rogers 2010: 105–107).

6.10 Three Schools of Innovation

Having established the argument above about the unthought-of or undesirable consequences of innovation and the pro-innovation bias, this section will now focus on the three Schumpeterian schools of innovation, which address the economic, social and cultural issues of innovation. The logic for choosing these three main schools is because they cover all related aspects to innovation and its consequences i.e. economic, social and cultural. This discussion will then lay the foundations for outlining a new school of innovation and its theory from an Islamic perspective.

Amid the concept of innovation in economic theory was advanced by Schumpeter, he assumed only minor reliance of innovation on invention (Ruttan 1959). One of the earliest interpretations of Schumpeter's views that shaped the sequential model was brought forward by two American economists, Y. Brozen and W. P. Maclaurin (Brozen 1951). Maclaurin's sequential analysis of innovation was based on the interpretation that Schumpeter regarded the process of innovation as being pivotal for the understanding of economic growth. However, he did not give due consideration to the role of science. This analysis by Maclaurin's provided a measurable detailed technological advance process, which is established on defined elements. He divided the process into five steps in this order, pure science, invention, innovation, finance and acceptance or diffusion (Maclaurin 1953). Brozen (1951) on the other hand, developed two models, one of which explained the required factors for the utilisation of discoveries of science, and the other based on Schumpeter's three categories.

Many years later, these propositions were developed further into a series of linear models of innovation, such as the sequence model suggested by Ruttan, invention → innovation → technological change (Ruttan 1959). More contributions to the theory and process of innovation including product development cycle by economists were presented in the following years. The above analysis has lead in later years to the birth of various schools of innovation which are discussed below. The following discussion will elaborate on the nature of innovation, focal concerns, and apprehension of time from the point of view of each school of innovation.

6.10.1 The Corporate Entrepreneurial School: A Social Perspective—Innovation as Grassroots Impetuses

Tzeng (2009) argues that grassroots impetuses feature the pattern of corporate innovation. Classic sources of evidence according to him include:

Peters and Waterman's (1982) research on 62 successful companies in the United States. After conducting various interviews in 1979 and 1980 and a 25-year literature review, Peters and Waterman concluded that 'autonomy and entrepreneurship' were crucial to innovation. Corporate entrepreneurs enjoyed their autonomy in skunkworks[5] in order to avoid formal routines. Moreover, very successful companies carried out innovation in a 'championship process' rather than in 'formal product planning' (1982: 204).

Quinn's (1985) research on large-scale American, Japanese, and European companies: Quinn's investigation lasted for two-and-a-half years examining how Intel, Sony and Pilkington Brothers, among others, carried out innovation. Overall, he also concluded that innovation operates in 'skunkworks' (1985: 78) and that even though, 'innovation tends to be individually oriented' (1985: 83), it involves 'a high level of group identity and loyalty' (1985: 78). According to him, introducing a new product can be compared to 'raising a healthy child, it needs a mother (champion) who loves it and a father (authority figure with resources) to support it' (1985: 78).

Kanter's (1983) research on the most innovative firms in the United States: It took Kanter five years to conduct 234 interviews in 47 firms. She observed that 'the largest amount of innovation occurred in a peripheral rather than a core area'. In addition, innovation 'was self-initiated, this means that innovation was not directed from the top, but was initiated by 'the rebels' who bootlegged organisational resources (1983: 99).

Burgelman's (1983) research into a major diversified, hi-technology firm in the United States: Following 61 interviews and writing 435 pages of field notes, Burgelman concluded that innovation resides in the autonomous strategic impetus of individuals at the operational levels (1983: 241). Based on his conclusion, Burgelman suggested that the institutionalised approach to innovation might be inadequate (1983: 242) because innovations don't fit neatly into established categories (Burgelman and Sayles 1986: 139).

The above discussions lead logically to the following conclusions. Through engagement, corporate entrepreneurs can form 'networks of innovators' (Freeman 1991), reaching out beyond its organisational boundaries to access, channel, and integrate innovative technologies developed by themselves and others (Chesbrough 2003; Schilling and Phelps 2007). Through the conscious and purposeful engagement in networks, corporate entrepreneurs can creatively respond to different

[5]The designation "skunk works", or "skunkworks", is widely used in business, engineering, and technical fields to describe a group of people within an organisation given a high degree of autonomy and unhampered by bureaucracy, tasked with working on advanced or secret projects.

opportunities in real time. It can thus be argued that engagement is the discipline of innovation (Drucker 1998).

6.10.2 The Cultural School: A Cultural Perspective—Nature of Innovation: Deep Craft

High-tech innovation is deep craft in itself. As Arthur maintained, Advanced technology resides, in essence, in deep craft' (2001: 7), and deep craft is associated with a shared culture of beliefs, a shared culture of practices' (2001: 8). True technical innovation 'cannot be created by digging information out of books or journal articles' (2001: 11). Instead, it is actually the product of craftsmanship.

Graham and Shuldiner (2001) concurred with Arthur after investigating the 150-year history of Corning. They noted that first, deep craft is not a technique because it is 'a set of skills and sensibilities that cannot be reduced to a science' (2001: xiv). Second, deep craft is an intergenerational heritage in that it is 'shared through time, and the craft is renewed and reinvented in each era in accordance with its peculiar circumstances' (2001: xiv). Third, as it is driven by vision, deep craft is motivated by purposes that go beyond simple materialism (2001: xiv).

6.10.3 The Capability School: An Economic Perspective-Innovation as Institutionalised Capability

Innovation, as an institutionalised capability, characterizes technological change. This observation was made by four eminent historians. Among them, Chandler, a business historian, built his observation (1992) on his unparalleled historical research on the US economic system from the 1850s to the 1920s. On the other hand, economic historians Mowery and Rosenberg established their observation (1998) on their research which traced the paths of innovation in the US from 1900 to 1990. Historian Hounshell (1996) tracked the evolution of industrial research in the US from 1875 to the early 1990s (Tzeng 2009).

Systemic innovation is dependent on the dynamic capabilities of a firm (Wang and Ahmed 2007), which can be defined as the firm's ability to integrate, build, and reconfigure internal and external competencies (Teece et al. 1997: 516; see also Teece 2007). Institutionalised capabilities translate into routines, which are the so-called 'genes' in innovation (Nelson and Winter 1982: 134). Routines are most of what is regular and predictable about business behaviour (1982: 15). By this definition, there are three classes of routines relevant to innovation: (1) the operating routine, (2) the investment routine, and (3) the search routine (1982: 17). The most important of these is the search routine, which carries out innovation and resides in the research and development (R&D) department where innovations occur (Tzeng 2009).

The next issue that needs to be responded to, according to Tzeng (2009), is how to institutionalise and routinize innovation. Based on her empirical study of the Objectives, Strategies and Tactics (OST) system at Texas Instruments, Jelinek (1979) argued that institutionalising innovation means codifying program innovation. The purpose of institutionalising innovation is to render a previously ad hoc innovation into a routine, which is a repeatable economic event.

The essence of institutionalising innovation can be described by the following mechanisms. First, systems/routines capture knowledge: It is through administrative systems that planning and policy are made possible, because the systems capture knowledge about the task in question (1979: 139). Second, systems/routines generate innovation: As a system, the OST would generalize a procedure for acquiring the requisite new knowledge, creating a shared pattern of thought regarding innovation (1979: 141). Hence, innovation can be institutionalised (1979: 157).

Research has highlighted the importance of a long time commitment to financing the development of new technology of an enterprise (Lazonick and Prencipe 2005; O'Sullivan 2007). This commitment is presented by how the enterprise decides whether to innovate or not to innovate, which is based on evaluating and calculating the costs and benefits of each R&D project. Hypothetically, the earliest development follows the simple economics of basic scientific research, the expected revenue of the invention exceeds the expected cost (Nelson 1959: 300).

In order to make such calculations, the capability school treats information as a commodity and views innovation as the production of information (Arrow 1962). It also sheds light on the R&D boundaries of the firm (Pisano 1990). This way, the management of innovation boils down to managing intellectual property rights (Aghion and Tirole 1994). Thus, the recent development in theory involves sophisticated techniques of real option valuation (McGrath and Nerkar 2004). Hence, the management of innovation ends up being manifested into simply managing R&D project portfolios (MacMillan and McGrath 2002).

In practice, according to Merck's CFO Judy Lewent, an advanced R&D paradigm consists of option analysis, financial engineering and game theory (Nichols 1994: 92–98). The green light for innovation turns on under the following two conditions. First, expenditures on R&D should be assured. Nelson and Winter (1982: 310) once stressed the effects of spending on the ability of a firm to innovate, arguing the probability that a firm will come up with an innovation that is proportional to its R&D spending. Second, appropriation of R&D profits should be secured.

As Levin et al. (1987: 783) discussed, to have an incentive to undertake research and development; a firm must be able to generate appropriate returns sufficient to make the investment worthwhile. However, the appropriation of R&D profits is not secured whenever externalities of innovation occur. The profits of innovation may spill over the boundary of the firm, thus becoming public. Once public, the profits of innovation are no longer economically appropriable (Nelson 1992). Thus, market failure will discourage firms from conducting R&D activities (Tzeng 2009).

6.11 Conclusion

The objective of this chapter is to identify weaknesses in the current financial system, and the approach taken towards innovation in general and financial innovation in particular. It is clear as shown herewith that there is a pro-innovation bias in the academic research and there is a critical area of innovation in general and financial innovation in particular, that has been ignored due to the perception of innovation being generally good.

Thus, there is an urgent need for this area to be researched and put under the spot light for scrutiny. In order to do that, this chapter looked at the aim, objective, process, factors, elements, structure, intended and unintended consequences of financial innovation and highlighted how some financial innovations can be harmful to the financial system, economy and society as a whole. It appears that there is a complacent understanding among regulators, policy makers and players in the banking and financial system to keep whatever action proposed to address this clear weakness, in the approach taken towards financial innovation, to the minimum. This implies that this situation of financial crises and irresponsible practices in the financial system will keep occurring, if it is not dealt with fundamentally and structurally urgently.

The three main schools of innovation as described by Tzeng (2009), their perspectives and building-block ideas are summarised in the Table 6.2 below. This table will be developed further by adding a fourth school of innovation that its principles and foundations will be analysed in the next chapter (Chap. 7).

Financial innovation should be driven by the needs and demands of users, but that is not the case in the recent years. Financial innovation today, even after the severe financial crisis of 2008, are and have been driven by competition among financial institutions, risk shifting, to circumvent regulation and legal constraints and profit maximisation rather than market demands and consumers' needs. This approach ignores the welfare of society, ethical financial and banking practices, average consumers and users of financial services and the impact on economic

Table 6.2 Summary of the three main Schumpeterian schools of innovation

	Corporate capability school: economic perspective	Entrepreneurship school: social perspective	Culture school: cultural perspective
1. Nature of innovation	Institutionalised capability	Innovation as grass-roots impetuses	Innovation as deep craft
2. Inherent logic of innovation	Evaluate	Engage	Envision
3. Relationship among members	Instruction-based relationship	Identity-based relationship	Intergenerational relationship
4. Focal concern	Affiliated institutions	Authentic voices	Affective identification
5. Apprehensions of time	Path dependencies	Improvisation	A deep sense of temporality

development. It focuses on the benefit of very small group in society in contrast to the benefit of all or at least most stakeholders in the society.

This view of financial innovation diverted the cycle of innovation as developed by the early economists with the objective of addressing particular financial needs in the market. However, as we have seen, it works, currently, in reverse; financial institutions create false financial needs in the market to sell their financial innovations for their sole benefit of profit maximisation, risk shifting and resolving liquidity issues. This practice refers to what some academics and regulators called as socially useless or harmful financial innovation.

The reasonable way forward, having diagnosed the disease, is to offer the remedy as painkillers do not make the disease go away and will not solve the problem. This remedy would require a cultural change in our financial system and banking practices that should be based on self-imposed moral and ethical criteria. This possible remedy will be explored in more details in the following chapter (Chap. 7) by analysing innovation from an Islamic perspective. This would then help outlining the religious school towards innovation as described in the theory of Islamic economics and finance.

Chapter 7
Financial Innovation Theory from an Islamic Perspective

7.1 Introduction

The previous chapter (Chap. 6) discussed innovation in the traditional economics theory and outlined the innovation approach for three main innovation schools. It also explored the issue of innovation bias in the literature and the role of financial innovation in financial crisis as an influencing and exacerbating factor. The financial innovation theory from an Islamic perspective, however, goes beyond the basic principles of its conventional counterpart. Its basic principles on which it could be built are deeply rooted in the teachings of Shariah, namely the Qur'an and *Sunnah* of Prophet Muhammad, in general and the particular general Shariah rulings of the principles of jurisprudence (*usoul al fiqh*).

Unlike its conventional counterpart that is driven purely by man-made rules, which could be influenced by worldly desires of profit maximisation for the benefit of a small group. The financial innovation theory in Islam takes into account a more holistic approach. This approach perceives any financial innovation as a worldly financial activity, which should benefit the wider society and simultaneously as an act of worship of God when based on good intention and being developed in accordance with Shariah and its objectives.

This is very important differentiation in the characteristics of the financial theory from an Islamic perspective, which is, usually, ignored or forgotten in current financial practices of IFIs. This chapter aims to articulate these distinctive features and characteristics on which a religious financial innovation theory is developed and built. This theory then will be the cornerstone for exploring the cycle and processes of any financial engineering and product development in IFIs.

This academic endeavour will set the foundations for a rapidly growing interest-free banking system and would ensure that it will not be diverted from its true path and what it stands for. The jigsaw pieces of this theory are already there, they just need to be rationalised and put together within a framework to serve their purpose and make sense. This chapter will aim to do just that by outlining the Islamic school

S. Alamad, *Financial Innovation and Engineering in Islamic Finance*,
Contributions to Management Science, DOI 10.1007/978-3-319-52947-9_7

of innovation from an Islamic economics theory perspective as a comparable alternative to the three outlined main traditional schools of innovation in the previous chapter. The chapter concludes then with analysis by identifying the key aspects of the Islamic school of innovation for a more resilient ethical approach towards financial innovation.

7.2 Four Schools of Innovation

Having established the argument in the previous chapter about the unthought-of or undesirable consequences of innovation, the pro-innovation bias and analytically discussed the three main Schumpeterian schools of innovation, we will now focus on establishing the fourth school of innovation. This discussion will then lay the foundations for establishing an innovation school from an Islamic perspective. For the benefit of this chapter we will summarise the three Schumpeterian schools of innovation and their Islamic counterpart that are analysed below. Thus, the four schools of innovation at glance are:

a. The capability school: sees innovation from an economic perspective. Innovation as an institutionalised capability influences technological change. The decision whether 'to innovate or not to innovate' is based on an evaluation of the firm requirements and objectives. Within firms, which are composed of routines, relationships among members are instruction-based; outside the firms, affiliated institutions serve as the engines of innovation. Technological change evolves in a path-dependent way.
b. The corporate entrepreneurial school: sees innovation from a social perspective. Grassroots stimulus presents the pattern of corporate innovation. In addition, grassroots stimulus emerges from a sense of identity and, as such, engages many actors. Authentic voices drive identity-based relationships. Therefore, innovation as a grassroots impetus impulses improvisation in action.
c. The cultural school: sees innovation from a cultural perspective. High-tech innovation, per se, is deep craft. Vision is the driver and the core of deep craft and its fabric is intergenerational relationships. Affective and clear identification is the pre-requirement of innovation. For this reason, innovation, as deep craft, is a product of a deep sense of temporality.
d. The Islamic school: sees innovation from economic, social and cultural perspectives. This research proposes to name this school the hybrid school of innovation, which in a way incorporates elements from the three schools above and adds to it. Innovation as institutionalised capability characterises a positive change. Whether to innovate or not to innovate is based on an assessment of objectives sought from the intended innovation, how this will be done and its consequences on all affected stakeholders directly and indirectly.
   Grassroots impetus forms the pattern of institutional innovation, and flows from a deep sense of righteousness and social welfare derived from a firm belief

in God. A deep rooted vision in Islamic teachings and the oneness of God as the creator who entrusted humanity with this universe to do good deeds, live together and benefit each other is the core of deep sense of identity. For this reason, innovation is a catalyst for social welfare wedded to a strong concept of accountability. This school is explored and analysed further in the next sections of this chapter.

7.3 Definition of Innovation from an Islamic Perspective

According to Lisan Al Arab and Al Qamous Al Muheat, to innovate is to bring about something new that does not have any resemblance for the first time, an idea, act, practice, product etc. Ibn al Atheer mentioned that innovation is of two types, a good one (innovation of guidance (*huda*)) and a bad one (innovation of misguidance (*dhalaal*)), if the innovation is in accordance with and does not contradict the Qur'an and the *Sunnah* of prophet Muhammad, then it is a good acceptable innovation (Ibn Mandhur 2009).

However, if the innovation contradicts the Qur'an or the *Sunnah* of Prophet Muhammad, it is a bad and non-acceptable innovation. Any innovation that does not fall in either type would fall under the permissible (*mubah*). As an example of a good financial innovation is the establishment of *bait al maal* (the state treasury) by the second caliph Omar Ibn al Khattab.

7.4 The Islamic School of Financial Innovation

Innovation in Islam should be performed with the objective of bringing something beneficial to individuals and society as a whole. Islam has warned those who innovate with bad intentions, who do not give due consideration, when innovating, to the wider society and environment, or initiate something bad in society, that these actions are a punishable sin. Islam has encouraged innovation to address any new issues by making it as one of the five primary sources of Shariah. This is embedded in the concept of *Qiyas* (analogical reasoning and rationalisation) and *Ijtihad* (an individual scholarly interpretation to come up with an answer or a solution to address pressing issues) (Al Khun 1994: 29).

Ijtihad has been encouraged by the Prophet Muhammad (peace be upon him) when he said whoever attempts to make a legal reasoning or judgement (makes *Ijtihad*) and his or her conclusion is correct, will gain a double reward from God, and those who tried their best and their judgement is proven to be incorrect, will get one reward for their attempt (Al Khun 1994: 29).

However, this attempt to reach a ruling, about a financial issue e.g. or financial innovation, should be sincere, based on employing all efforts to reach the right conclusion within the parameters of Islam and the permissible and impermissible in

Shariah. Furthermore, innovation should be with the objective of brining good and benefiting the society as a whole. If innovation is for the benefit of an individual (s) only, it stops to being considered as a good innovation when it clashes with the overall benefit of the society and its welfare (Khallaf 1942).

Islam however advocates accountability; punishment and rewards are all based on actions and intentions. Prophet Muhammad (peace be upon him) said 'whoever makes a good innovation, he or she will be rewarded for it and will even get the same reward as those who followed it, and whoever makes harmful innovation (bad innovation that contradicts the teachings of Islam) he or she will be held accountable for it and he or she will even get the same sin as those who followed it' (*Majma' al zawa'ed* 1980: 173). Thus, the criteria for a financial innovation to be acceptable in Islam is that innovation, in general, and financial innovation, in particular, should be in accordance with Islamic teachings, undertaken for the good of all stakeholders, accompanied with a good intention and is not socially useless or harmful.

7.5 The Mechanics of Financial Innovation: The Role of Jurisprudence

Jurisprudence emerged as a natural result of changes in the Islamic society after the death of Prophet Muhammad (peace be upon him). During his life, he was the point of reference for any new legislation addressing arising issues that require an Islamic view. With the Islamic state expanding rapidly to other parts of the world, new issues, which did not exist at the time of the prophet (peace be upon him), were faced by Muslims.

These new situations required taking certain approaches by early Islamic jurists to extract Shariah rulings based on the Qur'an and the *Sunnah*, but not covered by either of them. Therefore, the word jurisprudence means in Arabic, the efforts made to form one's own judgement (*ra'y*) about an issue that requires a Shariah legal opinion (Khallaf 1942).

The legitimacy of this approach is derived from an event when the prophet (peace be upon him) sent one of his companions, his name Mu'az Ibn Jabal, to Yemen as a judge and teacher. When he came to take leave of the Prophet, Ma'adh was asked how he would govern. Ma'adh said, according to the Quran. The Prophet thereupon asked what he would do if he did not find the solution to the problem in the Quran, to which Ma'adh said he would govern according to the *Sunnah*. But when the Prophet asked if he could not find it in the *Sunnah* also, Ma'adh said: I will exert myself to find the solution. The Prophet thereupon patted his back and told him he was right. Thus, the prophet (peace be upon him) guided him about the method to be used in the absence of a clear ruling in the Qur'an and the *Sunnah*. This method was the power of reasoning to reach a ruling or a judgment (Khallaf 1942).

Therefore, jurisprudence is based on various sources and employs certain principles in deriving the required Shariah rules. These sources are called by the Islamic scholars, the primary sources of legislation in Islam. The first and foremost of these sources are the Qur'an then the Sunnah. Whenever there are explicit rules in both of them there would be no room for the power of reasoning or self-judgment. However, when a clear rule is absent in both of them, the understanding of the Qur'an verses, their purposes and the interpretation of the *Sunnah* including *Ahadith* (sayings) of the prophet (peace be upon him) and their intention, which the contemporary Islamic scholars call the spirit of Shariah, should be employed. This is in order to guide the Islamic jurists towards arriving at the required Sharia rule. Hence the core of jurisprudence is the Qur'an and the Sunnah (Wilson and El-Ashker 2006: 35).

The other primary sources on which Islamic jurisprudence is based are: consensus of jurists' opinion *(ijma')*, analogical reasoning based on established precedents *(qiyas)* and the interpretation of an individual jurist *(ijtihad)*. There are also secondary sources of Shariah[1] that could be considered when making a Shariah legal opinion in relation to financial innovation (Khallaf 1942).

7.6 The Application of Normativity Through Social Practices: Bourdieu's Theory

A sophisticated post-structuralism sociological approach is provided by the work of Pierre Bourdieu. Bourdieu provides a powerful account both of the features of legal reasoning (as discussed above regarding the tool of *ijtihad*) and of the requirements and processes of its production. This provides an explanation that avoids the dilemma between idealism and economism, in order to reconcile both of them (McCahery and Picciotto 1995: 180). The body of legal doctrine, as Bourdieu argues in his theory, is a symbolic order which at any moment could delimit what is possible. Nevertheless, legal doctrine appears, due to its autonomy, abstract and formal nature, to be a closed and coherent system, which generates outcomes from its own embedded internal logic; it does not process the principles of its own dynamics (McCahery and Picciotto 1995: 179).

Islam provides a full and comprehensive code of conduct covering all aspects of life including economics and finance (Naqvi 1981). Therefore, an analogy can be made between the Islamic approach and Bourdieu's normativity theory as the basis for analysing a financial innovation theory from an Islamic perspective. Bourdieu's normativity theory uses the normative practices that are embedded in a legal structure which is observed, enforced and supervised by a legal symbol. This theory could form the basis of an innovation theory from an Islamic perspective. This is

[1]The secondary sources of Shariah would include *Maslah* (the consideration of public interest), *'Aurf* (custom) and *Istihsan* (approval of a good practice that does not contradict Shariah).

because of the similarity represented by the framework, which incorporates principles and requirements ordained by a divine authority, God, who sets those instructions.

This framework emerges from normative Islamic practices, to be embedded as part of the financial innovation cycle, rather than a man-made rules or laws for normative social practices in accordance with Bourdieu's normativity theory. The theory framework for both has some congruencies however; the legal authority for each is different. Furthermore, the social practices and behaviour in one, the Islamic innovation theory, is derived from a firm religious belief in a divine authority while the other is derived from a legal authority, which is not necessary to be a form of firm belief in the law or conviction.

One may ask what the relation would be between Bourdieu's theory and financial innovation. As mentioned above, the aim is to demarcate the financial innovation theory from an Islamic perspective. This is achieved by drawing on Bourdieu's theory of generating normativity through social practices, which fits perfectly with financial innovation in the theory of Islamic economics.

This is largely, because the generation of innovation theory from an Islamic perspective must be based on the Islamic legal structure and law, which are derived from the main sources of legislation in Islam. These sources are the Qur'an and the *Sunnah*; the principles on which financial innovation theory can be outlined are derived from both of them, and then embedded in economic, social and cultural practices. Islam provides the legal framework for the conduct and practices that should be embraced by Muslims as part of their life, regarding economic activities and financial innovation. This approach, in relation to financial innovation theory, is considered to be inseparable part of any Muslim fulfilling the requirements and instructions ordained by the higher authority, God the creator. Islam has succeeded in establishing an inner consciousness, self-supervision and accountability in those individuals conducting economic and financial activities within society. For instance, there is not any legal body to enforce *zakat* and punish and imprison those who do not pay their *zakat*, despite *zakat* being a compulsory obligation in Islam. *Zakat* should be paid to the deserving poor and needy, as detailed in the Qur'an and Sunnah, which set the criteria for those deserving the payment of *zakat*, in an Islamic society. This is in contrast to the way civil law deals with those who do not pay taxes imposed by government. Muslims calculate their annual *zakat* payment due on their wealth, according to the applicable percentage (2.5%) and pay it as a religious duty without being supervised by a legal authority (Naqvi 1981).

Bourdieu (1987: 833) provides a very strong argument on how the legal sphere is constructed. However, he is less clear in his argument on why abstract formal rules play such an important part in the production of social relations. In his view, legal rationality provided by the system (in our case the system here is the divine injunctions as ordained by God) offers predictability and calculability. For Bourdieu, the power of law is derived from the effectiveness and authority of legal symbols in giving the 'seal of universality' to social practices (1987: 845). Legitimacy is imposed in the social order through symbolic domination. Although

Islamic jurists can provide competing interpretations, they must operate within the hierarchy of both institutions and norm-sources, which defines the authority of legal decisions (McCahery and Picciotto 1995: 179).

Bourdieu (1987: 818) stresses the notion of social practices of participants by introducing his key concept of his theory of the 'habitus', which translates into durable differences in the outlook of differently situated groups. It provides an understanding of how humans internalise power structures and actively reproduce them. He explains this concept by stating that the juridical field tends to operate like an 'apparatus' to the extent that the cohesion of the freely orchestrated 'habitus' of legal interpreters is supported and strengthened by the discipline of a hierarchized body of participants (professionals), who utilise a set of an already established procedures.

In order to put this concepts into contexts and elaborate a little bit more, the habitus is defined as 'the system of dispositions to a particular practice, an objective basis for the regulation of behaviour, and hence for the regularity of modes of practice. Then, if practices can be predicated, this is because the effect of the habitus is that agents who are equipped with and will behave in a particular way in certain circumstances (Bourdieu 1990: 77, also in McCahery and Picciotto 1995).

Groups bring a different cultural understanding to existing power structures through an act of creative syncretism, through an institutional innovation. This symbolic action activates both of Laitin's two faces of culture, as the change in symbolic works both signal different goals and to mobilise collective action to achieve them (Bourdieu 1989). This process of aligning ends and means through symbolic action is identified by Smith as strategic constructivism (2006: 26). Bourdieu's concept of habitus portrays actors as being quite conditioned structurally; for instance, he rejects exclusionary portrayals of cultural elites, arguing instead that they are simply expressing in cultural terms their true position in objective relations. Bourdieu's formal name for his approach is structural constructivism (Bourdieu 1989).

Using symbolic power to align ends and means is clearly evidenced in the case of Islamic banking as an innovation of Islamic finance. Once the framework of Islamic finance is established, the mobilisation of capital within that framework is supportive of religious and cultural objectives (Smith 2006: 28).

Islamic finance deploys both of Bourdieu's symbolic strategies; the subjective side represented in the application of Islamic law to finance that creates a distinction between it and the existing conventional finance. From an objective perspective, Islamic finance has become a powerful symbolic notion of identity that encouraged Muslims to re-evaluate their financial dealings. Also, Islamic financial institutions began to expand for a share in the market to meet the rising consumer demands (Bourdieu 1989).

Therefore, the repertoire of behaviour is structured and limited by the habitus, even though it permits a range of innovation, which follows a practical logic. Bourdieu argues that, in order to avoid the twin charges of determinism and functionalism, the concepts of the field and of habitus must be understood as interactive notions (Bourdieu 1992: 102–115). This raises a question of whether the Islamic theory of financial innovation would be compatible with the conventional counterpart.

As discussed in the previous chapter (Chap. 6, Sect. 6.8) and is elaborated in Sect. 7.7 below, not all financial innovations have been beneficial to society not mentioning the negative effects on economy. Financial innovation from an Islamic perspective is limited and controlled by certain parameters and requirements that must be met and are by nature embedded as a habitus in the economic and social practices. This does not, in any way, suggest that it would be restrictive and limited because of these restrictions, as this view will be eliminated when we discuss these exclusions in innovation theory from an Islamic perspective, which would, potentially, be harmful to the society.

7.7 Socially Useless Financial Innovation

This view has been advocated by Turner who argued that many forms of financial innovations, which are of concerns, have a great potential to generate large negative externalities. Those financial innovations would produce not merely redistribution of an unchanged economic cake, but harmful instability in overall patterns of economic growth (2012: 36). Turner further argues that financial innovation might be of *zero* social value, even if it did not generate actually negative externality effects. However, factors which can make financial innovation a driver of systemic financial instability will produce not just *zero*, but negative effects on society. The higher the share of complex financial services, the greater the danger that highly skilled people are taking part in financial activities, which produce large private returns, but only have a merely distributive social impact (2012: 60).

Rajan echoes this argument, he explains that when producing and using financial innovations and products, we should ask ourselves if we are producing a socially useful financial innovation, however with few exceptions, making money ('profit maximisations' in the Islamic view regarding the principles of innovation theory) is the *raison d'etre* of the financier. This absence of naturally arising checks and balances creates a potentially legitimate role for regulatory interventions (2010: 121–133).

It is proven that regulatory intervention is not always effective as it requires a cultural change in grassroot economic and financial practices. This is however different in the Islamic theory of financial innovation as it is already orchestrated on a firm religious belief and a world view instructed by God as the Creator, which forms the legal framework that governs such financial practices.

This theory of a hidden power that drives behavioural and cultural activities is what Adam Smith (1789), referred to as the 'invisible hand'. This view was based on the assumption that innovation incentivised by self-interest would serve the social good. Smith's theory was originated in the eighteenth century, when he described his theory about the 'invisible hand' in the context of a very simple and basic financial market. However, the question that is posed here is whether this theory applies today, or it has become redundant as the financial system has developed and advanced. This question is particularly relevant, when considering the absence of real competition in the financial and banking system, the widespread occurrence of monopolistic power and the failure by the relevant financial and regulatory authorities to curb this abuse of power.

Thus, it is believed (Al Saead 1970: 112) that the Islamic economics and finance system provides a better alternative to the 'invisible hand' theory. This alternative is manifested by a multi-layered approach, which is: the divine accountability of an individual's financial behaviour, followed by a self-supervision, supervision by appointed credible and trustworthy Islamic scholars to monitor and approve financial innovation and products offered by Islamic financial institutions.

Finally, the supervision of Muslim society, who would boycott any financial practices that are perceived to contradict the principles of Shariah. This reaction by society in response to bad financial practices that contradict Shariah is considered one of the main risks that would threaten the very existence of an IFI and damage its reputation. This concept will be analysed in more details in the sections below.

7.8 Economic Thought in the Qura'an and the Sunnah, Basic Philosophy for Financial Innovation Theory

Three cardinal ideological concepts and three main principles could be considered to establish the basic philosophy of Islamic economic thought, which also apply on the theory of financial innovation from an Islamic point of view. The three concepts are: the concept of unity, the concept of viceregency of human being on earth and the concept of free-will and responsibility. The principles are considered to be the principle of moderation, the principle of economic efficiency and the principle of social justice (Ahmed 1980; Naqvi 1981).

7.8.1 The Concept of Unity, Tawhid

The concept of unity emerges from the first pillar of Islam which emanates from Muslims' firm belief in the oneness of God with the belief in Prophet Muhammad (peace be upon him) as His messenger. This concept has many implications, some of which are: the unity of the creator (God), the unity of His attributes (*sifat*), the unity of His work and creation and, as a consequence, the unity of the universe as fully integrated in this unity of God (Al Saead 1970: 112). Nothing can be viewed in separation of His will or work, nor could be seen in isolation of His existence. The whole creation should be seen as a 'whole', and be viewed as an integrated part of the holiness of the oneness of God (Wilson and El-Ashker 2006: 37).

The key to the economic, including financial innovation, philosophy of Islam lies in a person's relationship with God, His universe and His creation. This philosophy, as a common factor with other Abrahamic religions like Judaism and Christianity, is the basis of the moral appeal to humans to surrender themselves to the will of God (Al Najjar 2003: 134). Islam even goes beyond this exhortation and makes it clear that all life is essentially in unity because it also provides the practical way to conduct all facets of human life, including economic and finance activities, in accordance with God's will. There should be unity of ideas and actions in a person's existence and consciousness (Asad 1993). Muslims believe that their success in the hereafter depends on their performance and actions in this life on earth, because all people are accountable to God. This, therefore, adds a new dimension to the valuation of people's deeds, including the generation, conduct and practices of any financial innovation or activity, in this life (Siddiqi 1981).

The consequences of the whole-ness of the universe, as discussed above, dictates that any economic activity undertaken by an individual or a group of individuals should not be harmful to the interests of others, nor should it be damaging other sources of goodness in the universe. Moreover, this also means that no abuse or misuse of economic resources in pursuit of 'maximisation' of benefit to some individuals or a group of individuals by sacrificing the benefit to others (Wilson and El-Ashker 2006: 37).

A definite relationship between all humans is therefore prescribed in Islam. This is the relationship of brotherhood and sisterhood and equality (Abu-Sulayman 1976). Thus, the users of economic resources should always maintain a well-defined balance. Any deviation from this rule must be immediately rectified by the individuals themselves in the first instance, then by the state, which has the right to rectify the damage, if the individual has failed to put things right. If the harm caused was deliberate and persistent, God's retribution is promised in return in this life and in the hereafter for the wrongdoers and abusers of the system (Al Aqla et al. 2004: 16).

The Qur'an says "Whoever breaks the covenant of Allah after contracting it, severing that which Allah has ordered to be joined and causing corruption on earth. It is those who are the losers" (Qur'an, 2: 27). However, if they rectify their actions, God is always forgiving and is generous in His reward for the repentant. The Qur'an says "Except for those who repent and correct themselves and make evident [what they concealed]. Those, I will accept their repentance, and I am the Accepting of repentance, the Merciful", (Qur'an, 2: 160).

Hence, unity is a coin with two faces: one stresses the fact that God is the sole creator of the universe, and the other emphasises that people are equal partners or that each person is a brother or sister to the other. As far as economic thought and the theory of financial innovation is concerned, this means cooperation and equality of effort and opportunity, all for the well-being of people and society as a whole (Rice 1999).

7.8.2 The Concept of Vicegerency, al Khilafah

The concept of vicegerency is the core of the Islamic philosophy on which the Islamic economic thought and the theory of financial innovation revolves. Stressing this fact, man is the centre of the universe and God's deputy on earth (Al Aqla et al. 2004: 12), the Qur'an says, "He it is who has created for you everything on earth", (Qur'an, 2: 29), and "When your Lord said to the angels, I am placing on earth one that shall rule as my deputy", (Qur'an, 2: 30), also "It is He who had made you vicegerents on earth", (Qur'an, 35: 39).

This dictates that the deputy has to perform his duties in accordance with his superior's instructions. God has laid down His instructions for utilising economic resources on earth and innovating financial products from these resources in the manner He wishes it to be performed (Abdul Meneam 1979: 38). Ibn Taymiyyah (1994: 53–54) and Al Mydani (1996: 5–10) argue that the use of the word '*khilafah*' is not correct as it means that the '*khalifah*' is the successor of his predecessor, normally, after the death of the predecessor. This is not appropriate as it negates one of God's divine attributes as the only living being Who never dies.

Al Tha'alibi (1997: 536) in his interpretation of the Qur'an also emphasises this notion. Thus, we tend to use the word trusteeship instead of '*khilafah*' and the word trustee instead of '*khalifah*'. This is to ensure a balanced approach of the concept of vicegerency that takes into consideration the reservations of some Islamic scholars on the use of those words from a linguistic and Shariah perspectives due to their perceived meaning in that context.

Although, material prosperity is desirable, it is not an end per se. What is critical is the motivation, the desired "ends" of economic activity or financial innovation. Having established the right motivation, all economic activity assumes the character of worship (Siddiqi 1981). In other words, man utilises and controls economic resources as a trustee on the basis of a trusteeship between him and God, the creator and provider of these economic resources (Ahmed 1976: 163–164). Resources must also be disposed of in such a way as to protect everyone's well-being (Al-Faruqi 1976).

We as humans are, therefore, accountable to God, for any violation of these rules by virtue of the principles of trusteeship and stewardship we would deserve His punishment. This concept has many implications for all economic factors on earth, consumption of economic resources, development of these resources including financial innovation and product derived from it and the distribution of values and benefits among all participants (Wilson and El-Ashker 2006: 38). It is also worth mentioning that the notion of trusteeship is also common to the Jewish and Christian faiths; Green (1993) refers to Psalms 24:1, "The earth is the Lord's and the fullness thereof".

7.8.3 *The Concept of Free Will and Responsibility*, al-Iradah wa al-Masu'wliyyah

7.8.3.1 Free Will and Trust (*Amanah*)

Free will is clearly stated in the Qur'an, it is the ability of human beings to choose, select and decide. Man has the freedom to choose between good and evil, and his destiny is only known to God through His eternal wisdom and knowledge of the characteristics of the man He created. We, therefore, as humans have a free will to act in harmony with God's code of conduct, or in other words the straight path, or to divert from it, and God knows that in advance (Al Zarqa 2012: 48–51). This fact is emphasised in various places in the Qur'an, "Have We not given him two eyes, a tongue and two lips, and shown him the two paths?" (Qur'an, 90: 8–10). This means that it is up to us which path we choose to follow.

Man has also accepted to bear the burden of God's trust (*amanah*) on earth while no one else dared to do so, Qur'an says, "We offered Our trust to the heavens, to the earth and to the mountains, but they declined to bear it for fear of its burden, and man assumed it", (Qur'an, 33: 72). Hence, the delegated authority given to us by God is manifested in the free will and in the established trusteeship between God and us (Al Najjar 2003: 67). Having also assumed God's trust, a big responsibility comes with it to maintain this trust in the manner God expects us to observe as we will see below in the following section.

7.8.3.2 Responsibility

Responsibility imposes limits to man's freedom of choice and dictates accountability for his actions. Authority with free will, on one hand, portrays one side of the trusteeship agreement, responsibility, on the other hand, represents the other side of this relationship between God and us (Al Aqla et al. 2004: 16). This contractual relationship governs the way on which economic resources are owned by man as a trustee, and also establishes the conditions for its management (Hamed 2000: 178). Any breach or violation of these conditions makes man accountable to the ultimate owner, God. The limitations to our freedom in utilising economic resources on earth is two-fold, we should seek efficiency in resource production, and ensure social justice in resource distribution (Ahmed 1976: 88). These elements should be observed constantly when we consider financial innovation, in order to be within the parameters set for an Islamic theory of financial innovation as a diversion from this theory will have its consequences as explained above.

7.8.3.3 A System of Reward and Punishment

In order to complete operational mechanism of the trusteeship agreement where the fulfilment of duties and responsibilities will be assumed in the Hereafter and judged accordingly. Therefore, a system of reward and punishment has to be established (Al Zarqa 2012: 36). The Qur'an says, "And every man's augury have we fastened to his own neck, on the Day of Judgement We shall bring out for him (his) scroll, which he will see spread open. Read thine (own) record, sufficient is thyself this day to make an account against you", (Qur'an, 17: 13–14). Qur'an also says "That Day, the people will depart separated [into categories] to be shown [the result of] their deeds. So whoever does an atom's weight of good will see it, and whoever does an atom's weight of evil will see it", (Qur'an, 99: 6–8).

7.9 Islamic Economic Principles: The Fundamentals for an Islamic Theory of Innovation

The principles of Islamic economics are essential for the study of financial innovation from an Islamic perspective. They set the broad structure for a possible conceptual framework for financial innovation. These principles are explored further in the following sections.

*7.9.1 The Principle of Moderation (*I'atidal*) in Financial Innovation*

The principle of moderation implies that human behaviour, the economic and even non-economic should be exercised with moderation, avoiding any extremism. Consumption should be in moderation, Qur'an says, "Let not your hand be tied to your neck (in not spending) nor let it be stretched fully (in spending extravagantly) so that you may not end in poverty and regret", (Qur'an, 17: 29).

The concept of moderation, therefore, is based on Islamic ideology and it applies not only to the utilisation of resources, but also to religious devotion in obeying God (Wilson and El-Ashker 2006: 40). Muhammad (pbuh) instructed Muslims to be moderate in all their affairs; he described Islam as the "middle way." A balance in human endeavours is required to ensure social well-being and the continued development of human potential (Rice 1999).

Ahmed (1976) argues that Islam recognises what Marxism sought to deny: the contribution of individual self-interest through profit and private property to individual initiative, drive, efficiency and enterprise. At the same time, Islam condemns greed, unscrupulousness and disregard for the rights and needs of others, which the secularists, sometimes encourage this worldly aspect of capitalism. The individual profit motive is not the chief propelling force in Islam (Siddiqi 1981). Social good should guide entrepreneurs, businessmen, banking and finance professionals and even financial regulators and policy makers in their decisions, besides profit. A relevant saying of Prophet Muhammad is "work for your worldly life as if you were going to live forever, but work for the life to come as if you were going to die tomorrow", (al Qasimi 1976: 68).

Like some other religions, Islam places a greater emphasis on duties than on rights. This is because, if self-interest is automatically held within bounds and the rights of all members of society are undoubtedly safeguarded, duties then, relating to justice and trusteeship, for instance, are fulfilled by everyone. Therefore, society is the primary institution in Islam and not the state (Cantori and Lowrie 1992).

Chapra (1992) argues that it is crucial to focus on human beings themselves, rather than on the market or the state, in order to create equilibrium between scarce resources and the claims on them in a way that realises both efficiency and equity. This argument by Chapra is necessary for demarcating the theory of financial innovation in Islamic economic thought; as the well-being of humans is the focus in this theory rather than the market or an individual institution. It should also consider any adverse consequences on society rather than being driven by self-interest and profit maximisation.

Islamic jurists and the Islamic law or 'Shariah' directs governmental power. In particular, Muslims believe that the Qur'an contains a final and unambiguous statement of the truth, added to and complemented by what had gone before in previous Divine revelations (for example, the messages delivered to prophets Moses and Jesus). The duty of the Muslim community, therefore, is to preserve this message (Cantori and Lowrie 1992). Thus, Muslims have a profound horror of anything regarded as innovation in matters of religion that is not permitted or based on the innovation theory that has been discussed herein, including what modern Christians interpret as necessary adaptations of religion to changing times (Eaton 1994).

7.9.2 The Principle of Economic Efficiency in Financial Innovation

This concept complements the previous concepts of unity and trusteeship. Economic resources should be used in the most economically efficient manner to maximise the value of output in relation to that of the input regarding financial innovation. The input is provided to us by God in the form of natural and economic resources, which along with other factors of production; generate the increase in the wealth of nation in the form of its gross national product (Wilson and El-Ashker 2006: 41). Thus, indulgence in luxurious living and the desire to show-off is very disliked and condemned. Islam does not tolerate conspicuous consumption (Hamed 2000: 158).

Islam differentiates clearly between two important things *israf* and *tabzir*. *Israf* means extending the level of consumption beyond the level of acceptable basic needs. *Tabzir*, on the other hand, is the unnecessary use of economic resources, which means wastage of economic resources at all levels of consumption. *Tabzir* is not limited to the level of extravagance; it goes even further beyond that to include the wastage in the consumer behaviour in satisfying his or her very basic needs of these physio-sociological wants (Hamed 2000: 57).

Keynes' (1972) observations on this subject, as Rice (1999) advocates, may be useful to draw on. He asserted that even though "the needs of human beings may seem to be insatiable," they would fall into two classes, those needs which are absolute in the way that we feel them whatever the state of our fellow human beings may be, and those that are relative ones in the way which their satisfaction ranks us above or makes us feel superior to others. According to Chapra (1992) Islamic jurists' categorisation of necessities (*daruriyyat*), conveniences (*kamaliyyatt*) and refinements (*tahsiniyyat*) would fall into Keynes' first class of needs. These are any goods and services which fulfil a need or reduce a hardship and make a real socio-economic difference in human well-being.

Therefore, resources would not be allowed to be diverted to the production of luxuries until the production of necessities was ensured in sufficient quantities (Siddiqi 1981). The definition of luxurious or extravagant is related to and measured against the average standards of consumption in a society, the idea being that a large shift from the standards would not be permissible (Rice 1999).

Therefore, there is a clear distinction, as discussed above, between *israf* and *tabzir* as the former refers to the extensive use of resources, while the latter is the wasteful use of these resources (Wilson and El-Ashker 2006: 42). The Quran says "Verily resource wasters (*mubazzirin*) are brethren to Satan and Satan is the worst unbeliever", (Qur'an, 17: 27). *Tabzir* attracts the wrath of God, for which the penalty is His retribution. Hence, both production and consumption functions in society are, with no doubts, affected by this basic notion in Islamic economics about *israf* (extension) and *tabzir* (wastage) (Abduh 1974: 42). Islam teaches us that no one is allowed to destroy or waste God-given resources. This is very relevant to ethics concerning the theory of financial innovation and its economic impact on the environment, economy, culture and society.

When Abu Bakr, the first ruler of the Islamic state after Muhammad, (peace be upon him), sent an army on a war assignment, he exhorted the leader of the army not to kill indiscriminately or to destroy vegetation or animal life, even in war and on enemy territory. Therefore, there was no question of this being allowed in peacetime or on home territory. Trusteeship is akin to the concept of sustainable development. Models of sustainable development do not regard natural resources as a free good, to be plundered at the free will of any nation, any generation or any individual (UNDP 1994).

*7.9.3 The Principle of Social Justice (*al-A'adalah al-Ijtima'iyyah*) in Financial Innovation*

Social justice as a principle in Islam is embedded in all economic activities. Islam emphasises equality among people regardless of their race, gender, faith, social class and wealth (Abdul Meneam 1979: 54). Prophet Muhammad (peace be upon him) said "People are as equal as the comb's teeth", (Sahih al-Bukhari), and also said "the noblest of you are the best in character", (Sahih Muslim).

Islam is certainly clear in its objective of eradicating all forms and traces of inequity from society, injustice, exploitation and oppression. This objective should be observed with due consideration in the financial innovation theory to ensure financial innovation is established on emphasising social justice and avoiding any form of exploitation of any stakeholder, including the environment, in the financial innovation cycle. The Qur'an also explicitly condemns vicarious guilt or merit and teaches the greatest possible individualism (Chapra 1992), "... no bearer of burdens can bear the burdens of another; ... man can have nothing but what he strives for ...", (Qur'an, 53: 38–39).

This individualistic outlook on the spiritual destiny of humanity is counterbalanced by a clear rigorous conception of society and social collaboration in all aspects of the financial innovation cycle (Al Zarqa 2012: 230–239). In their acquisition of wealth, however, people should not lie, deceive, cheat, cause harm or damage; they must uphold promises and fulfil contracts. This underpins the economic theory of financial innovation in Islam by advocating a universal view rather an individualistic selfish one.

Islamic teachings show us the right path by teaching us that all wealth should be productive and people may not stop the circulation of wealth after they have acquired it, nor reduce the momentum of wealth circulation (Al Hamshari 1985: 83). This Islamic worldview of financial innovation, in contrast to the conventional worldview, is the product of a divine guidance that brings together economic activities and self-accountability if the above is not incorporated in every stage of financial innovation.

This firm commitment of Islam to justice and brotherhood and sisterhood stipulates that Islamic society takes care of the basic needs of the poor and needy. Individuals are required to earn a living and only when this is unachievable does the state intervene. The institution of *zakah* in Islam, which is, a tax on wealth comprising compulsory alms-giving for specially designated groups in society, facilitates the care of all members of society. The rich are not the real owners of their wealth; they are only trustees in accordance with trusteeship agreement with God. Thus, they must spend it in accordance with the terms of this trust by very important requirement to fulfil the needs of the poor.

The word "*zakah*" means purification and as such, income redistribution is not only an economic necessity, but also a means to spiritual salvation (Naqvi 1981) and gaining God's reward ("... of their wealth take alms so that you might purify and sanctify", (Qur'an, 9: 103). Therefore, economics in general and the theory of financial innovation in particular is effectively integrated with the principle of justice.

7.10 Application of the Basic Islamic Philosophy in Financial Innovation

The above mentioned Islamic ideological concepts and principles aim to serve one purpose, which is the proper utilisation and management of economic resources to satisfy our needs, and to preserve the environment around us and our social unity and coherence.

The emphasis is therefore on the human being as the real wealth of society. An excessive obsession with the creation of material wealth can obscure the ultimate objective of enriching human lives. Humans are thus the ends as well as the means. Unless humans are motivated to pursue their self-interest within the constraints of economic well-being (the application of the "moral filter"), neither the "invisible hand" of the market (Smith 1789) nor the visible hand" of central planning can succeed in achieving socioeconomic goals or deliver beneficial sustainable financial innovation as theorised herewith (Chapra 1992).

The overall objective of Islamic ideology in relation to economic activities is not based, therefore, on the concept of 'maximisation' of any sort of utility, profit or wealth, but on the concept of preserving the universe (Wilson and El-Ashker 2006: 44). Adopting the concept of 'maximisation' in Islamic economics and financial innovation would, definitely, conflict with the basic Islamic ideological concept of moderation. The goals of the financial innovation theory, in particular, and the economic thought, in general, in Islam are not primarily materialist. They are based on Islamic concepts of human well-being and a good life, which emphasises brotherhood/sisterhood, socioeconomic justice and requires a balanced satisfaction of both the material and spiritual needs of all humans (Abduh 1974: 74).

7.11 The Origins of Shariah Supervision and Governance

As we have discussed in Chaps. 4 and 5, the development of Islamic economics and finance has gone through various phases. During this period of development, the ethical conduct and Shariah supervision in the financial market has also evolved. This is to ensure that the Islamic financial principles and philosophy, mentioned earlier in the previous sections of this chapter, in relation to the utilisation and deployment of economic resources are conducted in accordance with the legitimate ethical use of those resources.

Financial innovation and engineering, as part of the economic and financial activities, should also adhere to those prescribed Shariah fundamentals. Therefore,

Shariah governance and supervision has also developed accordingly, this was due to the expansion of the Islamic state and the use of new, different financial instruments.

Hence, the concept of establishing a Shariah Supervisory Board or Committee (SSB) that ensures proper Shariah governance within IFIs, since its emergence in the 1970s, is not a new phenomenon. This Shariah governance is rooted back to the concept of *Hisbah* (accountability and supervision), which was applied in various forms within the Islamic state in the past.

Hisbah was defined by al Mawardi and Abu Ya'la al Farra' as "Enjoining what is good when no one else is doing so, and forbidding what is evil if it spreads", (1973: 240). Al Shiraazi added to that definition "and reconciliation among people", (1946: 6). Therefore, the *Muhtasib* (supervisor) should be a jurist and a Shariah scholar, in order to be able to assess the validity of a financial transaction or a financial innovation and to prevent any prohibited financial transactions or harmful financial innovations.

Moreover, he should be able to identify void sale contracts, those contracts that are disliked in Shariah, different forms of cheating in financial transactions, misleading, uncertainty in contracts, ignorance in commodities' prices or fees charged for services, manipulation of the market, taking an advantage and exploiting people's needs, delivering or offering defective financial products or not being in accordance with the agreed product specifications (Al Shiraazi 1946: 12).

Hisbah emerged at the time of Prophet Muhammad (pbuh), although, it was not known by that name then. There was not a need during that era for this Shariah supervision as the Prophet was still living among the people, as his teachings and his conduct had positively influenced the Islamic society, shaping it into one with the best ethical and behavioural conduct and this was reflected in the market place, in particular.

At that time, the Islamic state had limited and simple financial activities that did not require a sophisticated system for Shariah supervision. This was the case until the end of the era of the righteous guided caliphs, who followed the example of the Prophet Muhammad in conducting the *hisbah* themselves. However, when they were busy running the affairs of state, they entrusted the task of market supervision to the most devoted, righteous, honest and trustworthy individual of the companions, as this was a role viewed as having great importance (al Mawardi 1985: 256).

When the Islamic state substantially expanded during the Omayyad and the Abbasid eras and Muslims mixed with other nations that had different traditions and financial systems to what Muslims have had used to, a new approach of Shariah governance became eminent. Thus, the need to establish the concept of *hisbah* as an independent institution that has its own system, setting up the requirements, qualifications, obligations, power and authority of the *Muhtasib* was founded (Al Shiraazi 1946: 13).

Hence, Islamic scholars supervising IFIs, should meet the requirements mentioned above for the *Muhtasib* of being righteous, honest, trustworthy, expert jurists who have mastered the required Shariah sciences to be able to interpret a Shariah ruling, judge a financial product, guide the IFI and ensure Shariah governance is maintained. This is not expected to be carried out by the management of an IFI or executives, because they would not have the required qualifications and knowledge, and there will be a clear conflict of interests. Thus, the SSB is an independent from any executive body in the IFI and has the authority to approve or disapprove proposed actions, products or services by financial institutions after they consider them for compliance with Shariah.

7.12 Conclusion

The objective of this chapter is to identify the fundamentals and main characteristics of the financial innovation theory from an Islamic perspective as an attempt to articulate this theory. The chapter discussed various elements within the Islamic philosophy of economic thought and principles outlining the Islamic school of financial innovation and its approach.

The theoretical framework for a theory of financial innovation from an Islamic perspective has been inspired by contributions from various theories, research studies and the three main Schumpeterian schools of innovation. This has been the basis for also outlining the Islamic school of innovation, its philosophy, theory and methodology.

Table 7.1 below provides a comparison between the three main Schumpeterian schools of innovation as described in the previous chapter (Chap. 6, Sect. 6.10) verses their counterpart the school of innovation from an Islamic perspective that we have called it the hybrid school in this chapter, their perspectives and building-block ideas are summarised in Table 7.1 below, which is an extension to Table 6.2.

Table 7.1 A summary of the four schools of innovation, perspectives and building-block

	Corporate capability school: economic perspective	Entrepreneurship school: social perspective	Culture school: cultural perspective	Islamic school: socio economic perspective
1. Nature of innovation	Institutionalized capability	Innovation as grassroots impetuses	Innovation as deep craft	Innovation as a religious grassroots
2. Inherent logic of innovation	Evaluate	Engage	Envision	Empower
3. Relationship among members	Instruction-based relationship	Identity-based relationship	Intergenerational relationship	Socially-based relationship
4. Focal concern	Affiliated institutions	Authentic voices	Affective identification	Affiliated society well-being
5. Apprehensions of time	Path dependencies	Improvisation	A deep sense of temporality	A deep sense of evolution and contemporarily

The concept of unity, the concept of trusteeship, the concept of free will and responsibility, the principle of moderation, the principle of economic efficiency and the principle of social justice, among others, form the building-blocks and foundations of financial innovation theory in the Islamic school of innovation. Given this holistic approach and world view of innovation theory in Islam, the Islamic finance and banking system would be very much welcome as an ethical approach. This theory promotes regulatory induced financial innovation rather than vice-versa and provides a theoretical framework that should be looked at and taken seriously.

Thus, the financial practices are structured around intrinsic checks and balances. This what makes the banking culture in Islamic finance, to some extent, self-regulating unlike the conventional system where the ethical framework has to be imposed and monitored by a regulator, such as the Financial Conduct Authority (FCA) in the UK and other regulatory authorities.

Regulation is intrinsic to Islamic finance, Islamic finance is derived from rules/regulations of Shariah, without Shariah there would be no Islamic finance. Whereas, in conventional finance, the rules are an external addition to financial practices and may be hugely variable, depending on economic circumstances, availability of resources, political ideology and many other factors.

The next chapter (Chap. 8) examines a selected derivative product, namely futures contracts and the possibility of engineering this product to be compliant with Shariah requirements. The analysis carried out in Chap. 8 and then in Chap. 9 would outline and set the scene for a framework for financial innovation and engineering in Islamic finance and the process it goes through. The structure of the discussion in this chapter focuses on the thinking process in analysing and deducting an Islamic finance juristic informed-view regarding a financial product under consideration.

Chapter 8
Futures Contracts as an Underlying Product of Financial Engineering in Islamic Finance

8.1 Introduction

The previous chapter (Chap. 7) aimed at articulating the distinctive features and characteristics on which a religious financial innovation theoretical framework could be developed. This framework would be the cornerstone for exploring the cycle and processes of financial innovation and engineering in IFIs.

The main characteristics of Islamic finance and IFIs have been discussed and highlighted in previous chapters (see Sect. 2.7, Table 2.1 of Chap. 2). The current practices of IFIs in relation to financial innovation and engineering are diverse, as they are influenced by different approaches taken by each individual IFI, or specific influences from the country in which the IFI operates. It is then not unreasonable to assume that, given this diversity, these practices are not always based on well-established financial innovation and engineering processes.

As a result, the Shariah compliance and governance of such variables also differs and is often not appropriately structured. Shariah is intended to govern the activities and policies of IFIs in a similar way to the way it seeks to govern individuals and their actions. It puts emphasis on the importance of honesty, transparency, justice and fair dealing, documentation, accountability and ethics. This religious imperative to infuse Shariah into IFIs necessitates that IFIs have to follow a certain prescribed code of conduct for its operation. This code of conduct avoids *inter alia*: cheating, exploitation, misleading, injustice, harmful actions to the society etc. (DiVanna et al. 2009; Warde 2010).

This Chapter aims to analyse futures contracts as a derivative product in the financial market and the possibility of engineering this product to be compliant with Shariah requirements. The analysis carried out in this Chapter would be complemented with a further analysis undertaken in Chap. 9 regarding another derivative product (options contracts). The combined analysis of both chapters would portray a full picture for a framework for financial innovation and engineering in Islamic finance and sets out the thinking process in order to reach a

S. Alamad, *Financial Innovation and Engineering in Islamic Finance*,
Contributions to Management Science, DOI 10.1007/978-3-319-52947-9_8

conclusion regarding the contemplated financial innovation. This analysis of the thinking process would set the structure of a framework for financial innovation and engineering in Islamic finance.

The term financial engineering is associated with innovation. It implies a search for new and innovative solutions to financial problems. In the conventional sense, it often connotes the design of new financial contracts for management of risk, providing a better match between corporate and investor needs and leading to enhancement of efficiency of the financial system. Options are an important tool of financial engineering often used in the design of new financial contracts or in developing innovative strategies and solutions for financial problems, such as management of risk implying a right without obligation. A conventional financial option is often traded as a separate contract in itself.

Islamic transactions have been singled out as the most important area of contemporary research in relevant Islamic studies. It has been given within the current literature higher consideration of research. This is due to the critical importance of Islamic finance transactions in the generation of wealth and the raising of productivity in contemporary Muslim countries. In recent decades, researchers have increasingly focused on specific themes with the objective to develop new operative formulas to stimulate profitable business in the market place. Futures trading is one such theme wherein original, independent juristic reasoning (*ijtihād*) is strongly required to enhance the prospects of economic success.

Trading in futures is a relatively new phenomenon which emerged in the early 1970s and has rapidly expanded ever since (Kamali 2000: 16). New products and trading formulas in the various sectors of trading in commodities, options, financial futures, and stock index future, have increased dramatically. In terms of trading volume, futures trading has far exceeded trading levels in conventional stocks, and it is currently the single most voluminous mode of commerce on the global scale. Futures trading is believed to be economically beneficial because it facilitates better production planning in the agriculture and agro-based industries. In these sectors it is also utilized as a hedging device against violent movement in the price of commodities over a period of time.

Buyers and sellers of commodities can make a contract to deliver a product at some future time at an agreed price, thus taking the uncertainty out of their operation.

8.2 Definition of Futures

Gough (1994: 108) explains that in Futures contracts the buyer and the seller can agree on the amount, quality and date of delivery, and both parties will put down deposits to protect each other from one side defaulting on the deal. This is known as a 'futures contract'. Futures are a kind of insurance policy, or 'hedging instrument' against the risks of price volatility, business can simultaneously trade in futures and in the cash market.

8.3 Financial Futures

Gough (1994: 109) mentions that shares, bonds, and currencies can be treated as commodities, and futures contracts can be made on them. Margins on financial futures can be considerably less than the 10 per cent or so required as a deposit on commodity futures. This increases the risk, unless you are using financial futures to hedge against changes to large liquid investments you have elsewhere. In this case, you are behaving in the same way that a hedger in the commodities business does.

For example, suppose you are dealing in futures based on long gilts (e.g. long term gilts), in this case, the contract size is £50,000, suppose that the price when you buy is 100-28 (i.e. 100 28/32). Gilts move in 32nds of 1 per cent; each 32nd is called a 'tick'. The margin you must deposit is £500. If you are certain that gilts are going to go up and you want to buy gilts at a future date when money becomes available, you might buy the futures contract now to hedge against the expected higher cost of the gilts when you have the cash to buy them. If you are wrong, all is not lost, because the lower cost of gilts will approximately balance the loss you make on the futures contract (Gough 1994: 110–111).

You can close out a futures contract either by delivering the gilts on the due date or by selling an identical contract. Most people do the latter. However, if you are speculating, the situation is rather different. Suppose the underlying value of your gilts contract dropped by 50%; you would not have lost £250, but £25,000, all on your £500 initial deposit. The rules of the system say that investors' contracts have to be checked daily for losses and profits; if you are losing, you will get a 'margin call' for more money to cover the losses, and you can close out the contract to stop any further losses (Knott 1998: 169).

According to Lee (1998: 118) broker is one of the players in the financial futures. Lee defines broker as, any person engaged in the business of effecting transactions in securities for the account of others but does not include a bank. The other players in the financial futures are owners of very large portfolios, such as, investment trust fund manager, pension funds and other institutions trade in financial futures to hedge against the chance that share prices will fall.

It has been argued that the commodity futures market differs from the forward market. In the former the actual delivery hardly ever takes place. Not more than 1% of the contracts actually mature into a physical delivery. The rest of the contracts are purchased and sold in the future by book transfers. The future market is highly organised (Khan 1988: 98). The maturities for different commodities are specified and all prices are quoted for those maturities. The grades of each commodity are also precisely defined. In actual practice, the settlements are made through clearing houses. The dealers pay into or receive from the clearing house without even knowing the name of the other party. In the final analysis, it is a zero-sum game. Losses of the one are gains for the other (Khan 1988: 98).

It is further argued that the futures market does not visualise physical delivery of any commodity. The non-delivery aspect of the market gradually evolved in response to the actions of certain large buyers, who would continue buying large quantities of the same maturity. Ultimately, the sellers were 'cornered' because of shortage in the actual market. As a redress to this situation, the sellers were allowed to deliver the grade of the commodity, other than the one agreed to. Thus, the buyers were pressured to accept unwanted grades (Khan 1988: 99).

In order to protect the buyers from this pressure, they were allowed to re-sell the futures contracts without getting delivery. Consequently, the forward contract led to manipulations by the buyers, which led to options for the sellers to vary the grade or place of delivery, which led to the buyers not accepting the delivery. As a result, the vicious circle was completed. The futures market in commodities is designed to keep the prices in the spot market stable. However, its real benefit is reaped by hedgers and speculators.

8.4 Hedging Mechanism Through Derivatives

As mentioned earlier that the objective of futures is to hedge risky trading positions as a risk management tool. So it is necessary to talk a little about hedging what it is, and who is the hedger. The important function of hedging or risk management will be considered in this section. There are many kinds of hedging; however our focus here is on hedging using options as a financial engineering instrument.

8.4.1 Objective of Hedging

Before we talk about the objective of hedging let us first define who the hedger is? According to Blake (2000: 14) hedgers are specialist financial intermediaries who wish to lay off risks that they currently face or expect to face in the future.

The objective of hedging or risk management is to transfer risk from one individual or corporation to another individual or corporation. The hedger is the person off-loading the risk, while the person taking on the risk is the speculator or trader. In order to hedge successfully and so transfer all risk, the hedger will have to select a suitable instrument, i.e. one whose price mirror closely those of the underlying cash market securities. The two most suitable hedging instruments will therefore be instruments that are derivative upon cash market securities, mainly financial futures and options (Thomsett 2001: 17–20).

8.4.2 Hedging Using Options

Hedging using options can be a more flexible substitute to hedging using futures. Futures are used when the amount and timing of the exposure are known with certainty, a futures contract locks in the price of a specific amount of an asset at a specific future date. While options can be used when either the amount or the timing of the exposure is not known with certainty (Blake 2000: 618–620), options can also be used when the hedger wants to protect against adverse price movements. But, would like to benefit from favourable move in one direction, but possible loses when prices move in the opposite direction (Kamali 2000: 184–185).

8.4.3 Hedging Interest-Rate Risk with Financial Futures

Financial institutions, such as, banks, insurance companies, pension funds, finance companies and mutual funds make use of two basic kinds of hedging strategies involving forward markets and futures markets. This hedging is to reduce interest-rate risk, the micro hedge and the macro hedge. When a financial institution hedges the interest-rate risk for a specific asset it is holding, it is conducting a micro hedge. And when the financial institution is hedging interest-rate risk on its overall portfolio, it is conducting a macro hedge (Eakins 2000: 650). To illustrate this point, suppose that a person owns some shares, which he does not want to sell, but he expects them to fall in the short term. He can buy a put option in the shares to protect them against a fall in value. In general, this kind of hedging is costly and unnecessary for the smaller investor (Gough 1994: 119).

8.5 Futures from an Islamic Perspective

Futures contracts are quite old, although their use in organised exchange markets is recent and goes back only to the 1970s. In futures, the seller promises to deliver something in the future (commodity or stock or even an index), while the buyer advances part of the price and makes a legal commitment to take delivery of the underlying subject of the contract at a future date. A large quantum of commodity trade is carried out in futures markets. The commodity futures market is a highly competitive market in which the individuals or firms deal in specified commodities.

Many participants in the futures markets have no intention of ever taking or making delivery. They enter into future planning to close their position before delivery dates, albeit they are legally obliged to deliver at the date of delivery. This contract is quite similar to *salam* which is permissible in Shariah. In Islam the price is advanced while the delivery takes place in a future date. Unlike options, the underlying subject of future contracts is the commodity not the right or obligation; it is in this sense similar to *salam*.

It is argued that the dissimilarities are, however, overwhelming:

a) It is a condition for the permissibility of *salam* to advance and pay the whole price at the moment of contracting. This never takes place in futures. The price is paid at the time of delivery to an investor for a speculative reason. Thus, it does not make sense to pay the amount in full up-front. Moreover, the seller of options contracts does not need finance in contrast to a *salam* contract (El Gari 1991: 34).

b) It is also argued that the underlying commodity in a *salam* contract is not to be sold before the delivery date. If this happens then the seller engages in a prohibited contract in under Shariah in relation to selling a commodity that is not owned by the seller. In modern exchange contracts, the commodity is often sold many times before its delivery date. As a matter of fact, most of the profits are made by those who speculate between the two dates.
c) One may argue that what is being sold in each transaction is a new *salam* agreement, therefore, there is no sale of the commodity prior to delivery. The holder of a future contract, therefore, can agree another future contract for the same quantity and dates of delivery. This can be acceptable only if there is enough distinguishing characters of each contract (i.e. in term of quantity and dates), which is rarely the case. Hence, it is just a formula to cover up a transaction that does not comply with Shariah requirements (El Gari 1991: 34).

The Islamic position on futures market is quite clear. To start with, the commodity is non-existent, and then it does not involve physical transfer of commodities, moreover, successive sales are made without anyone's actually owning the commodity. Therefore, from the Islamic point of view, all the transactions in this chain are unlawful (Khan 1988: 99). Khan explains the rationale of the Islamic view regarding this matter as follows; in the futures market a number of intermediaries make money from futures contracts without spending any time, providing a workplace or any form of utility to the commodity. Thus, some people earn without giving anything in recompense (*'Iwad*). The situation is closely similar to the one in which a person claims *riba* (usury) without giving anything in recompense (Khan 1988: 99).

This point of argument might not stand as even if the seller is perceived not to provide any work or efforts in selling the commodity, this does not render the transaction void or similar to an interest-based agreement as long as the Shariah requirements for a sale contract are met. Having the right understanding of the contract in questions and any Shariah implications is a key for the financial engineering process from an Islamic finance perspective, in particular in derivatives.

It is often argued in the literature from an economics perspective that the futures markets are more economical and efficient than the cash market. This is because the former do not involve any physical transfer or storage costs. This argument is relevant in the context of speculators only. From the point of view of the economy as a whole, the physical transfer of commodities at each stage may involve a lot of human activities.

Eventually, a number of people get jobs for activities like storage, transport and packing. They in fact, add time, place or form utilities as well. Therefore, in terms of economic activity, the emphasis on physical or constructive transfer of commodities by each seller in the Islamic commercial law has a more encouraging effect as compared to the contemporary futures market, which has a restrictive effect on the market. Nonetheless, the futures markets may have some other problems as well. These problems are discussed in the section below.

8.6 Problems Related to Futures Markets from an Islamic Finance Perspective

Firstly, in futures markets small investors hardly ever win and they can hardly make economical bargain (Goss and Yamey 1978: 238).

Second, large firms in the futures market persuade the new-comers to get into losing bargains with the help of their own employees who deal as if they are 'independents'. Thus, the unwary new-comers are deprived of their capital (Khan 1988: 100).

Third, futures trading allows the sellers to change the grade and place with concurrent change in the agreed price. So, eventually, everything changes. Even the time is not an exact date, whereas a month during which it could be any date (in certain commodities, specially metal, the time is specified exactly). Therefore, the transaction gets very close to the sale of uncertainty (*bay̒' al-gharar*), which has been prohibited under Shariah. This suggests that a different principles or adjustment is required for the financial engineering process of this derivative product, in order to be acceptable from a Shariah perspective.

Fourthly, brokers in futures markets also carry out 'dual trading', which means to conduct a business on their own account first, if it is beneficial for them, and then they fill the order of the client. No regulation has been able to eradicate this (Hewson 1985: 25–26).

Fifthly, despite all the safeguards which futures commodity exchanges try to provide against manipulations, market 'insiders' are always able to make use of the information before it is in the public domain. Fabrication and dissemination of rumours by powerful traders is also carried out to earn huge profits. On all these grounds, the Islamic economy does not accept futures trading in commodity exchanges (Khan 1988: 101).

8.7 *Al-Gharar* (Uncertainty) in the Futures Market

The existence of *al-gharar* in the transaction of future trading in the stock market is apparent as there is no physical transfer in underlying commodity of the transaction during the conclusion of the business contract. The above future trading is not the same as the legally binding Islamic business transaction of *salam* sale. The physical delivery hardly ever takes place; only about one per cent may take delivery. This is a kind of uncertainty in such transactions, which is disallowed in Islamic finance (Salamon 1998: 30).

It has been reported that Abu Sayeed al Khodri reported that the messenger (peace be upon him) said: "Whoever advances a commodity for so commodity, let him not transfer it to others before he possesses it" (Fazlul Karim 1994: Vol. 2, p. 290). A final point regarding using *al salam* sale to financially engineer an Islamic finance instrument, that provides an alternative to futures contracts, is that futures contracts are binding at the time of contracting, but its effects take place in the specified time in the future (Al-Zuhaylī 2002: 3100).

8.8 Conclusion

This Chapter explored futures contracts as a derivative product in the financial market and the possibility of engineering an alternative Shariah compliant structure that achieves the economic and commercial objective of futures contracts, but it meets Shariah requirements at the same time.

This Chapter has set out the discussion around the process that a financial innovation would go through to assess its suitability from an Islamic commercial law perspective. Following viability of the financial innovation the financial engineering process comes into play to work out the best fit for purpose structure from a Shariah perspective. This structure could be based on two or more Islamic finance principles in order to achieve the required outcome. A further analysis then would follow to ensure that such engineered structure and the combination of various Islamic finance principles does not breach any Shariah rules or requirements. This process does not always mean that an acceptable Shariah engineered solution for the financial product can be achieved though.

The analysis carried out in this Chapter would be complemented with a further analysis undertaken in the next chapter (Chap. 9), which examines another derivative product (options contracts). Chapter 9 follows the same analytical process in order demonstrate the thinking process and key elements for a possible framework for financial innovation and engineering in Islamic finance.

Chapter 9
Options Contracts as an Underlying Product of Financial Engineering in Islamic Finance

9.1 Introduction

The previous chapter (Chap. 8) paved the way for the discussion around the process that a financial innovation would go through to ascertain its acceptability from a Shariah perspective. Following viability of the financial innovation the financial engineering process starts in order to find the best fit for purpose structure from a Shariah perspective.

This Chapter aims to complement the analysis undertaken in Chap. 8 regarding futures contracts. The analysis of options contracts, as a derivative product in the financial market and the possibility of engineering this product to be compliant with Shariah requirements, is provided in this Chapter. The analysis carried out in this Chapter would further outline the building blocks for a framework for financial innovation and engineering in Islamic finance and continues to establishing the thinking process in order to reach a conclusion regarding a contemplated financial innovation. This analysis of the thinking process regarding options contracts would provide further insights for financial innovation and engineering in Islamic finance.

Options on equity securities have been traded for many decades. However, until 1973 the market was very informal. A person who wished to purchase an option on IBM stocks would contact one of option dealers, generally small firms that specialised in the product. The option dealer would seek out another party willing to sell the option (Kamali 2000: 183–184).

9.2 What Is an Option

Fink (1998: 618) defies an option as the right, but not the obligation, to buy a particular item at a predetermined price on or before a specific date. Thomsett (2001: 17) illustrates, an option is a contract that provides you with the right to

S. Alamad, *Financial Innovation and Engineering in Islamic Finance*,
Contributions to Management Science, DOI 10.1007/978-3-319-52947-9_9

execute a stock transaction that is to buy or to sell e.g. 100 shares of stock. This right includes a specified fixed price per share that is good until a specified date in the future. Currier (1987: 206) explains that options are contracts which give their owners the right to conduct a specified transaction, such as buying or selling a certain number of shares of given common stock at a set price within a stated period of time.

Also when you own an option, you do not gain any equity in the stock, and neither do you have a debt position. You have only contractual right to buy or sell 100 shares of a company's stock. Since you can buy or sell 100 shares of stock at the current market value, this raises a question, why do I need to purchase an option to gain that right? The answer is found in the fixed stock price that you get with the option contract (Thomsett 2001: 18). That is the key to the option value. In other words, when you own an option, the price at which you can enter into a stock transaction is frozen for as long as the option remains in force.

Therefore, no matter how much price movement takes place. As an owner of the option you have fixed the price for your purchase or sale of stock, and that fixed price when is compared to the market price of the stock, ultimately determines what the option is worth as time passes. According to King (1999: 180) options are contracts which resemble forwards and futures in that two parties agree to do, a deal on a future date at terms that are agreed in the contract.

9.3 A Brief Historical Review of Options

The major change in trading of equity options occurred in 1973, when the Chicago Board of Trade (CBT), which dealt in commodities, set up the Chicago Board of Options Exchange (CBOE), when for the first time equity options began to trade on an exchange. CBOE is founded as first US options exchange and trading begins on standardised listed options. April 26, the first day of trading, sees 911 contracts traded on 16 underlying stocks. This centralisation of the market led to an increased interest in options, and many other bourses in the US followed suit and established similar facilities for options trading (Colburn 1990: 3–5).

Trading in put options begins in 1977. SEC places a moratorium on options expansion pending an in-depth review of the rapidly growing derivative securities market. Essentially, these markets are systems for the reduction of risk in trade between large companies and institutions, overlaid with a large number of speculators who hope to make profits from price fluctuations (Gough 1994: 107). Before 1973 the parties to an option contract would have to agree on three important aspects of the contract:

1. The exercise price. The buyer might have wanted the contract exercised, say, at £3.00 per share but the seller at £3.50 a share.
2. The length of the contract. The buyer may want the option to extend to 9 months, the seller only 6 months.

3. The premium. All the three elements were subject to negotiation and agreement. Nevertheless, with the listing and centralization of equity options, the need to negotiate the first two (A and B), was eliminated since they were now determined by the exchange on which the contract was traded (Kamali 2000: 185–186).

9.4 Types of Options

9.4.1 Call Option

A call option as a contract provides the buyer of which (who pays the price) the right to buy a specific number of shares in a certain company for a fixed price during a particular period. In addition, it is the obligation of the seller (who receives the option price) to sell these shares to him when he so decides (El-Gari 1993: 13). To illustrate this point, assume that shares in company X are going to rise in the next 3 months. You can buy a three-month call option on 1000 shares at, say, 184p; the premium will be 18p per share, so you will pay £180 plus dealing costs for 1000 shares. If the share price is at 187p after 3 months, you could exercise the option to buy in the hope that the share price will carry on to rise. You will have spent 180 + 1840 = £2020, so, not counting dealing costs, the shares will have to be above 202p for you to make a profit (Gough 1994: 118).

9.4.2 Put Option

A put option as a contract is whereby the person who pays the price enjoys the right to sell a certain number of shares against a fixed price during an agreed period of time. He is involved in the transaction by option, as he is not bound to sell the obligation 'to buy' undertaken by the person who receives the price (El-Gari 1993: 14). Assuming a company X's shares will fall in the next 3 months. You can buy a put option for 18p per share for 1000 shares at 184p. If the shares go down to, say 150p, you can exercise your option by putting it on to an option dealer, forcing him to buy your shares for £ 1500 and pass them on to him. The cost to you, excluding dealing chargers, is 1500 + 180 = £1680, so your profit is 1840 − 1680 = £160. Since your broker can conduct both transactions quickly, you will not need to come up with all the money to buy the shares (Gough 1994: 118–119).

9.4.3 Double Options

Double options are combined sell and buy, put and call options, with a premium which is nearly double a normal premium. When you are betting that the share price will move out of the range represented by the premium cost (Radwān 1996: 354).

9.5 Why Options Are Popular

Trading in options has become popular for variety of reasons.

(a) 2.4.1 Options can be bought for a fraction of the money required to buy the underlying assets.
(b) Investors who do not have enough funds or who do not want to lie up large sums of money in futures contracts can, by buying options, acquire control over large quantities of commodities and their associated contracts.
(c) They can exercise the options and buy the underlying assets in case, market prices move in their favour, and then sell them on at a profit.
(d) In the event of an unfavourable move in the market prices, the option holder simply does not exercise it and forfeits the premium.
(e) Options are also used by speculators as a hedging device against open positions both in the stock and futures market (Kane 1988: 281).
(f) That the development of the secondary market, where transactions of selling and buying stock occur, with associated futures and business activities by executing the appropriate transactions (Spencer 2000: 79).

9.6 Useful Economic Purposes Served by Options

Some may argue that there are useful economic purposes achieved and fulfilled through options trading. These useful economic purposes served by options are summarised below:

(a) They bring about an increase in the liquidity of the market.
(b) Investing in the stock market involves a high level of commercial risk due to price fluctuations and the influence of the modes of other investors on the market.
(c) Since decisions in the stock market almost depend upon future expectations, any event believed to influence the economic situation will certainly affect the market trends. For this purpose investors need a method, which is similar to insurance. Options can play such a role.
(d) Options give the investors the opportunity to rearrange his investment portfolio by choosing the most suitable options for his preferences relating to the risk-return trade off.

(e) Options contracts lead to reduction in the effects of fluctuations in the prices of securities to which these contracts apply (Gastineau 1988: 123).

Furthermore, options provide a means of shifting risk from parties who are presently exposed to it for a price. The major categories of options are calls, puts, stock index options, interest-rate options and options on futures. Options have an important role to play in any stock market, such as:

- They increase the market liquidity,
- Stabilising the market by reducing fluctuations in price.
- They provide insurance like protection to legitimate investors.
- And finally they improve the choices open to investors, hence attract more people since preferences will be served better (El Gari 1991: 30–31).

9.7 Market Analysis of Options

Blake's (2000: 273) analysis concludes that the effect of a futures contract is to fix today the future price of some security. This means that with a futures contract, all future distribution of the security price is concentrated at a single point, namely the current future price. That is for many reasons exactly what is required, however, for others it is overly restrictive. An investor may be more certain of price rises than price falls, but may nevertheless wish to protect against price falls. Buying an option contract is the solution in this case. The initial purchase of an option is known as an opening purchase.

Thus, options are versatile, which can be used in a large number of ways. Strategies that can be applied to options are virtually limitless and new products are introduced frequently in the market. Options are mainly sold (or written) by companies or financial institutions which hold inventories of commodities or financial instruments. Therefore, profits can be realised with little assumption of risk by writing options against these inventories (Kamali 2000: 183).

An option gives to its holder the right, but not the obligation to buy or sell an underlying security at a fixed price (the exercise price or strike price). This right is given by the issuer or writer of the option (Black 1975: 36–72). A call option on GBP gives the holder the right to buy GBP in the spot market at an exchange rate equal to the strike price. A call option on GBP futures gives the holder the right to receive the amount by which the futures price exceeds the strike price. If the GBP futures option is exercised, the holder also obtains a long position in the GBP futures contract (Hult et al. 2004: 76–78).

If options are properly priced and an investor is able to buy and sell securities costless at the end of every relevant trading period; options cannot improve portfolio outcomes beyond what could otherwise be achieved using stock and safe assets alone (Rendleman 2002: 212). It is also argued that options which are priced fairly may improve portfolio outcomes over what would otherwise be an optimal allocation of stock and safe assets. Provided that options reduce stock-safe asset trading costs, or reduce constraints imposed on investors, either directly through market structures, or indirectly through the investors own rational choice (Klob 2000: 386–387).

9.8 An Assessment of Options from an Islamic Finance View

The theory of contracting in the Islamic commercial law discusses the notion of options within the framework of a sale contract. One type of options may provide the contracting parties a right, either to confirm or to cancel the contract within a stipulated period. Such options for either or both the parties may apparently be seen by some as violating a Shariah norm that a valid contract comes into existence with the acceptance of the terms of contract by both parties. Permissibility of these options is, however, justified on grounds of several larger benefits to society. Through options, the parties to the contract are granted a reassessment or cooling off period over which they can rationalise their decision or reverse the same. Thus, the possibility of conflicts between the parties to the contract because of their abrupt, irrational or wrong decisions is minimised.

Another important reason may be that under the conditions of excessive *gharar* or uncertainty regarding the article of exchange, price etc., and options for the parties are provided to reduce *gharar* and bring it within legitimately acceptable limits. The rational underlying options may be at times, to undo a wrong committed on a party to the contract. For example, Islam attaches great importance to the role of information in the market. The release of inaccurate or misleading information in the market or about certain financial products is forbidden.

9.9 Options in the Islamic Literature

Different terms of options were used by Arab writers. The most commonly used term is the phrase *al-amaliyyāt al-shartiyyah* (lit, 'deferred conditional transactions'), (see e.g. Radwān 1996; al-Barwari 2005). There are three types of options that have been discussed by Arab writers: simple options whether call or put, known as *amaliyyāt shartiyyah basītah*. Double options, *amaliyyāt shartiyyah murakkabah*, which combine call and put options and entitle the option holder to act in either or both capacities. And finally, double quantity options, or *amaliyyāt shartiyyah mudā'afah*. In this section options and futures will be analysed from an Islamic perspective, as well as the issue will be measured according to the scale of Islamic law (*fiqh*) and the sources of law (*usūl al-fiqh*). In addition to, reviewing the opinion of Islamic jurists and economists to determine whether they are permissible or not and on what basis of Islamic financial engineering the permissibility or prohibition is based.

9.10 Some Possible *Sharī'ah* Objections to Options

The forms of options of both kinds call and put options, which have been discussed earlier, have some Shariah objections and criticism as summarised below:

- It is argued that options contracts do not serve any useful purpose, but are only a method of gambling by way of sale and purchase of securities. The possibility of using this type of contract for gambling purposes is not ruled out. However, this element does not accompany the option concept by necessity (Vogel and Hayes 1998: 227).
- The acceptable options in Islamic finance are affiliated to sale contracts. Therefore, they relate to it and they are not separable from it, and thus, they have no independent existence of their own. Therefore, it cannot have a price of its own. However, this objection is based upon the assumption that the said option is similar to the option known in Islamic jurisprudence, which is giving the right to one of the contracting parties or both to sign the contract or terminate it. In such sales, acceptance of a proposal is allowed for a period of time, which is equivalent to the period of the option given (Kamali 2000: 192–193).

9.11 *Khiyār* as a Form of Option

It is important to point out the significance of the availability of options contract, considering that they supplement the operations of exchange markets. It is, therefore, not useful to say that it is better to ignore them since their existence could create juristic problems. It is useful to understand the real implication of such contracts and the purposes that they serve and then examine them to achieve what is being sought by methods allowing us to avoid the legal problems and engineer a possible Shariah acceptable alternative.

As we mentioned earlier, option is both a right and an obligation. Thus, whosoever pays the price of an option has the right of sale or purchase during a fixed period of time in respect of stocks or other securities. The person who receives the price will be bound to sell or buy the shares during a fixed period of time. The price of such shares will be fixed and agreed upon in the first part of the contract (Radwān 1996: 348–351). The subject of options is addressed within the purview of *fiqh* (jurisprudence) doctrine of *al-khiyārāt* (options).

The origins of *al-khiyārāt* are clearly traceable in the *Sunnah* (prophet Muhammad practices), but the elaborated details and sub-divisions of *al-khiyārāt* into various types have all been developed, as a matter of initiative and *ijtihād,* in the juristic writings of the early Islamic scholars. The basic concept of options which occurs in the *sunnah* and in the manuals of jurisprudence, was intended not as a new trading formula or a risk-management tool, but as a way to ensure propriety and fairness. In addition to, protecting the integrity of consent in the completion of contracts (Kamali 2000: 192).

9.11.1 *Main Typical Types of* al-khiyārāt *(Options) as Validated by the* Sunnah

(a) Option of stipulation (*khiyār al-shart*), according to al-Mawardi et al. (1985: Vol. 5, p. 248) this option grants the buyer the option within a time frame to either ratify the contract or revoke it. Al-Sharbini (1994: Vol. 2, p. 56) has added that the ruling of the *sunnah* has evidently envisaged the eventuality where the buyer does not possess sufficient knowledge of the subject-matter turns out to be defective in a way that is not obvious to the naked eye.
(b) Option of defect (*khiyār al-ayb*), this option materialises only as a result of a clear provision in the contract (Al-Dardeer 1972: Vol. 3, p. 166). Thus, Islam grants the buyer an option on account of material defect, in which case the buyer is automatically entitled to seek revocation of contract on that basis (Al-Bāhoutī 1983: Vol. 3, p. 224).
(c) Option of viewing (*khiyār al-ru'yah*), is when Shariah grants the buyer an option on account of material defect when he sees the object he has bought for the first time (Ibn-Jazzi 1984: 264).

9.12 Options and Islamic Jurisprudence

The idea of conventional 'options' does exist in the Islamic commercial law, albeit it is distinct from the above described concept of options attached to a sale contract. As mentioned before an option in Islamic finance is affiliated to a sale contract (and to other permissible contracts which are optionable). The option is part of the conditions of the sale and not separable from it.

Thus, it cannot have a price of its own and it cannot be traded separately. An option is defined, therefore, as giving the right to one of the contracting parties (or both) to follow through with or call off the contract within a specified period of time (El Gari 1991: 31). Therefore, acceptance of the proposal to sell or buy is allowed for a period of time, which is equivalent to the period of the option given. According to Abu Hanifa the period is 3 days, but the majority of the other three schools of thoughts' scholars allow an 'appropriate' length of time, which could be more or less than 3 days. According to El Gari (1991: 32) the idea of options in

Shariah is not unrelated to the stock market options. The dissimilarities, however, are enormous:

Firstly, stock market options create a right (enjoyed by the buyer) and an obligation maintained by the seller. They are independent contracts autonomous from the sale or purchase of the underlying stocks.

Secondly, even if we say that options are new contracts and that Shariah does not restrict transactions to only standard contracts, we need to determine the permissibility to ascertain the subject matter of this contract. The underlying construct in an option contract is a 'right' and an 'obligation' that are sold and traded in the market. The problem here is that Shariah does not recognise these abstract matters to be the substitute of a sale contract in the process of financial engineering of an Islamic alternative to options to be used in IFIs. Though some rights in Shariah are subject to inheritance and some are subject to cash settlement, such as the right of the wife on her husband in case of divorce, but they are not transferable to a third party through a sale transaction. Therefore, a market for option trading as it stands would not be acceptable under Shariah.

Thirdly, if we assume that the option contract is not separable from the sale contract of the underlying stock, i.e. the naked options. We are still faced with the problem of paired contractual obligations; the transaction consists of two sale contracts in one, which results in the invalidity of both (El Gari 1991: 32).

9.12.1 Call Option

Many traders in call options operate without intending to exercise them, but to profit from changes in market price. Furthermore, some option writers sell what is called 'naked option', i.e. writing options on stocks they do not own, just for the purpose of making profit. Options as a speculative device are, clearly, unacceptable in form of contract under Shariah. One, nevertheless, should not overextend the definition of speculation. There are many legitimate uses of options in stock markets. In particular, the hedging aspect of options is quite in line with the recognized needs of individuals and IFIs, which is not contradictory to Shariah. The problem remains, however, that an option contract should not have an independent existence of a sale or lease contracts. This means that what is paid for an option is part of the total sale price of the underlying goods or asset.

There is, however, one form of sale contract in Islamic jurisprudence which allows an option at a price. The sale of down payment or advance (*'arbūn*) allows the buyer to advance a small percentage of the agreed upon price so that he can have time to decide. If this decision was not on the affirmative, then this advanced payment is kept by the seller. It is worth noting here that the option is only for the buyer, the seller is obliged to honour his commitment. This shows that the amount paid, while it is a percentage of the total price, it is in reality a price of the option (see Radwān 1996; El Gari 1991; Kamali 2000). It is noteworthy, that what has been suggested, as a financial engineering solution for options, on the basis of a down payment is in accordance with the Hanbali School of jurisprudence, but not the other three schools.

9.12.2 Put Option

Put options are contracts which give their owners the right to sell a specified stock at a set price within a given time period. An investor who expects prices to decrease can sell a put to protect his investment. If expectation takes place he can exercise the contract. Hence, selling above the market price, which has gone down, while there is, obviously, plenty of space for speculators, the need for such a contract is legitimate in most cases. Once more, the substance of the put option is not the underlying stock, but the right and obligation of properties which are not compliant with Shariah.

9.12.3 Index Option

If the purpose of transacting in stock markets, from savers point of view, is to profit and since the latter depends on ability to predict the direction of the market, then there is no need to buy and sell. Rather, it is sufficient to cash the difference between what is expected and what really took place. It is because of this index options are quite popular, where one can speculate on the whole market, as if he buys and sells every stock in the exchange market. Obviously, this is pure gambling.

What one buys or sells, when he buys an index option, is a chance to win an amount of money not specified (the difference between current price and future price). Gambling in Shariah is not permissible even for charitable purposes, not mentioning profit making. Buyers and sellers of options are not necessarily part of the shareholders of the corporation and, as such, may not be participating in any way in the running of the underlying corporation. They are essentially betting on the expected performance of the corporation in very much the same way gamblers bet on horses in horse racing (see Radwān 1996). There is a clear difference between the two. In the option case, the gainer and the loser are the investors themselves, not the corporation.

9.12.4 Right as an Object of Sale

The view of some Islamic scholars is that an option is a promise to sell or purchase an item at a specified price within a stipulated time, such a promise in itself is permissible. The promise is also binding on the promisor. However, this promise cannot be the subject matter of a sale or purchase contract (Usmani 1996: 10–11).

As the resolution of the Islamic Fiqh Academy, Jeddah (the 7th Session of the Council on 9–14 May 1992) asserts "Option contracts as currently applied in the world financial markets are new types of contracts, which do not come under any one of the Shariah nominated contracts. Since the subject of the contract is neither a sum of money nor a utility or a financial right which may be waived, the contract is not permissible in Shariah".

One of the counter values in the trading of options is a right or a privilege granted to a party in contrast to a tangible object or *māl*. The scope of *māl* also generally includes intangibles, such as a service and usufruct (Obaidullah 1998: 76). The subject matter of an option is a right (*haqq*) that is pure and simple (*al-haqq al-mujarrad*). This right is neither a tangible commodity nor a usufruct; it cannot therefore be a proper subject matter of a contract.

There is an argument, however in favour of introducing options trading on other grounds, concurs with this viewpoint. Provided that the right does not have a tangible or material quality, but it is indeed intangible that may not be sold or bought, considering that it is not a property. It is only similar to a preemptive right (*shuf'ah*, right of custody and guardianship) all of which, while allowed in Shariah, are intangible rights that are not allowed to be sold or relinquished against monetary compensation (Abu Sulayman 1992: 32–33; El-Gari 1993: 13).

A few Islamic scholars however, would prefer to include any kind of benefit (*manfa'ah*) in the definition of *māl*. Since options involve a benefit (a right without obligation) for the purchaser, trading of such benefit is observed to be permissible. Ahmed (1996: 6–15) argues that the Islamic Investment Study Group of the Securities Exchange Commission, Malaysia in its report finds call warrants to be acceptable because it "has the characteristics of an asset. This asset satisfies the concept of tangible right (*haqq māli*) and right of ownership (*haqq tamalluk*), which is transferable based on the majority of Islamic jurists' (*fuqaha'*) views other than the Hanafi School. Therefore this right can be classified as an asset and can, consequently, be traded.

9.13 The Framework of *Khiyār al-Shart and Damān* (guarantee)

The option of stipulation (*khiyār al-shart*) is an option manifested in the form of a condition stipulated in the contract. It provides a right to either of the parties, or both, or even to a third party to confirm or to cancel the contract within a stipulated time period. The permissibility of such option is inferred directly from the following *hadith* of prophet Muhammad (peace be upon him) reported by al-Bukhari and Muslim (al-Bukhari 1985: Vol. 3, p. 805), when Habban Ibn Munqidh complained to the prophet that he was the victim of frequent fraud in some earlier transactions, the prophet (peace be upon him) is reported to have said "When you conclude a sale you may say that there must be no fraud (misleading) and you reserve for yourself an option lasting 3 days".

According to another *hadith* reported by al-Bukhari and Muslim (al-Bukhari 1985: Vol. 3, p. 807), the prophet said: "the two contracting parties have a right of option as long as they are not separated or the sale was a sale of option". This *hadith*, therefore, proves the basic validity of *khiyār al-shart* along with *khiyār al-majlis*.

There is a consensus among jurists belonging to all major schools of thought regarding the permissibility of *khiyār al-shart.* According to Al-Nawawi, the strongest basis for *khiyār al-shart* is consensus (*ijma'*) and that is enough. However, there is some divergence of opinion among Islamic jurists on whether options and other contractual stipulations are valid as a matter of principle, or these are merely tolerated by way of exception (Obaidullah 1998: 77). Al-Zuhaylī (2002: 26) reported that Imam Abu Hanifa and Imam Shafi'ī viewed such option-related stipulation as a mere exception, which is permissible for a period of 3 days only, while Imam Ahmed Ibn Hanbal did not impose any limit.

As far as the general framework of contractual stipulations and conditions is concerned, the general Hanafi and Shafi'ī position relating to all contractual stipulations including options is that these should be in harmony with the essence of the contract (such as, the seller in a deferred sale seeking a mortgage or guarantor). The Malikī position is more liberal, which validates stipulations even with financial value (such as, buyer stipulating that the goods be transported to certain locality).

Islamic scholars from the Hanbali School have been quoted extensively on this matter, such as Ibn Taymiyyah and his disciple Ibn Qayyim al-Jawziyya. This is to highlight their liberal views, which lay emphasis on the basic freedom of contract and the parties' liberty to make stipulations as they please. They assert that the *sunnah* entitles the parties to insert stipulations in contracts so as to meet their legitimate needs and what may be deemed to be of benefit to them (Kamali 2000: 191–204).

Some modern Islamic scholars, though in minority, prefer to examine the same under the framework of option of stipulation and find option trading to be permissible. They argue that charging a premium by the option writer may be treated as compensation within the framework of guarantee (*damān*).

Kamali (2000: 191–204) is the major proponent of this line of thinking. As stated above, he asserts the *sunnah* as the basis of stipulations in contracts. It is pertinent to quote the views of another scholar Ahmed Muhayyuddin Hassan on this issue. Hassan argues that the basic notion of *khiyār al-shart* is anomalous to the norm and is merely tolerated, which is why it is basically confined to 3 days. The way in which options are designed and traded on the other hand turns the restrictive terms of *khiyār al-shart* into a basic permissibility (Obaidullah 1998: 78), which makes a departure from the stated guidelines of Shariah and diverts the legitimate financial engineering aspect from its objective.

The counter-argument attempts to contradict the same by asserting that this is essentially the same argument that Hanafi and Shafi'i jurists have advanced on the subject and has, in fact, been addressed and effectively refuted in the writings of the

Hanbali jurists, in particular Ibn Qayyim al-Jawziyya, who has departed from the earlier position and reached the conclusion that options and contractual stipulations are valid as a matter of principle, and not by way of exception (Kamali 2000).

The following *hadith* is quoted in support of this position. "The prophet (peace be upon him) bought a camel from Jabir Ibn Abdullah and agreed to Jabir's stipulation that he wished to ride the camel to Medina and deliver the same afterwards". According to another *hadith* the prophet (peace be upon him) said "One who sells a slave who owns property, the property shall belong to the seller unless the buyer stipulates otherwise". Another *hadith* asserts that the prophet (peace be upon him) said "whoever sells a palm tree that has borne fruit, the fruit belongs to the seller unless the buyer stipulates otherwise". On the basis of these *ahadith*, the Hanbali jurists Ibn Qayyim al-Jawziyya asserted that, this is nothing other than sale combined with an extraneous stipulation (*bai' wa shart*), which is explicitly validated by authentic *sunnah* (Kamali 2000: 195–201).

When a conditional sale (*bai' wa shart*) with options as conditions (*khiyār al-shart*) is combined with compensation (*damān*) for the party at a disadvantage, the result seems to be very similar to the conventional options framework (Obaidullah 1998: 79). As options are derivative instruments which derive their basic rationale from associating with another transaction or contract. The notion of granting the trader a choice whether to ratify or cancel an underlying contract is therefore essential to options. For instance, in case of a call option of stock X maturing after 3 months, the underlying contract may involve purchase of 100 stocks of company X at a price of £5 per share. This may be viewed in the jurisprudent framework of the Islamic commercial law as *bai' wa shart* contract for purchase of 100 stocks of company X with a condition of option (*khiyār al-shart*) for the buyer to either ratify or cancel the contract on or before 3 months from the day of contracting (Kamali 2000: 162–90). In *khiyār al-shart* context, the counter values need not change hands at the time of contracting, similar to the conventional options trading practices. Additionally, when the buyer compensates the seller for being at a disadvantage for granting the option, the framework is complete and the conventional options trading apparently perfectly fits into the framework of Islamic jurisprudence (Kamali 2000: 162–80).

However, it is perhaps the additional component of compensation (*damān*) in the above framework, which is questionable. Not many contemporary Islamic scholars have any objection to the validity of a sale with a condition (*bai' wa shart*). This is of course where the condition is stipulation of option (*khiyār al-shart*); or even when the contractual price (*thaman*) is inclusive of any compensation for the benefit provided by the seller for being at a disadvantage. However, conventional option trading would imply separation of the compensation component and its up-front payment to the option writer or seller under a separate contract (Obaidullah 1998: 80).

As noted from the earlier discussion, a promise or an obligation cannot be the subject matter of a sale contract according to an overwhelming majority of Islamic scholars. The adjustment and treatment of conventional options in the combined framework of *khiyār al-shart* and *damān* is also questionable on another ground.

Also, in the classical Islamic law, before *damān* can be invoked, one needs to show some illicit act or negligence by the party required to compensate. It is a kind of tortuous liability and reference to the same in the context of a sale of a right contract seems to be clearly misplaced. Kamali also fails to cite a single reference of the well-known Islamic jurists of the past on the use of *damān* in the *bai' wa shart* framework (Edge 1988: 40).

9.14 Similarity Between Options and *Bai' al-'Arbūn* (Down-Payment Sale)

'Arbūn refers to a sale in which the buyer deposits earnest money with the seller as a part payment of the price, but agrees that if he fails to ratify the contract he will forfeit the deposit money, which the seller can keep. It is, therefore, argued that a call option is similar to *bai' al-'arbūn* in the sense that the seller does not return the premium or advance payment to the buyer in case the latter does not exercise the purchase option and confirms the contract (Vogel and Hayes 1998: 156).

However, in case of a call option, the buyer loses the option premium even if the option is exercised and the contract is confirmed. In case of *bai' al-'arbūn*, however, the option premium is adjusted in the sale price when the contract is confirmed. Interestingly, similar to the case of a sale with a condition (*bai' wa shart*) all schools of Islamic jurisprudence except the Hanbali School find *bai' al-'arbūn* unacceptable (Obaidullah 1998: 80).

These scholars have found the retention of earnest money or premium by the seller akin to misappropriation of the property of others. They have primarily relied on the following simple and straightforward *hadith,* which is mentioned earlier, narrated by Ibn 'Abbas "the prophet (peace be upon him) prohibited the sale of '*arbūn*" reported in Imam Malik's *Muatta*'.

The followers of Imam Ibn Hanbal however, find this kind of transaction permissible in Islamic law. Imam Ibn Hanbal considered this *hadith* to be weak and based the validity of '*arbūn* on the practice of the Caliph Umar. It is reported in *al-Mughni* from Nafi' bin al-Harith, the Caliph's officer in Mecca that he purchased from Safwān bin Umayya a prison house for four thousands *dirhams* on condition that if the Caliph approved of it, the deal would be final, otherwise he (Safwan) would be given four hundred *dirhams,* (Vogel and Hayes 1998: 156).

Al-Qaradawi (1973: 114) has examined the evidence relating to *bai' al-'arbūn*. He quoted another *hadith* in support of such contract recorded in *Nayl al-Awtar*. "The prophet was asked concerning the sale of *'arbūn* and he declared it permissible". Al-Qaradawi observes that the issue should consequently be determined on rationale grounds. This ruling of Ibn Hanbal is more suitable to our own times and in greater harmony with the spirit of Shariah, which seeks to remove hardship and facilitate convenience in financial transactions for people.

El Gari is one of those who argue in favour of adapting transactions of call options using the framework of *bai' al-'arbūn*. According to him, the followers of Ibn Hanbal argue in favour of this type of sale, which is one of the old rules of this particular school of *fiqh*. He quotes the *athar* (practices of companions) reported in al-Bukhari from Ibn Sirin when he said: "A man told the operator of a caravan, I would like to join your passengers, but if I did not depart with you on a certain day, you would be entitled to a sum of one hundred *dirhams*. When he did not depart on the set date, he willingly agreed to comply with the condition" (El-Gari 1993: 9–16).

Abu Sulyman is also of the view that charging a price for call options whereby the buyer may then decide to exercise the option and make it a part of the price does not affect the validity of this contract. Provided that, it is valid in other respects, but may be seen in the category of *'arbūn* sale (Obaidullah 1998: 81). He questioned the validity of conventional options trading on other grounds by discussing the basic purpose behind the two transactions. This purpose is so different as to make drawing an analogy between them totally superfluous; as such an analogy will be no more than a discrepant analogy (*qiyas ma' al-fariq*), which is invalid.

It may be noted here that any argument on the validity of options because of its similarity with *bai' al-'arbūn* is relevant only for call options. As far as a put option is concerned there seems to be little support in its favour for the financial engineering of a Shariah compliant derivative products.

9.15 Conclusion

This Chapter was structured to complement the analysis undertaken in Chap. 8 regarding futures contracts. The analysis of options contracts provided in this Chapter provides an in-depth insight into the subject of financial innovation and engineering in Islamic finance. It critically explored this matter to present the thinking and practical process of reaching a conclusion about whether a financial innovation is compatible with Shariah requirements and can be engineered to comply with such requirements.

The analysis carried out in this Chapter further has added to the building blocks for a framework for financial innovation and engineering in Islamic finance that we have established in previous chapters. Largely, Islamic scholars have avoided to divulge in derivative products and preferred to avoid and adopt a conservative view about it. This is perhaps for two reasons; the first is complexity and the diverse practices of derivative products, which would form a challenge for a typical Islamic scholar to fully comprehend its structure and workings to form a Shariah view about its permissibility. The second reason is the concept associated with derivative products of being completely not compliant with Shariah as they involve usury, speculations, prohibited types of sales and major uncertainty.

This approach has started to shift gradually as the Islamic finance industry grows and enters new markets. The need to engage with other markets and possibly establish an Islamic financial market raised a necessity to explore new financial instruments and tools more in-depth in order to provide acceptable financial tools for hedging, risk management, liquidity and other financial market products for IFIs. This need has revived the innovative thinking and financial engineering in IFIs.

The next chapter (Chap. 10) provides a practical framework for the analysis of a financial innovation under consideration from a Shariah perspective and the rules of the Islamic commercial law. It helps understand the evaluation process of assessing a potential financial innovation and possible Shariah-engineered solutions to structure the contemplated financial product in a Shariah compliant way.

Chapter 10
Outlining a Framework for Financial Innovation and Engineering in Islamic Finance

10.1 Introduction

The previous Chapter (Chap. 9) was structured to complement the analysis undertaken in Chap. 8 regarding futures contracts. The analysis of options contracts provided in Chap. 9 provides an in-depth insight into the subject of financial innovation and engineering in Islamic finance. It explored this subject to present the thinking and practical process of reaching a conclusion about whether a financial innovation is compatible with Shariah requirements and can be engineered to comply with such requirements.

The analysis carried out in this Chapter (Chap. 10), however, builds on the discussion in the previous chapters in order to demark the framework of engineering Shariah compliant solutions for a financial innovation to be offered by IFIs. This does not mean, however, a solution as an outcome is guaranteed to be the conclusion of such analysis. The thinking process is to explore whether such a financial innovation can be structured in a Shariah compliant way by engineering various solutions or combining more than one Islamic finance instruments.

This Chapter is organised in logical way that ensures the flow of the analysis provide in the previous structure and is divided into sections. Some sections identify Shariah prohibitions associated with options and futures, others explain the logic behind the Shariah prohibitions and the analysis of the role of options and futures in the financial market. The Chapter then concludes by attempting to adjust providing such a derivative products on possible engineered solutions and how this process is structured and rationalised from a Shariah juristic perspective.

S. Alamad, *Financial Innovation and Engineering in Islamic Finance*,
Contributions to Management Science, DOI 10.1007/978-3-319-52947-9_10

10.2 Affiliated Risk with Options Contracts

Options contracts bring into the market an additional element of uncertainty, over and above the inherent uncertainty, which every trader has to face. This additional uncertainty that is the product of call and put options increases the risk of both the buyers and the sellers. As a result, both of them become exceedingly keen to pass on their risk to someone else. It starts the chain reaction of transactions tempts much more numbers of non-genuine investors than the ordinary stock market. Hence, the number of people who tend to live on 'unearned income' rises further.

In contrast to this, the options regulations in relation to the sale of option (*baý' al-khiyār*) in the Islamic market pertain to specific cases, such as:

- where the commodity is not precisely defined, or
- where the time or place of delivery are not known, or
- where the deal is not yet finalised and the buyer and seller are still at the same place in which the contract is being completed, or
- where the price is not yet finalised (Khan 1988: 108).

All these situations where options to rescind an agreement have been allowed tend to minimise the uncertainty from the market place. The objective of this is to remove all possibilities where a party may agree to a bargain without knowing all the costs, risks and benefits attached to it. These provisions support the free market rule. Such approved options from a Shariah perspective do not allow one party to make money due to ignorance of the other party.

10.3 *Al-Gharar* (Uncertainty) in the Option Market

Al-gharar (uncertainty) literally according to Ibn Al-Jawzīyyah (n.d., Vol. 1, pp. 357–361) and Salih (1988: 49–83) means danger, hazard, peril and other words that provide a similar connotation. Mu'jam al-Wāsit gives the precise definition of *al-gharar,* which means uncertainty that is present in the contract in any business transactions and which is concerned with the lack of clarity and ambiguity concerning the time, price, quantity, quality, and security of the subject matter of the transaction (Al-Nawawī n.d., Vol. 10, p. 156).

The Islamic injunctions on the subject of *al-Gharar* sale are abundantly available in the tradition of Prophet Muhammad (peace be upon him). Al-Nawawī (n.d., Vol. 10, p. 156) has mentioned that "Abu Hurairāh reported that the messenger of God forbade a transaction determined by throwing stones and the type which involves some uncertainty". Al-Qaradāwī (2003: 253–255) explains that the prohibition in Shariah on *al-gharar* sale is based on the probability that this type of transaction or sale may lead to future dispute and conflict between the parties involved. However, if the existence of uncertainty is something minor, common and bearable and it involves a needed item, then Islam shows its flexibility (*rukhsah*) by allowing the transaction to be carried out.

The aspect of *al-gharar* is present in the options sales with respect to the question of uncertainty of the participants' future position. Their participation in the market is not based on the economics of a financial transaction and its fundamentals; instead it is based on the sentiment of the market. This aspect of detaching themselves from the economic reality or economic fundamentals is in itself *al-gharar* (Al-Dhareer 1997: 29). This situation is more visible when the speculators buy options for both rights, the right to buy and the right to sell. This position certainly represents a clear *gharar* because the buyer or seller is unsure of the sentiment of the market. Firstly, they are not sure concerning the 'information' or more precisely, the rumours gathered, and secondly, they are not able to predict the trend of the price movement in the future.

The majority of Islamic jurists (they are the four schools of jurisprudence, *Malikite, Hanafite, Shafaite*, and *Hanbalite*) agreed that the ability to deliver the subject-matter of sale is a condition for the validity of the sale. It is, therefore, invalid to sell what one cannot deliver, such as a stray camel (the traditional example in the books of jurisprudence) of unknown whereabouts because this entails uncertainty (*gharar*), and this is the case in options contracts. The *Zāhiris* (school of jurisprudence but they are not popular like the other four schools, *Malikite, Hanafite, Shafaite*, and *Hanbalite*) have, however, disagreed and held that the ability to deliver the subject-matter is not a condition for the validity of the sale (Salamon 1998: 27).

Among the examples mentioned by Islamic jurists for the inability to deliver is the sale of a debt against another debt, the sale of that which one does not have in possession, and the sale by a buyer of what he has bought before he takes possession. Imām Muslim (1976: Vol. 3, p. 801) has mentioned in his book that Ibn 'Abbās, God be pleased with him, reported that God's messenger (peace be upon him) as saying: "He who buys food grain should not sell it until he has taken possession of it". A thorough review of options contracts, apparently demonstrates that options are affiliated with a lot of uncertainty which cannot be ignored.

The other aspect of *al-gharar* in the transaction of option sales is seen with respect to the question of the 'option cost', the option money paid to the dealers. The position of the money is also uncertain, whether it belongs to the buyer or seller. Provided that, the way option dealing is carried out is similar to the operation of betting or gambling; if the expectation is correct, they will gain profit, otherwise they will lose their 'betting money' (Salamon 1998; Al-Dhareer 1997).

10.4 The Issue of *Riba* (Usury) Associated with Options

One may examine the case of interest rate options or bond options, currency options, equity options, options on other Islamic contracts, and the more complex asset or put the main contract to scrutiny. There is a general consensus on the view that the entire range of debt securities involves *riba* (usury), and thus, is considered illegitimate in the Islamic commercial law. Hence, options relating to such securities are also not permissible.

Employing the same view in relation to currency options, it could be argued that currency options are also ruled out, since an overwhelming majority of Islamic jurists equate currency exchange with *bai'-sarf,* in which spot settlement or *qabd* by both parties on the spot is insisted upon. Some Hanafi scholars however, seem to permit deferment of settlement of the transaction in currencies belonging to different countries from one end. These divergent views were presented at the Fourth *Fiqh* Seminar organized by the Islamic *Fiqh* Academy, held in India in 1991.

Considering the issue of equity options from the same point of view as discussed above, the equity stocks must meet some additional criteria to conform to Islamic norms. All business activities of the company issuing the stocks should be *halal* and permissible. Accordingly, options on stocks of companies belonging to the breweries, entertainment, interest-based banking and finance and other similar industries where the major line of business is unlawful (*haram*) fall into the forbidden category. An issue on which some differences of opinion exist among Islamic scholars relate to the permissibility of stocks of a company that is engaged in lawful business, but which also finances part of its assets through interest-bearing debt. Various certificates are obviously permissible, as these have been created with the explicit purpose of meeting Shariah requirements (Obaidullah 1998; Salamon 1998; Al-Dhareer 1997).

10.5 The Rationale of Prohibiting Conventional Options

Throughout the Islamic literature of contemporary writers concerning option contracts it was clear and noteworthy that some of the writings about options consider the conventional practices of options in the market to be similar to the Islamic options (*al-khiyārāt*). However, based on the analysis provided herein in relation to the process of engineering an Islamic alternative for futures and options contracts we tend to disagree with this opinion. This is due to the fact that there is no similarity between the two versions of options contracts, on the contrary, they are completely different in their framework and application.

As there is a confusion The analysis undertaken here is the required framework for assessing whether a financial innovation can be engineered to be compliant with Shariah, if not, then how this could be achieved in a Shariah compliant way. We have chosen futures and options contracts, as a practical example to demonstrate the depth of the process for assessing financial innovation and engineering in Islamic finance, due to the complexity of such contracts as a derivative products.

Due to this complexity about this issue we will clarify this point further; Islamic options (*al-khiyārāt*) are not in themselves the contracted subject matter. The subject matter of the contract should be a commodity or an asset against a price in a sale contract or semi-sale contracts, *al-khiyārāt* are then associated with the sale contract as a complementary sub-division to the sale contract. *Al-khiyārāt* have been allowed in the sale contract in order to minimise uncertainty of the underlying subject matter, and to avoid dispute among the contracted parties.

Therefore, *al-khiyārāt* cannot be traded and contracted as independent contracts. In contrast, conventional options contracts, as practiced in the financial markets, are the underlying subject matter of the contract, which is not a commodity, tangible asset or usufruct from an Islamic finance perspective. Furthermore, options and futures contracts involve excessive uncertainty that cannot be forgiven or allowed in Shariah. They are considered to be a sale of what is not possessed and a sale of non-existent item, which are prohibited in the Islamic commercial law. This is because, they are sold in the market many times to many buyers without a real ownership of the underlying sale subject, where everyone buys and sells options or futures, which he does not possess or have an ownership of it. This kind of sale is called in Shariah a sale of debt for debt (*bai' al-kali' bi al-kali'*), which is prohibited in the Islamic commercial law.

According to Chicago Board Options Exchange (CBOE) 2013, CBOE options contracts volume was an all-time record of 968,249,301 contracts (up 30% over the previous year 2012), Provided that, if there were to be defaults or a crisis, which likely in financial markets, it would cause a significant harm and collapse in the financial system, given the volume and value of the options market. Following the market collapse in 2008 and some of the analysis provided about the causes of this financial crisis, the rationale to prohibit such contracts under Shariah in the form they are practiced today in the financial markets may be clearer.

10.6 Muslim Economists Point of View

Let us review now some opinions of Muslim economists about the permissibility of option contracts. Ahmed Muhyyi Addīn (1995), Ali al-Qrādaghī (1993), Ali Ma'bad al-Jarihī (1989), Samir Radwān (1996), and the mainstream Islamic jurists and the *Fiqh* Academy in the 7th Conference in Jeddah (No. 63, 7/1) have not allowed call and put options. Because it is not a tangible asset and not a usufruct, it is only a promise which is non-contractual and cannot be sold or purchased from a Shariah perspective. Thus they are invalid contracts.

On the other hand, some Muslim economists believe that options contracts are permissible, such as, Ahmed Yusuf Suliyman (1982), he argues that the condition which the contractual parties agreed upon is a valid condition, and the price of this condition is a right of the seller and non-refundable to the buyer. In favour of options contracts El Gari (1991: 31) discusses that many *sharī'ah* scholars, however, think the whole concept of 'option' trading does not serve any useful purpose. Rather it is a scheme, the aim of which is to legitimise the practice of gambling. Their judgment is, therefore, against allowing options (El Gari 1991: 31; Sulyman 1982).

It is not denied that options are quite prone to be used for gambling. One, nevertheless, should not ignore the useful ends they serve. According to this view, the seller of a share should be the original owner of the shares, and it should not be short sale to gamble on the price movements. The options should be exercised in the last day of its maturity (European options not American options) and the contracts should be finalised in the first hour of market opining price. Concerning put options the price is considered as a price of service, which is done by a third party to sell the seller's shares.

10.7 Options from *usūl al-Fiqh* (The Sources of Law) Point of View

In order to provide a full and more comprehensive approach to the framework of financial innovation and engineering in Islamic finance relating to the derivative products, we reflect on aspects of *usūl al-Fiqh.* The section analyse the issue of options and futures from the viewpoint of *usūl al-Fiqh.* We will consider the issue of conventional options contracts according to principles of *istihsān* (a stronger guiding Shariah reasoning) and *maslaha mursalah* (common good) of *usūl al-Fiqh.*

10.7.1 Istihsān

According to Zidan (1974: 193–197) Al-Bazdawī defines *Istihsān* as, when there are two analogies concerning the same matter the stronger one is preferred. Imam al-Hulwanī al-Hanafi states that an analogy should be left out in favour of another based on a stronger evidence from Qur'ān, *sunnah*, or consensus (*ijma'*). In other words, it is the process of allowing exceptions to strict legal reasoning or guiding choice among possible Shariah outcomes, when consideration of human welfare so demand if it does not contradict a clear Shariah text.

Applying the definition of *istihsān* on the issue of options contracts we find that there are many *ahādith* state that all contracts which involve uncertainty, two sales in one and sale of what is not owned are all disallowed. Hence, this evidence is stronger than any analogy could be drawn on the issue of options or futures sale, thus, *istihsān* supports the point of view which considers options invalid contracts.

10.7.2 Al-maslaha al-mursala *(Common Good)*

The principle of *al masalih mu'tabara* in *usūl al-Fiqh* means to bring the good and avoid the harm. However, there are the acknowledged interests/common god (*masalih mu'tabara*) and rejected interests (*masaleh mulghat*), beside these two kinds there are the common good (*maslaha mursala*), which is neither acknowledged nor rejected by Islamic law. In other words *al-maslaha mursala* is to bring the good and avoid the harm when there is no statement about the issue in any of the four sources of Islamic law (*Qur'ān, sunna, ijma'*, and *qiyās*).

Islamic jurists have different views about the use of *al-maslaha al-mursala* in financial transactions as an evidence to support a specific view. and mention that the Shafi'i and Hanafi schools consider al-*maslaha al-mursala* as a guiding principle, the Maliki and Hanbali schools went even further and consider it as a Shariah legal evidence and one of the legislative sources in Shariah. However, the Zahiria school does not consider *al-maslaha al-mursala* at all (Zidan 1974: 198–200; al-Nadawī 1991: 164–182). There are some restrictions and conditions for *al-maslaha al-mursala* to be applied, some of them are mentioned by Al-Ghazali, these conditions are:

(a) It must not contradict a text in the Qur'ān.
(b) It must not contradict the *Sunnah.*
(c) It should not contradict with an existing analogy (*qiyās*)
(d) It should not neglect another interest or common good which is more important (Al-Būtī 2000: 110–118).

Therefore, it is clear from the definition and conditions of applying *al-maslaha al-mursala* on the issue of options contracts that it contradicts with many *ahādith* in the *sunnah,* which states that all contracts that involve uncertainty, two sales in one, and a sale of something is not owned or does not exist are disallowed and invalid contracts. Thus, it is a cause of dispute among the contracting parties, as it was explained earlier. Moreover, considering options contracts from the perspective of common good leads to neglecting a more important public interest or common good, which is to save the property (*māl*) that is one of the five necessities in Islam (*al-daruriat al-khams*).

10.8 Financial Contracts with Embedded *Khiyār al-Shart*

It is clear from the discussion above that the permissibility of options as an independent contract is highly questionable. However, when an option is embedded in another exchange contract as a condition, the same appears to be valid in the Islamic commercial law. In this section we examine whether *khiyār al-shart* or option as a condition has any potential economic benefit as a tool of risk management, even though the framework is primarily ethical in nature.

Obaidullah (1998: 86) states that there is a general agreement among all jurists that the options would continue for a known and limited period of time. Al-Zuhaylī (2002: 26) mentions that according to Imam Abu Hanifa and Imam Shafii, the period of time during which the condition of option remains in force cannot exceed three days.

According to them the stipulation of condition is an external element to the nature of a contract of exchange, which should be binding and obligatory immediately after its conclusion. It was justified by the prophet's permission which must be strictly construed, and hence, cannot be extended to a period beyond what has been specified.

However, according to Imam Muhammad and Imam Abu Yusuf, prominent jurists of the Hanafi School, such stipulation may continue for any length of time, since three days may be too short period under certain circumstances to make a decision for the parties involved. According to the Maliki School, the nature of the object of transaction would determine the maximum permissible period of time. According to the Hanbali School, the time period must be known, free from any uncertainty and known to both parties at the time of contracting and there is no limit on the maximum permissible time period (Al-Zuhaylī 2003: 33–35).

10.9 Managing Price Risk with *khiyār al-shart*

The importance of risk management in present day business can be hardly overemphasised. A factor which significantly contributes to risk is price volatility. Since a complete discussion of risk management possibilities for an IFI is beyond the scope of this book, we analyse and demonstrate the possible use of *khiyār al-shart* as part of the financial innovation and engineering framework in Islamic finance for managing risks and specifically price risk in the context of commodity markets.

It is difficult to see the usefulness of *khiyār al-shart* for managing risk in financial markets, such as the stock market, which is characterised by volatile prices (Obaidullah 1998: 91). In previous example it has been showed that the risk due to price movement could be hedged by purchasing a call or put options with a given exercise price.

Let us now consider an alternative scenario in the *khiyār al-shart* framework. Individual A can now enter into a purchase (sale) contract and stipulate a condition of option for itself for a period of 3 months. The delivery of price (stock X) can now be deferred until the expiry of the 3 months. At the end of 3 months, if the price of stock X moves up (down) then he can confirm the contract of sale at the known contractual price and thus be immune from price risk. However, if the price of stock X moves down (up) then individual A can rescind the contract and sell it in the market, thereby not losing the profit potential.

Thus, *khiyār al-shart* may provide a benefit for the party holding the option at the cost of the counterparty. However, the disadvantage caused to the counterparty can be compensated in the form of higher contractual price or *thaman* and needs not be paid separately upfront to the counterparty. It is this feature that provides an effective curb on speculating on price differences and thus, differentiates Islamic options from the conventional ones.

An alternative financing mechanism for repeated purchases from a single supplier in the Islamic framework is known as *bai'-istijrar*. The difference between *bai'-istijrar* and *bai'-salam* relates to whether sales are made from a single and regular seller or not. In the former case, it is considered as *bai'-ajil* where payment of price can be deferred. In the latter case, the price must be paid by the buyer at the time of contracting. With *bai'-istijrar*, however, the IFI is exposed to price risk, since the contractual price is set at the time of entering into the contract or beginning of the financing period (Qureshi 1988: 10).

10.10 *Istijrār* Sale with *Khiyār al-Shart*

Bai' al-istjrār is defined as the commodities which a person extracts or takes from the seller and pay its price after the commodities have been consumed. This kind of transactions is known among people, however, there are different opinions about it where some Islamic scholars see it as a sale transaction, while others consider it a guarantee for the consumed goods with the seller's consent according to customs or traditional practices (Al-Zuhaylī 2002: Vol. 4, p. 3096). An *istijrar* sale with *khiyār al-shart* for both parties would be a complex instrument, which has some similarities with certain traditional financial engineering products, such as, the average price (Asian) option, barrier option, and range forward contracts. All these financial innovations pertain to transactions in currencies although these could also be used for commodity or stock transactions.

Asian or average price option as a contract is where the payoff depends on the average price of the underlying asset during the lift of the option. The payoff from an average call is max (0, pavg-P*), and that from an average price put is max (0, P*-Pavg). In this framework, Pavg is the average price and P* is the strike price. It may be noted that in case of *istijrar*, the payoff for the IFI is the same as for an average call (even though the IFI is the seller and a call option is a right to buy) and that for the client-firm is the same as for an average put option (even though the client firm is a buyer and a put is a right to sell) where P* is the contractual price (*thaman*). This apparent contradiction is because the options in our framework imply an option to rescind the contract; and disappears once we consider the implications of options for the parties in terms of payoffs (Obaidullah 1998: 94).

It may be noted that the above options appear as features in *istijrar* involving a real and physical transaction, and not separate contracts in themselves. If the options are separate contracts, which are fully transferable, there is a possibility of speculation on the direction of price movement.

10.11 Exclusions from Option Contracts

We have discussed earlier whether options contracts can be engineered in a Shariah compliant way on the basis of their compatibility with Shariah requirements. We have discussed various reasons why a Shariah compliant alternative cannot be engineered and other possibilities on which a solution may be engineered to be acceptable from a Shariah perspective. The following are few extracted reasons from the earlier discussion addressing why options and futures contracts must be excluded from the Islamic financial market.

(a) Options and futures contracts are not comparable to *salam* sale. They are considered as one of the business techniques, which do not conform to the Islamic finance requirements. An option contract, which gives the right to buy or sell shares in a stipulated time in the future at the current price, is not comparable to the specified requirements in the Islamic law for *salam* sale. In a *salam* sale only one aspect is being deferred or non-existent at the time of the contract that is the commodity, while in options contracts the deferment takes place for both counter values, the payment and the delivery of the subject matter.
(b) Bringing into the market additional uncertainty is another reason for incompatibility. As they pass the risk to others through exercising a put or call option. This practice would form a chain of transactions which give speculators an opportunity to make profit from the prevailing uncertainty; as a consequence, the tendency for market manipulation becomes enormous. This contradicts the rules of market conduct and financial transactions requirements under the Islamic commercial law.
(c) Options and futures contracts are created to serve the speculators, which are usually carried out in a short time (usually 3 months). This reflects a strong motive of speculation rather than investment. At the same time as the contract allows the participants to pay a fraction of the full price, it leads to more uncertainty and instability in the market.
(d) Options contracts are similar to gaming as the participants can indulge in the contract if they expect a price movement upwards or downwards or even if they are unsure about the direction of the price movement. The situation of forfeiting the option money if the option holders abandon the contract, another aspect that is not in conformity with Shariah requirements. This forfeiting condition of the option money if the contract holders abandon the contract is forbidden in Islam as this is equivalent to the contract of al-'arbūn sale which is clearly prohibited by the prophet (peace be upon him) in his *hadīth* in *al-Muatta'* (1951: *Kitab al-Buyū'*, p. 1) (Qureshi 1988: 10).

10.12 Conclusion

The conclusion we would draw shows that there are no effective derivatives of Islamic debt contract, which could replicate conventional risk-hedging and leveraging contracts as practiced today, such as swaps, futures, and options. Similarly, in the equity security sector, there are no risk-hedging or leveraging contracts in Islamic finance truly comparable to available conventional derivatives that aim to maximise profit, due to incompatibility between both of them.

Previously they were classified as financial instruments and were, therefore, ineligible to be bought and sold. Now a number of Islamic scholars classify them as specific claims on real assets, thus making secondary market trading in them acceptable. This is at least a start towards the future formulation of equity derivatives, which are acceptable in the Islamic commercial law.

The rationale of the Islamic law is as follows; in the futures market a number of intermediaries make money without adding any time, place or form utility to the commodity. Thus, some people earn without giving anything in recompense (*I'wad*). The situation is closely similar to the one in which a person claims *riba* (usury) without giving anything in return or exchanging an asset.

Islamic scholars and economists are involved in a continuous process of designing and developing new financial instruments and finding innovative solutions to financial problems within the Islamic framework. This is important since many of the traditional financial engineering products, such as, the conventional options or products with embedded options may not be permissible. A major justification for financial engineering is provided in terms of the need to manage risk. It is indeed a challenge to demonstrate that risk management solutions do exist in the Islamic finance framework.

The different approaches that Islamic scholars have taken in order to verify the validity of options trading in Shariah set a cornerstone in the foundation of a financial innovation and engineering framework in Islamic finance. While some have preferred to subsume trading in options and futures under the Islamic legal concept of contractual stipulations, or *al-khiyārāt*. Others have drawn an analogy with *'urbūn* (down-payment) in which an intending purchaser gives the seller a deposit as good faith money. This down payment however, is non-returnable in the event that the buyer does not proceed with the sale.

It is fair to say, based on the analysis provided, that options as independent contracts may not be suitable forms of hedging or managing risk from an Islamic finance perspective, the primary reason being that these are not Shariah nominated contracts. Furthermore, they can be used for speculation on price movements and would generate effortless income, which violates Islamic norms of financial ethics. At the same time, the problem that confronts every participant in various markets, such as, the commodity, securities, and currencies markets arising out of volatility in prices may be addressed by designing instruments of risk management within the Islamic framework of *khiyār al-shart*. We have discussed that such a tool of risk management cannot be used for speculation on price differences.

The potential of Islamic options is vastly untapped. While discussing several possible uses of *khiyār al-shart* for risk management, we also analysed and demonstrated how a specific contracts can be designed by combining *bai'-istijrar* with *khiyār al-shart* as a possible acceptable alternative for engineering a Shariah compliant financial product. The possibilities discussed herein are, by no means, exhaustive, however, they provide a clear path that sets the framework and key building blocks for financial innovation and engineering in Islamic finance. In the framework of *khiyār al-shart,* e.g. may lay some interesting solutions to financial problems that need to be explored further in the future.

The next chapter (Chap. 11) presents the findings of a practical analysis of a case study based on a documentary analysis of various financial products currently on offer from IFIs. This analysis is based on the discussion in the previous chapters and the framework we established in this Chap. 10. The documentary analysis method, undertaken in the next Chapter, compliments the analysis conducted in Chaps. 8, 9 and 10 for more robustness and rigorous findings.

Chapter 11
Case Study: Analysis of Selected Shariah Compliant Financial Products

11.1 Introduction

The previous chapter (Chap. 10) built on analysis in the previous chapters in order to paint the picture for the framework of engineering Shariah compliant solutions for a financial innovation to be offered by IFIs. This framework for financial innovation and engineering was established in the previous chapter with a clear demonstration of the thinking and analytical processes from an Islamic juristic perspective.

This Chapter presents the findings of a practical analysis of a case study. This analysis is based on the discussion in the previous chapters and the framework we established in Chap. 10 in terms of the considerations and steps that should be followed by IFIs in the financial innovation and engineering process. The documentary analysis method, undertaken in this Chapter, compliments the analysis conducted in Chaps. 8, 9, and 10 for more robustness and rigorous findings.

It examines current practices in the Islamic finance industry as a whole and IFIs, by analysing existing financial products and innovation in the market against the framework that has been outlined in the earlier chapters. This framework takes into account the philosophy and objective of the Islamic economic thought and the Shariah requirements for financial innovation and engineering as conceptualised in the process of analysing futures and options from an Islamic finance perspective. This framework was developed, as a result of the research findings that were also based on data collected from IFIs, which provided an in-depth insight into current practices in relation to financial innovation and engineering in IFIs.

The documentary analysis aims to cover a wide range of existing financial products, for a representative view of the existing practices. Thus, the aim of the analysis was to include a sample of main financial activities undertaken in the Islamic finance industry. The activities were divided into four segments, retail, investment and commercial, derivatives and *sukuk* issuance. By doing so, it is assumed that all areas of financial activities, which included an investment account,

S. Alamad, *Financial Innovation and Engineering in Islamic Finance*,
Contributions to Management Science, DOI 10.1007/978-3-319-52947-9_11

a home finance product, a derivative product and a financial market product (*sukuk*) are covered.

The documentary analysis is based on collecting all available documents associated with the financial product being analysed, this includes prospectus, terms and conditions, product structure and processes, product information and Shariah compliance certificate if available. It does not include internal NPD processes as this would not be available to analyse the steps followed by the IFI in developing the financial product due to confidentiality, this element, therefore, was covered in the data collected from IFIs that provided more insights about such processes.

The available documents from various IFIs were reviewed thoroughly and the analysis process was based on a set of criteria that were extracted from the outlined framework from the analysis of earlier chapters for financial innovation and engineering. The documentary analysis process aims to obtain data from major Islamic banks, in relation to product development, to be analysed. This method analyses 4 main types of Shariah compliant financial products in the market, one investment product for savings account, one asset product for home financing, a derivative product and a *sukuk* (Islamic equity certificate) issue. At least documents from 5 IFIs were collected for each product. This included documents and prospectus related to each type of the selected financial products, Islamic legal opinions and certification of those financial products.

11.2 Scope of the Documentary Analysis

The documentary review and analysis examine specific areas of the document being analysed that are related to the book's objectives. The objective of the review is to investigate current practices of financial innovation and engineering as implemented in the product development process of IFIs. The judging criteria of the analysis are based on the developed framework for financial innovation and engineering in previous chapters.

The elements of the assessment criteria may vary depending on the type of the product being analysed and the Islamic finance principle that underpins the structure of the product. The general assessment criteria are:

- Embedding one or more of the Shariah objectives in the process of the product structure whether implicitly or explicitly.
- A social welfare view of the impact of this product (this element might be difficult to gauge as it would not be usually included in the publicly available documents).
- Assessment of the suitability of the selected Islamic finance principle or structure.
- Compliance of the structure with all requirements of the Islamic finance principle employed to offer that product.

- Whether the structure provides a Shariah compliant product or a Shariah inspired product in form and substance.

11.3 Findings of the Case Study Through Documentary Analysis

Based on the collected data, as mentioned above, and using the outlined framework for financial innovation and engineering as a measurement tool, we assessed how the fundamental principles are enmeshed in those financial products and banking practices. Then, this data was analysed to identify certain variables and relationships among them, in order to provide an assessment of the role of these different relations in the current financial innovation and engineering environment. This method has added value in answering the questions raised in this book as shown below in the coming sections.

11.3.1 Documentary Analysis of an Investment Product

The documents selected for the analysis of an investment product is a *wakala* agreement for investment that belongs to Islamic banks based in the Middle East. *Wakala* is an agency agreement for investment, (see explanation of *wakala* principle in Chap. 2, Sect. 2.4) it is used by Islamic banks for inter-banking placements, when banks deposit funds with each other, or to provide deposit savings products to retail and corporate clients. The document analysed is the Master *Wakala* Agreement for Investment, which sets all the terms and conditions of the transaction and the transaction documents.

11.3.1.1 Shariah Objectives

The documents do not specify adhering to certain Shariah objectives, it seems that current practices do not suggest that either. However, that would, usually, be imbedded within the document somehow and would require to be extracted based on the analysis of certain sections of the documents. The analysis identified two Shariah objectives incorporated whether intentionally or not, when the document mentions 'that the transaction and each related document are for only investment in a Shariah compliant manner and all parties agree to abide by the rules of Shariah'. This incorporates the Shariah objectives of preservation and maintenance of the religion, by avoiding interest-based transactions and using Shariah compliant transaction instead. It also incorporates the Shariah objective of safeguarding wealth, by investing the funds provided by the investor to grow it and make profit in accordance with Shariah.

11.3.1.2 Social Welfare Impact

The social impact of this financial product is also not mentioned clearly in the documents. However, it is implied by the way the *wakala* contract works, as there is an investment relationship between the parties which results in purchasing and selling commodities, that complies with the Shariah requirements of undertaking activities that are not harmful, and where other stakeholders in the society would benefit as well. It is worth noting that what they would consider harmful, would be based on the level and robustness of their internal Shariah compliance controls.

11.3.1.3 Suitability of the Selected Islamic Finance Principle or Structure

The *wakala* principle is suitable as a structure for this type of product, although another suitable structure is *mudaraba* (see definition of *mudaraba* in Chap. 2, Sect. 2.4).

11.3.1.4 Compliance of the Structure with All Requirements of the Islamic Finance Principle Employed

The structure as detailed in the master agreement seems to fulfil all requirements of the *wakala* principle. However, if this structure is used in the context of a retail deposit, as defined in the Financial Services and Markets Act (FSMA) 2000, it means that the IFI has to guarantee the principal amount deposited. This is a clear breach of the Islamic finance principle of *wakala,* where unless there is a clear negligence or gross misconduct of the IFI, the IFI is not liable for any loss in the principal amount because it acts as a trustee. Other IFIs make a specific disclaimer to address this issue in their terms and conditions in order to comply with both Shariah and regulatory requirements, they state:

> If your deposit amount returns a loss, we shall offer to make good the amount of any shortfall that you may have suffered. We are required by current UK bank regulations and policy, pursuant to clause xx, to make this offer to you. If you choose to accept this offer, you shall be entitled to receive payment from us of the full amount that you had previously deposited with us. You are entitled to refuse this offer from us.
>
> We would like to draw your attention to the guidance offered by our Sharia Supervisory Committee. Their guidance is that if you accept our offer to make good the amount of any shortfall (set out in special condition xx), you will not be complying with Sharia principles. (An extract from a UK based Islamic bank's terms and conditions for a wakala investment product).

This issue presents one of the regulatory restrictions that form a challenge for introducing Islamic finance innovation and financial products that are Shariah oriented.

11.3.1.5 A Shariah Compliant Product or a Shariah Inspired Product in Form and Substance

The structure of this product seems to go beyond just being compliant with Shariah to the category of being inspired in form and substance, as this structure is not a complicated one. A Shariah compliance certificate of the product was also available which explains the structure and corresponds to the legal terms. There is, however, an issue though in relation to how it can ensure that the trustee is going to follow Shariah guidance when undertaking the investment transactions. This issue is, (Rammal 2006), covered by the Shariah governanceDocumentary analysis:investment product: of the IFI and the internal Shariah compliance audit reviews which perform these checks.

11.3.2 Documentary Analysis of a Home Finance Product

The analysis of this type of financial product, offered by IFIs, is based on all available product documents that are part of the offerings. Islamic home finance is based on three main different structures a *murabaha* based home finance, an *ijarah* based home finance and a diminishing *musharaka* with *ijarah* structure, (see explanation of each of those principles in Chap. 2, Sect. 2.4). For the purposes of this analysis, we have selected a structure based on diminishing *musharaka* with *ijarah* for a home finance, which is also considered financial engineering as it involves employing various contracts within the product. The reason for choosing this particular structure for the analysis is because it is very common structure and is more complicated than other available structures, as it uses various Islamic finance principles (financial engineering) to offer the desired financial product.

The structure works as follows, as described by the Islamic bank offering this product: the bank and its client contribute towards the purchase or refinance of the chosen property, by the client, as partners. The Islamic bank (IB) agrees to sell its share of the property to the client over a period of time, known as the finance term. The IB also leases its share of the property to the client, for which the client pays a monthly rent.

Therefore, the monthly payment consists of two elements: an acquisition payment, which is the payment the client makes to acquire the IB's share in the property; and a rental payment which is the charge for renting the IB's share in the property. Monthly acquisition payments will remain constant throughout the term of the finance and the rent element is variable. Once the IB's share is fully acquired in the property, the monthly payments cease and full legal ownership of the property transfers to the client.

The analysis is based on reviewing four associated legal documents, diminishing *musharaka* agreement, lease agreement, service agency agreement and legal charge agreement, in addition to the offer document and product leaflet.

11.3.2.1 Shariah Objectives

The documents do not specify adhering to certain Shariah objectives, although it is a good Shariah compliance practice to do so. However, this is imbedded implicitly within the document. Two Shariah objectives were identified, whether intentionally or not, when the diminishing *musharaka* agreement states that 'the transaction as a whole and each related agreement are for only enabling the IFI to provide finance in a Shariah compliant manner and all parties to the agreement agree to be bound by the rules of Shariah and never to claim interest payments from each other'.

This incorporates the Shariah objectives of preservation and maintenance of the religion, by avoiding interest-based transactions and providing clients with the Shariah compliant alternative. The second Shariah objective, that was met, is safeguarding wealth by ensuring that the customer share is paid towards a legitimate purpose under a Shariah structure that would financially benefit both the IFI and the client. The IFI financial benefit is made from the rent element in accordance with Shariah and the client acquires its home.

11.3.2.2 Social Welfare Impact

The social impact of this financial product is also not mentioned clearly in the documents. However, this is implied by the overall product structure, as there is an approved process as mentioned in the diminishing *musharaka* agreement to ensure that the client chooses suitable property that they can afford. Also, providing the client with a Shariah based finance solutions for housing that meet pressing needs in the market. This product provides a solution for financial inclusion of Muslim clients to be able to finance their homes in accordance with Shariah. Also, ensuring that this process will not generate a negative or harmful outcome to other stakeholders in the society.

11.3.2.3 Suitability of the Selected Islamic Finance Principle or Structure

As mentioned above there are more than one structure available in the market for offering home finance. The diminishing *musharaka* with *ijarah* (DMI) structure is believed to be more appropriate and flexible than the other two structures, i.e. *murabaha* and *ijarah* only structures. This is because (Khir et al. 2008: 229) of the flexibility of the pricing structure of a DMI structure, which works better for possible adjustments of the product and its profit, i.e. rental rate, throughout the finance term, in order to facilitate refinancing, releasing equity, reducing the finance term, lump sum payments by the client to increase its equity or early settlement. Also, this structure is believed to be more suitable from a profit rate risk management perspective, as the rental rate charged by the bank could be adjusted according to agreed intervals based on a benchmark or an index. This would work better for both the IFI and the client at the same time.

11.3.2.4 Compliance of the Structure with All Requirements of the Islamic Finance Principle Employed

Components of a DMI for home financing are:

1. The unilateral promise made by the client to purchase the IFI's beneficial interest in the property over the finance term. This is, usually, countered by an open offer from the IFI to sell its beneficial interest to the client.
2. A lease agreement that specifies the terms of the lease and particulars of rental payments. It also stipulates the roles and responsibilities of each party, the IFI in our case shifted its responsibilities under the lease in relation to maintenance of the property to the client under an agency agreement.
3. A service agency agreement which appoints the customer as the IFI's service agent in the IFI's beneficial share of the property, this suggests that the IFI would pay its share of any costs incurred. However, nothing was mentioned in the document about this process in either the lease or the service agency agreements.
4. A legal charge agreement in order to secure the monthly payments, this should apply only to the rental payment but not the acquisition payments. Nevertheless, that was not the case in the reviewed documents and it is mentioned that a default on acquisition payments constitute an event of default. This could be due to regulatory guidelines in relation to regulated mortgages (in particular with the Mortgage Market Review (MMR), which became effective from April 2014, that was conducted by the UK regulator and tightened the rules on mortgage provides) and what constitutes an event of default. The rules do not differentiate between a Shariah compliant home finance and a traditional mortgage.
5. The approval of the diminishing *musharaka* model, by many Shariah scholars, was on the view that it is a form of *sharikat al-mulk* (partnership in a property) not as *sharikat al-'aqd* (partnership by contract). While the parties are not allowed to agree in advance a fixed price for the forward sale of partnership shares among themselves, as this would constitute a *riba* transaction, this does not apply in *sharikat al-mulk* (which the analysed product is based on) because the contract is not intended as a profit making venture for either party (El-Diwany 2010: 263). Other Shariah scholars disagree with this view, i.e. agreeing in advance a fixed sale price of the IFI's share in the property,

because the IFI is not using the market value or price of the property at the time of sale (El-Diwany 2010: 263).

11.3.2.5 A Shariah Compliant Product or a Shariah Inspired Product in Form and Substance

The structure of this product seems to be Sharia compliant; it does not go beyond that to the category of being Sharia inspired in form and substance. The implied complexity in the structure is a key factor for that and differences in the scholarly views in relation to the principle itself. It, however, meets the minimum requirements by Shariah as a Shariah compliance certificate of the product was also available, which explains the structure briefly. We would suggest a possible review of the structure of this product for enhancement of its structure, a better justification and further details in the Sharia compliance certificate of the structure.

11.3.3 Documentary Analysis of a Derivative Product

The document selected for the analysis of a derivative product is a sale and purchase of currency master agreement, or as also called FX currency swaps, which is used by many Islamic banks. The sale and purchase of currency under Shariah is subject to strict rules, as this type of contract should be used on spot basis and not as a future trade. This is because this could render the agreement as a *riba* transaction. The counter values of buying and selling money in a FX contract should be exchanged on spot, according to the applicable exchange rate at the time of executing the transaction. This is because money is classed as a usurious item in Shariah.

This transaction is used between counterparties IFIs to hedge their exposure to currency movements. It involves two spot currency exchange transactions, one at present and the other at a future date, with a binding unilateral promise. The document analysed here is the master agreement for the purchase and sale of currencies, which sets all the terms and conditions of the transaction.

11.3.3.1 Shariah Objectives

The master agreement does not specify its aim to satisfying particular Shariah objectives. However, it is assumed that would be imbedded within the document somehow. The analysis has identified two Shariah objectives incorporated whether intentionally or not and were extracted from the objective of the contract. The document states in the recital that:

B *The Bank and the Customer have agreed to enter into Transactions on the terms and conditions of this Deed.*

C *This Agreement is entered into by the Parties in compliance with Shariah principles.*

This incorporates the Shariah objectives of preservation and maintenance of religion, by avoiding dealing with interest-based transactions, to achieve the desired outcome by using Shariah compliant transaction instead. The other Shariah objective that was identified is safeguarding wealth, by using transactions that comply with Shariah in order to hedge the position of the IFI against being exposed to currency exposure and market movement. This is a way of risk management for currency exposure that protects against financial loss.

11.3.3.2 Social Welfare Impact

The social impact of this financial product is also not mentioned clearly in the documents. However, that is implied by the objective of undertaking this transaction. This objective is to sell and purchase currencies, which is a legitimate economic activity under Shariah as all involved parties will benefit from it. This is also achieved by analysing the outcome of this transaction, which is managing risks involved with the IFI's exposure to currency volatility in the market, and protecting its position in accordance with Shariah. If the IFI was exposed to this risk and collapsed, as a result of that exposure, this would cause great harm to the welfare of the society and the IFI's clients.

11.3.3.3 Suitability of the Selected Islamic Finance Principle or Structure

The existing structure, as a hedging mechanism for a currency exposure, is the only available Shariah compliant structure that serves this purpose. It delivers the required outcome as long as; there is a robust internal Shariah control in the IFI to ensure that the documentation and each transaction are executed properly in accordance with Shariah rules. There is, possibly, a room here for an alternative financial innovation that could serve the same purpose.

11.3.3.4 Compliance of the Structure with All Requirements of the Islamic Finance Principle Employed

The structure as detailed in the master agreement seems to fulfil all requirements of the sale of currency contract under Shariah, except for the following issues that were identified:

1. It should be made clear, as a Shariah requirement, at the beginning of this contract that it is for hedging purposes only, (Dusuki et al. 2012), in order not to be used for other purposes, such as pure profit making.
2. The contract failed to include the standard 'interest clause' that is required in each Shariah compliant financial contract, in particular those who are governed by a secular jurisdiction law, such as English law. The purpose of this legal clause is to ensure that neither party to the contract will claim from the other interest payment in any legal proceedings.
3. The contract also failed to address an important issue associated with this type of transaction, what happens if the transaction is not completed, for any reason, within the spot period of 2 days for settlement. This is an important issue that is omitted in the contract, because if the transaction was not concluded within the spot period, T+2 as practiced in the financial market, the contract will be void under Shariah rules, and a new transaction should be initiated on the same terms.

The above three issues are the main findings from the analysis of the document in question, which affects its full compliance with Shariah.

11.3.3.5 A Shariah Compliant Product or a Shariah Inspired Product in Form and Substance

The structure of this product seems to fall in the category of not meeting the very minimum of Shariah requirements. There are some serious Sharia non-compliance issues that need to be addressed, as mentioned above. In particular, issue No. 3, - Section 6.4 above, which form a substantial uncertainty (*gharar*) in the contract. Therefore, our view in relation to this contract is that, it does not satisfy Shariah requirements in either form or substance.

11.3.4 Documentary Analysis of Sukuk *(Equity Based Islamic Certificate) Issue*

The analysis of this type of financial product is based on reviewing the base prospectus of the some *sukuk* issuances and their Shariah *fatwa*. *Sukuk* is defined as "certificates of equal value representing undivided shares in ownership of tangible assets, usufructs and services, assets of particular projects or special investment activity" (AAOIFI, standard No. 17, 2014). The analysis was for a *sukuk* issued by a multilateral Islamic bank based in Saudi Arabia. The total *sukuk* issue is for a value of U.S.$6,500,000,000, the trust certificates are issued by a trust company incorporated in Jersey. The programme is based on issuing a series of trust certificates for the total value of the *sukuk*.

11.3.4.1 Shariah Objectives

The sukuk base prospectus does not specify considering certain Shariah objectives, although it is a good Shariah compliance practice to do so. However, this was integrated implicitly within the document. Two Shariah objectives were identified by analysing the base prospectus. It implies raising funds in a Shariah compliant way and observing preservation and maintenance of religion, by avoiding dealing with interest-based transactions to achieve the desired outcome. The other Shariah objective that was identified is safeguarding wealth, by using transactions that comply with Shariah in order to invest and manage the funds collected to generate income that is distributed among the certificate holders.

11.3.4.2 Social Welfare Impact

The social impact of this financial product was, to some extent, mentioned clearly in the documents. There was a clear reference to the assets purchased and possible use of it in social projects and improving infrastructure. That was implied by stating that the portfolio, which is the subject of the trust is a portfolio of assets created by the issuing IFI that would be separate and independent from all other assets of the IFI and shall comprise of:

> (a) at least 33 per cent. tangible assets comprising of leased assets, disbursing Istisna'a assets, shares and/or Sukuk; and
>
> (b) no more than 67 per cent. intangible assets comprising of Istisna'a receivables and/or Murabaha receivables, including, without limitation, the right to receive payment of any amounts due in connection with such assets, the right to demand, sue for, recover, receive and give receipts for all amounts payable, or to become payable, under the assets and/or agreements relating to the assets and the benefit of, and the right to sue on, all covenants in favour of the IFI and the right to exercise all powers of the IFI thereunder, the constituent elements of which may be supplemented from time to time with additional portfolio assets.

This major programme for issuing *sukuk* certificates to raise funds in order to finance big social projects is for the benefit of all stakeholders in that venture and the society as a whole. The IFI makes a clear reference to its socially responsible approach as it states that it carries out a number of other activities which have an impact on social and economic development. These include:

- human capital development, by way of providing scholarships and extending training
- opportunities to individuals engaged in development activities;
- undertaking research in Islamic economics, banking and finance;
- social infrastructure development; and
- various support activities for private sector development.

11.3.4.3 Suitability of the Selected Islamic Finance Principle or Structure

The *sukuk* issue is structured on the *wakala* Islamic finance principles, the issuing trust company appointed an agent to collect the income and distribute it to the certificate holders. The base prospectus sets clearly the method used and state clearly that it follows AAOIFI Shariah and accounting standards. The legal structure seems to be in accordance with the *wakala* principle as described in AAOIFI Shariah standards, and is reflected clearly in the terms and conditions. Therefore, the employed Islamic finance principle is believed to be suitable for the structure of the *sukuk*.

11.3.4.4 Compliance of the Structure with All Requirements of the Islamic Finance Principle Employed

The legal terms state that the trust certificates are limited recourse obligations trust certificates issued under the programme 'are not debt obligations of the Trustee'. Instead, the trust certificates represent 'an undivided beneficial ownership interest in the relevant trust assets'. This is completely in accordance with the principle of *wakala*. Recourse to IFI in respect of each series of trust certificates therefore, is limited to the trust assets of that relevant series of trust certificates, and the proceeds of such trust assets are the primary source of payments on the relevant series of trust certificates.

The analysis also covered examining if the *sukuk* is asset-backed or asset-based. According to Moody's (an international rating agency) definition, asset-backed *sukuk* are those whose "investors enjoy asset-backing; they benefit over some form of security or lien over the assets, and are therefore in a preferential position over other, unsecured creditors. In other words, in the event the issuer were to default or become insolvent, the noteholders would be able to recover their exposure by taking control of and ultimately realising the value from the asset(s). It also requires the element of securitisations to be present, true sale, bankruptcy remoteness and enforceability of security, (Lotter and Khalid 2007).

On the other hand, asset-based *sukuk* are those for which "the originator undertakes to repurchase the assets from the issuer at maturity of the *sukuk*, or upon a predefined early termination event, for an amount equal to the principle repayment. In such a repurchase undertaking, the true market value of the underlying asset (or asset portfolio) is irrelevant to the *sukuk* certificate holders, as the amount is defined to be equivalent to the certificate (Lotter and Khalid 2007).

In this case, certificate holders have no special rights over the asset(s) and rely wholly on the originator's creditworthiness for repayment. Thus, if the originator is unable to honour its obligation to repurchase the assets, the certificate holders are in no preferential position to any other creditors, or indeed in no weaker position to any other unsecured creditor, stressing the importance that the purchase undertaking ranks *pari passu* with any other of the originator's senior unsecured obligations (Lotter and Khalid 2007).

Similarly, in asset-backed *sukuk*, the *sukuk*-holders are the owners of the asset, and the actual performance of the underlying asset will determine the return to the *sukuk*-holders (Dusuki and Mokhtar 2010). Therefore, the analysis concludes that the sukuk issue in question, based on the analysis of its documentation, is asset-backed and fully in accordance with Shariah requirements.

Hence, there is a need to move towards more asset-backed *sukuk* in the market. In order to promote this, Islamic scholars will be the main driving force that will determine the growth of asset-backed *sukuk*. This can be achieved by Islamic scholars demanding that the Shariah requirements and the legal status of the *sukuk*-holders are aligned. Issuers who want to raise funds must be ready to part with their asset, and investors who want to invest in *sukuk* must be prepared to take asset risk (Dusuki and Mokhtar 2010).

11.3.4.5 Shariah Compliant Product or a Shariah Inspired Product in Form and Substance

We can therefore, based on the above analysis, say that asset-backed *sukuk* clearly fulfils the Shariah requirements and eliminates all the controversial Shariah issues that are associated with asset-based *sukuk*. Also based on the incorporation of Shariah objectives and commitment to social welfare by the IFI, the structure of this *sukuk* seems to go beyond Sharia compliant to the category of Shariah inspired in form and substance. This is based on examining and subjecting the *sukuk* issue to all the above criteria.

11.4 Summary of the Documentary Analysis Findings

This section provides a brief summary of the documentary analysis review and its main findings as discussed above. Table 11.1 below shows the main findings of the documentary analysis for each of the financial products.

11.5 Conclusion

This Chapter conducted a documentary analysis review of key financial products as offered in the Islamic finance industry. Various documents from around 5 IFIs collected for each product. The analysis provided great insight into current practices of IFIs, in relation to financial innovation and engineering. It shows to a great extent, based on the analysis we have undertaken for financial innovation and

Table 11.1 Summary of the documentary analysis findings

Criteria	Investment Product	Home Finance	Hedging / Derivative Product	Money Market Product / *Sukuk*
Islamic finance principle	*Wakala*	Diminishing *musharaka* with *ijara*	Sale and purchase of currency / *sarf*	*Sukuk al wakala*
Shariah certificate is available	✓	✓	✓	✓
Meeting Shariah objectives	✓	✓	✓	✓
Shariah objectives stated clearly	✗	✗	✗	✗
Considered social welfare	✓	✓	✓	✓
Social welfare stated clearly	✗	✗	✗	✓
Structure is Shariah compliant	✓	✓	✓	✓
Structure goes beyond minimum Shariah compliance requirements	✗	✗	✗	✓
Legal terms include 'interest waiver clause'	✓	✓	✗	✓
Asset backed	✓	✗	✓	✓

engineering, various levels of incorporating Shariah requirements in the process of NPD (new product development).

The analysis concluded that, although Shariah objectives are not referenced in the product structure or documentation clearly, it is integrated to some extent in different ways. A good practice for IFIs is to state clearly the Shariah objectives that the developed financial product satisfies, and the justification of how it is satisfied. The analysis also revealed a variation of the level of Shariah compliance and integration of its requirements, in relation to financial innovation and engineering, in the Islamic finance industry.

Next chapter (Chap. 12) provides a full account of the book's chapters setting out the discussion in accordance with the book's objective, conceptual framework and how they are linked to the findings, contribution and practical policy implications.

Chapter 12
Discussion and Conclusion

12.1 Introduction

In accordance with the main objectives of this book as stated in Chap. 1, Sect. 1.8, this study has explored the approach of the Islamic banking industry in defining and implementing a religious orientation towards financial innovation and financial engineering at all levels within the Islamic Financial Institutions (IFIs). It also examined various approaches exhibited in individual and institutional behaviour and practices of an IFI in relation to the enactment and application of religious theories into the processes of financial innovation and engineering.

This book investigated how IFIs are embracing religious guidelines in their structure to drive the processes of product development and its outcome in order to be compatible, at the same time, with the rapid growth of the financial system. This chapter extends further the discussion of the findings provided in Chaps. 8, 9 and 10 and outlines and discusses the findings of the research as presented in those chapters. It also states parsimoniously the contribution of this study to relevant theory and draws a conclusion. It further outlines policy implications of the research for various stakeholders, proposes a new financial innovation that was developed to resolve a social problem in the UK, and finally it suggests avenues for future research.

12.2 Discussion

The religious imperative to provide alternative financial services that comply with the principles and teachings of Shariah in IFIs was discussed in Chaps. 2, 3, 4 and 6 of this book (see also: Wilson and El-Ashker 2006; Ahmed 1980; Naqvi 1981). Chapters 4 and 5 explored how, financial innovations developed over 1400 years in the historical context of the Islamic civilisation and the key influencing factors that

S. Alamad, *Financial Innovation and Engineering in Islamic Finance*,
Contributions to Management Science, DOI 10.1007/978-3-319-52947-9_12

impacted its development, (Al Omar 2003; Lewis 1970; Hitti 1963). Chapter 6 discussed innovation bias and innovation from a conventional perspective with a view to three Schumpeterian schools of innovation, which paved the way for outlining the Islamic school of innovation in Chap. 7.

The process of financial innovation and engineering remains not clear enough as discussed in Chap. 7. This is due to the wide-ranging interpretation of Islamic commercial law and the lack of standardisation of such processes. This has created a major challenge for the Islamic finance industry and the compliance of the financial innovation with religious requirements that they must seek to adhere to (Asad 1993; Al Aqla et al. 2004; Al Zarqa 2012).

Chapter 7 concluded that the absence of a coherent conceptual definition of what constitutes religious orientation towards financial innovation is a major challenge. This conceptualisation would act as a tool to facilitate further examination of the incorporation of Shariah-induced financial innovation. This book also examines the role of Shariah rules and requirements in the financial innovation and engineering process as a dynamic concept. It demonstrates the pervasive and repetitive process back and forth in exploring a new financial innovation and the possible Shariah basis for engineering such innovation to meet Shariah requirements.

The different degrees to which Shariah rules are implemented or infused in financial innovation and engineering emphasises the IFIs' lack of agreed upon accepted standards regarding what constitutes religiously driven financial innovation. Albeit, they all, as the findings clearly show, agree to the importance of fully implementing Shariah rules in all processes, but the absence of a unified approach or framework is the missing factor in this formula.

Hence, the developed theoretical conceptualisation and need for a coherent definition, proposed by this study. These developments are needed to provide the ground for proposing a standardised framework for religious concept for financial innovation and engineering. In order to address this issue, this book built on the theoretical work in the literature as presented in Chaps. 6 and 7 in relation to the Islamic economic thought and its world view regarding economics and finance.

There has been some ambiguity, which emerged from the analysis undertaken herein, about the instruments that could be used for the development of a financial innovation, which are based on Shariah rules in its processes. Those potential instruments, as emerged from the analysis in Chaps. 8, 9 and 10, have been clearly identified within this section. The initial understanding is that those instruments are not any different from what an Islamic scholar uses to extract a Shariah ruling related to, e.g. an aspect of worship. The same methodology would be used for initiating a financial innovation or examining and judging whether a financial innovation is acceptable or not under Shariah.

Instruments that could help in developing financial innovation and engineering, as emerged from the analysis in previous chapters, are the Qur'an, *Sunnah*, *Ijma'* (consensus of qualified Islamic scholars regarding a financial matter), *qias* (analogical reasoning), *ijtihad* (individual scholarly interpretation), *istihsan* (approving something on the basis of the common good, the Hanafi school equivalent of social good), *al masaleh al mursalah* (common good) and *bab sad al tharae'* (blocking legal tricks and causes of prohibitions).

Maslaha (common good) is the most powerful instrument, *maslaha* is concluded by studying the Shariah text, however there is a potential that it could be misused as a tool. Islamic scholars have researched the theory of *maslaha* under Shariah (Suliman 1898; Al Nadawi 1993; Al Buti 2005) with the objective of ensuring it is not going to be misused in the process of developing a financial innovation or other matters.

This has led them to come up with Shariah controls for the use of *maslaha*. Thus, It should be part of the Shariah objectives, it should not contradict the Qur'an or *Sunnah*, it also should not contradict *qiyas* and it should not dismiss another *maslaha*, which is more important or equal to it (Al Buti 2005: 25–35). The above controls for the employment of the concept of *maslaha* should be carefully considered in the process of financial innovation and engineering, in order to be acceptable.

The main control for *maslaha* as a tool is that, it should not contradict Shariah and its text; it should be also a real *maslaha* and benefit and should not generate harm or something impermissible under Shariah. It is important for a *maslaha* to be considered a real *maslaha*, that it demonstrates its viability and benefit for a wider segment of society rather than a benefit for a small group. What is perceived as a *maslaha* for a small group in the society could be harmful for others. Therefore, *maslaha* cannot be used on its own as an instrument under Shariah for justifying whether a financial innovation is of a real benefit to the wider society or not, it should be supported with at least one of the Shariah objectives. This would ensure the objective employment of the theory of *maslaha* rather than the subjective view, which could eventually abuse the use of *maslaha*.

Thus, following the initiation of a new financial innovation and considering the financial engineering structure, by ensuring that the engineered structure complements the Islamic philosophical learnings and Shariah requirements, the NPD (new product development) process begins. The developed framework for financial engineering and NPD, shown in Fig. 12.1 below, was a result of the findings of the analysis conducted in this book and the detailed thought process (see Chaps. 8, 9 and 10), which collected data about the existing practices in the Islamic finance industry in relation to financial engineering and NPD.

Figure 12.1 depicts the NPD process in IFIs that is conceptualised on the theoretical framework and sets the detailed process for implantation of the identified financial innovation and the engineered structure that would deliver this financial innovation. This process shows the steps to be followed for what we believe to propose a best practice framework for financial engineering and NPD in the Islamic finance industry. The proposed framework above incorporates business and Shariah requirements for NPD process. It highlights the key controls for required checks and approvals based on progress of key milestones in the development cycle.

The new financial product would start to take much clearer shape in the product definition paper (PDP) where the structure of the product, the engineered Islamic

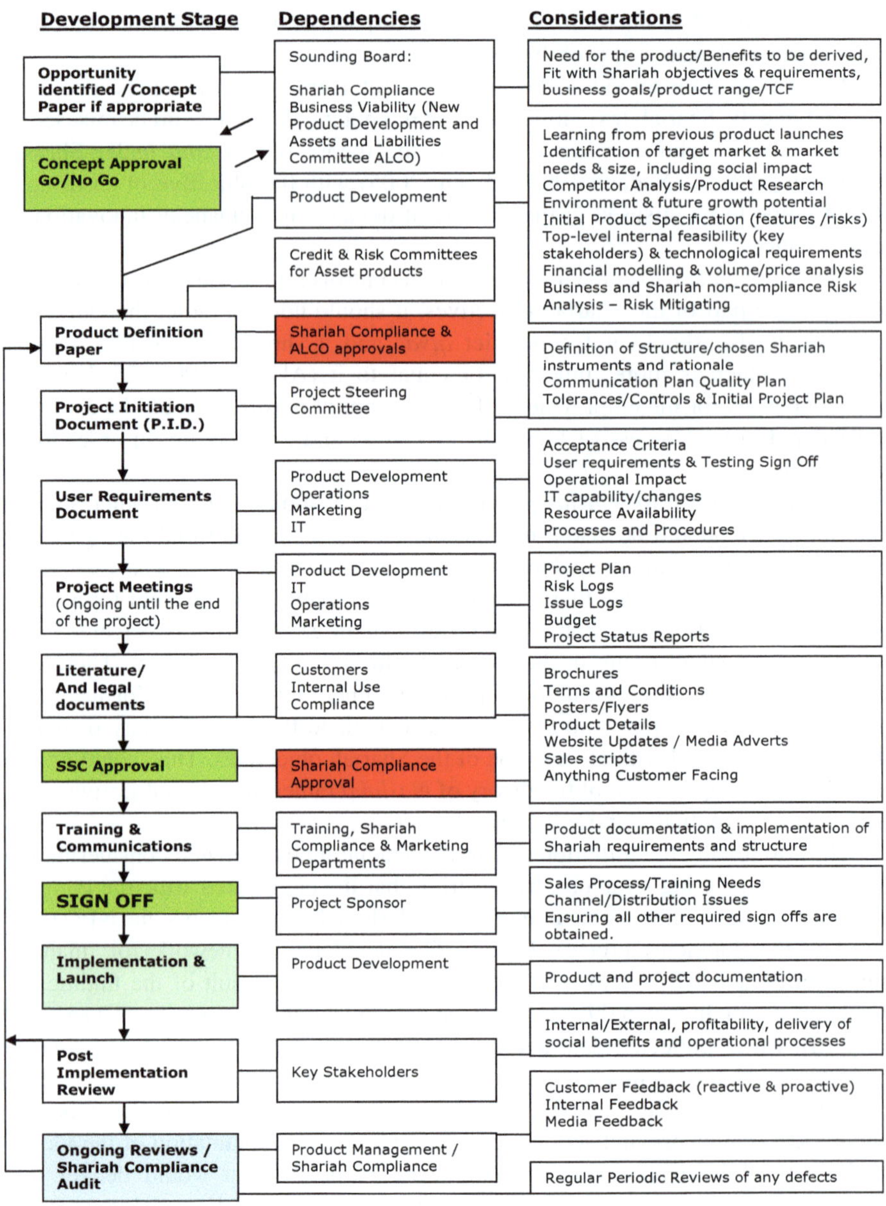

Fig. 12.1 A framework for financial engineering and NPD in IFIs

finance principles and the rationale for using the chosen structure are clearly defined and explained. The features, benefits, financial modelling, target market, customer research, sales process to ensure this process follows Shariah ethics and guidelines, and risk analysis is also one of the main components of the PDP. This process would be led by the product development team with close cooperation with other stakeholders in the IFI.

The Shariah compliance role would be to oversee the development process, review and approve the product documentation, ensure that the approved steps and requirements are maintained throughout the NPD process. Also, to monitor any diversion in the operational application from what was approved, and to undertake the post implementation audit review to check if the product is delivering the intended outcome from a Shariah compliance perspective. The product sponsor ensures that all required development work, required approvals and sign offs are obtained and all testing and operational processes are completed before providing the approval for the launch of the financial product. Customer feedback would be collated about the product and their experience to address any defects or issue that may arise post implementation.

The Financial Conduct Authority (FCA) in the UK started recently, in November 2014, enforcing conduct risk principles to be incorporated in the conduct of business in the financial market and financial institutions. The FCA sets their 2014/15 forward looking view of the conduct and prudential landscape for the firms they regulate and the consumers who are served by them. They look at what causes risk in the financial markets and how these factors affect the firms and consumers that participate in them. The FCA has divided the drivers of risks into three groups. The Inherent factors, Structures and business conduct features are the internal characteristics of financial markets and market participants and are influenced by the Environmental developments (FCA Risk Outlook 2014).[1]

IFIs are also required to comply with conduct risk principles in financial innovation and engineering processes; however, they are more prudent as they should also comply with Shariah principles. Ethical conduct in IFIs is an intrinsic feature of Islamic finance and it requirements, it is an internal core part of the operations of IFIs and the NPD process, rather than being an add-on or principles enforced externally by a regulator.

12.3 Book Contribution

This book has presented theoretical (Chap. 7), empirical (Chaps. 8, 9 & 10) and practical contributions (Chap. 11) that demonstrate the novelty and validity of the underlying study. By developing a relational view of the role of Shariah in the process of financial innovation and engineering, this book makes several contributions to existing theory and provides a platform for further research.

It also addresses the challenge to have a clear concept of what constitutes a Shariah acceptable financial innovation as a new phenomenon within the innovation field proposed in previous studies (Subramaniam and Venkatraman 2001;

[1]Financial Conduct Authority (FCA), 2014, FCA Risk Outlook, accessed on 24/05/2015, available from: http://www.fca.org.uk/static/documents/corporate/risk-outlook-2014.pdf.

Siguaw et al. 2006; Van de Ven et al. 1999; Amabile 1997; Worren et al. 2002; Burns and Stalker 1977; Zaltman et al. 1973; Hurley et al.'s 1998).

Thus, this concept of Shariah driven financial innovation and engineering suggested two directions for this book: firstly, a more in-depth investigation of the existing level of Shariah compliance, and secondly, exploring and examining the process of financial innovation and engineering as a dynamic Shariah-induced concept (Bartel and Garud 2003; Bechky 2003; Boland and Tenkasi 1995; Carlile 2002, 2004; Levina and Vaast 2005; Pawlowski and Robey 2004; Star and Griesemer 1989; Nicolini et al. 2012).

The third important contribution of this book is the proposed framework for understanding Shariah compliant financial innovation in the context of IFIs (Chap. 10). This focused view of Shariah compliant financial innovation and engineering is particularly important for three reasons. Firstly, a focus on explicit areas for financial innovation, such as product development or processes, would provide a new perspective on innovations. This implies that religious orientation towards financial innovation, as the research findings showed, encourages the integration of religiously guided innovation into all areas of an IFI to better create a long-term sustainable Shariah compliant financial model.

The fourth contribution of this book is from a practical perspective for IFIs and the Islamic finance industry as a whole. This contribution is developing an evaluative and measurement tool, provided by the book findings and the outlined framework, to examine existing financial products on offer. The findings of this book would enable IFIs to reflect on their current practices, processes, Shariah compliance framework for financial innovation and engineering in the NPD process. Furthermore, it would enable them to evaluate the financial products and services offered by them in the market.

This was demonstrated in Chap. 11 (using a documentary analysis method) where existing products were examined by employing the outlined framework for financial innovation and engineering. This developed theoretical and practical framework would offer the Islamic finance industry a useful tool from Shariah compliance governance for the financial innovation and engineering process, product development governance structure, standardised regulatory governance structure for financial innovation and engineering in IFIs and a tool for conducting audit reviews for the NPD process in IFIs.

12.4 Policy Implications

This section discusses the implications of the book findings for various stakeholders. Four main stakeholders have been identified who could benefit from the practical implication of the research findings; these are academics, regulators, the Islamic finance industry and banks and audit and risk managers. The policy implication for the identified stakeholders is detailed below. The key policy implication points to be mentioned are listed below:

1. The developed theoretical framework, which is based on the findings of the research, extends the existing theories to another field and concepts for further academic research.
2. The research findings provide an in-depth insight for academics, financial regulators, Islamic finance bodies such as AAOIFI, managers and students about the processes and structure of financial innovation and engineering in IFIs, in terms of their philosophy, governance, drivers and knowledge structure.
3. The developed practical framework and processes as emerged from the research findings could help all stakeholders understand the financial innovation and engineering process and appreciate its influencing factors.
4. The developed framework also provides financial regulators, central banks and Islamic finance industry regulators a practical framework that could form the basis to help them in formulating their own regulatory framework and policies in relation to IFIs.
5. The findings of the research along with the developed framework would aid bankers to understand their own processes in relation to financial innovation and engineering. They would also provide a useful practical tool for other professionals in the industry, such as risk, product development, audit managers and Shariah advisers, in their work.

Hence, the findings of this research study offer an in-depth insight into religiously guided processes and practices of financial innovation and engineering. The findings also address the lack of knowledge and research in the field of religious-based economics and finance model. The developed framework provides a measuring tool to assess financial practices of IFIs and their financial products on offer in the market.

Moreover, the findings of this research and the developed framework would provide the UK financial regulator, and other financial regulators beyond the UK, a valuable insight into the potential of standardised best practices of self-regulating and accountability driven by a religious-based banking culture. They would help financial regulators understand the dynamics of financial innovation and engineering in IFIs. Regulators and practitioners could use it as a measuring tool, or select suitable elements from the proposed framework to include it in their framework and testing of financial products and their design processes.

In the past the UK financial regulator's regulatory approach was based on the assumption that effective consumer protection would be achieved provided sales processes were fair and product feature disclosure was transparent. But, this approach has not been effective in preventing waves of severe customer detriment. They have therefore come to recognise that there are fundamental reasons why financial services markets do not always work well for consumers. In response, they started adopting a new regulatory approach which involves earlier regulatory intervention (DP 11/1 product intervention), engaging with firms to ensure that new products truly do serve the needs of the customers to whom they are marketed.

The UK regulator started to intervene earlier in the product value chain, proactively, to anticipate consumer detriment where possible and stop it before it occurs.

They are looking in more detail at how firms design products and their on-going governance procedures to ensure that products function as intended and reach the right customers. This, however, did not resolve the issue and the development and offering of financial products that were harmful and scandals attached to many banks and their products continued to take place.

The findings of this research would provide the UK financial regulator, and other financial regulators beyond the UK, a great insight into standardised best practices of self-regulating and accountability driven by a religious-based banking culture.

12.5 Case Study of a New Shariah Compliant Financial Innovation (Takaful Student Finance)

12.5.1 Background of the Financial Innovation

In September 2012 changes to higher education funding in the UK meant that British students were able take out student loans for tuition of up to £9000 for each year of study. These post-2012 loans carry a different rate of interest, above inflation, to student loans issued before September 2012.

The 2012 reforms regarding student loans have a real positive rate of interest. This could deter some prospective students who feel unable to use interest-bearing loans for religious reasons, particularly some Muslim students, from participation in higher education. Due to the 2012 reforms the UK Government mentioned that some students will not access higher education in these circumstances, some will access higher education and use loans but will be troubled by their situation, and others will restrict their choice of course or institution to try to minimise the sums involved.[2]

The UK Government was aware that some students, whose religious beliefs may forbid the taking out of a loan that bears interest, may be unable to take advantage of student loans because of this change. This could make it more difficult for them to benefit from higher education. At that time as an expert in the Islamic finance industry, I received many requests from Muslim students and community leaders in the UK to try and find a solution. I felt at that point that this responsibility falls on my shoulders as a British Muslim first and then as an expert in the Islamic finance industry to find a solution for this social problem. However, this solution would require bringing the government on board and working with them as the solution would need to be provided by them eventually.

The UK Government started exploring the possibility of making an alternative student finance product available. This finance product would be Shariah compliant and overseen by a Shariah advisory committee.

[2]https://www.gov.uk/government/uploads/system/uploads/attachment_data/file/523396/bis-16-265-success-as-a-knowledge-economy.pdf.

However, any such alternative finance product would not result in a student being in any way disadvantaged or advantaged over a student who took out a traditional student loan. Both the size of the finance and the repayment amounts would be equivalent between the two systems. The model of the proposed product could be applied for in the same way as a traditional loan: through the Student Loans Company (SLC). This was a real challenge in terms of finding a Shariah compliant solution that meets the required criteria by the government.

The UK Government sought the views of Islamic finance experts in the UK and beyond regarding the potential solution. I was contacted by the Government at the time, in 2012, through the Department for Business, Innovation and Skills (BIS) to help in finding a solution. This provided the platform for me to discharge my social responsibility and try to find a viable Shariah compliant product, and the work started to achieve this objective.

12.5.2 The Analytical Process That Led to a Solution for the Alternative Student Finance

I started the process of finding a solution by exploring and examining various possible Islamic finance principles and structures. For example, a Mudaraba structure was considered (see Chap. 1 for a detailed definition about the various Islamic finance principles), however it was not viable as both the product requirements and the Shariah requirements cannot be achieved with this Islamic finance principles. Similarly, with a possible Wakala structure both requirements cannot be achieved as both Mudarbah and Wakala are equity-based Islamic finance principles.

I explored then a service based structure by employing the Islamic finance principles of *Ijara* (lease). An initial structure was developed on the basis of lease of services, however, when the rental fee becomes due it would be consider a debt from a Shariah perspective and subject to the strict debt rules under Shariah. Thus, this possible structure was not viable too.

After that I considered a debt-based Islamic finance principle, a reverse commodity Murabaha (*Tawarruq*) which would generate student funding through a series of commodity transactions (such as the buying and selling of metals through brokers), but was ruled out. These transactions generate funds for the student along with the obligation for the student to make deferred payments to include the cost of student support plus the agreed profit.

Under a Commodity Murabaha transaction of alternative student finance the SLC would purchase a commodity equivalent to the support a student is entitled to receive (such as copper) from Broker A. The SLC then sells the assets to the student at cost plus a specified profit. Payment of the sale price is usually deferred. The student will enter into a contract to sell the assets to Broker B for the cost price.

The net result is to create a deferred payment obligation from the student to the SLC. The SLC and student will usually enter into a succession of such transactions to create monthly, quarterly or semi-annual payment obligations. This solution although it could work as an option, it was ruled out because of its complexity as a product offered to students.

Also, the deferred amounts that the student owes are subject to the strict Shariah rules regarding debts. This series of required commodity Murabaha transactions over a very long period of time is very time-consuming, operationally complicated and costly. Moreover, it is usually criticised by Shariah scholars for being Islamically disliked as it does not achieve any Shariah considerable Shariah objectives.

The above analysis, then led me to the conclusion that a solution that is structured on an equity-based or debt-based Islamic finance principle will not work. This was the trigger of a new financial innovation as solution that I engineered on the basis of a contract of gratuity in contrast to a contract of exchange.

12.5.3 Takaful as a Solution for the Alternative Student Finance

As mentioned above, the analysis of various possible contracts of exchange as a solution for the alternative student finance led to a new innovative idea and structure. Islamic mutual model was established in the early second century of the Islamic era (eighth century) when Muslim Arabs expanding trade into Asia all mutually agreed to contribute to a fund to cover anyone in the group who incurred mishaps or robberies during the numerous sea voyages. Forms of mutual insurance arrangements existed in the early years of Islam.

Islamic jurists acknowledge that the basis of shared responsibility in the system of *Aquila*, as practised between Muslims of Mecca and Medina, laid the foundation of Islamic mutual insurance. This financial innovation is based on what was known as *al-Nihd*, this concept is the basis of the Takaful structure and is chosen as the most appropriate solution for an alternative student finance product. It was a practice that originated in a group of travellers making a contribution of provisions towards a collective pot to either be shared out between the travellers equally or to allow the travellers to partake from the collective pot. The contribution itself was known as *al-Nihd*. This practice raised the question as to whether the contribution of the same type, for example, dates, resulted in the incidence of ribā if one received a share that was disproportionate to one's contribution.

It is, therefore, not a case of exchange which would result in ribā if it occurred in unequal amounts in the same genus or if either or both counter-values were deferred. It is also not a case of proprietary transfer through a gift, as gifting requires an offer, acceptance and possession. Rather, it is simply a case of retaining ownership of one's contribution and allowing others to benefit from it out of compassion and mutual cooperation.

Takaful is a Sharia compliant system of mutual contribution and protection, in which the participants donate part or all of their contributions to a common fund for a specified purpose. The word Takāful comes from the root *kafala*, which means to be or become responsible, answerable, accountable, or guarantee for assets owed by another person.

The Shariah requirements are principally achieved by substituting the compensatory basis of conventional interest-based student loans or other Islamic finance principles (that were also explored above) with one of a gratuitous offering, otherwise referred to as a donation. Within the Shariah, a contract made under the principle of a donation, without an element of exchange, removes the prohibited elements of ribā (interest) and the exchange of mutually deferred counter values and allows the toleration of uncertainty (*gharar*) or lack of information (*jahala*). Therefore, the proposed alternative student finance product is a Sharia compliant Takaful structure, as it does not involve any exchange and is instead initiated by a gratuitous offering.

This gratuitous offering was further engineered in order to achieve a requirement set by the government that aims to ensure contributions are made by the participating students who already benefited from this product. This was achieved by ensuring that the Takaful structure is backed up by a unilateral promise by the student to contribute back to the Takaful fund in accordance with the terms and conditions of the product.

The exchange factor is eliminated here under the Takaful structure (as shown in Fig. 12.2), whereas students mutually contributing for the benefit of all of the participants in the fund i.e. all of them, instead of having a contract of exchange for each one of them separately with the government (as the other party to the contract) on e.g. a Wakala basis or a Mudaraba basis.

Figure 12.2 above is explained and illustrated by the following example, a student would be expected to pay during the study until statutory repayment date of 6th April after finishing or leaving the course a contribution of RPI + 3% (that is collectable at the time when the student is required to make the payment), then based on income up to £21 k a contribution of RPI, between an income of £21 k and £41 k a contribution of RPI + up to 3% depending on income and an income over £41 k a contribution of RPI + 3%, subject to what has been mentioned above in terms of being in accordance with the Sharia requirements for the takaful model.

The contribution deducted from students would be based on a % of the salary according to the threshold set by the Government, which constitutes of two elements paying the specified amount taken from the Takaful fund and the agency fee. However, students make one takaful contribution to the fund and the two elements of the contribution are managed internally by the Takaful fund.

Following a successful transfer of the idea of the takaful-based alternative student finance into a full workable and viable structure, a public consultation was issued in 2014.[3] The consultation was received with a widespread acceptability

[3]https://www.gov.uk/government/consultations/sharia-compliant-student-finance.

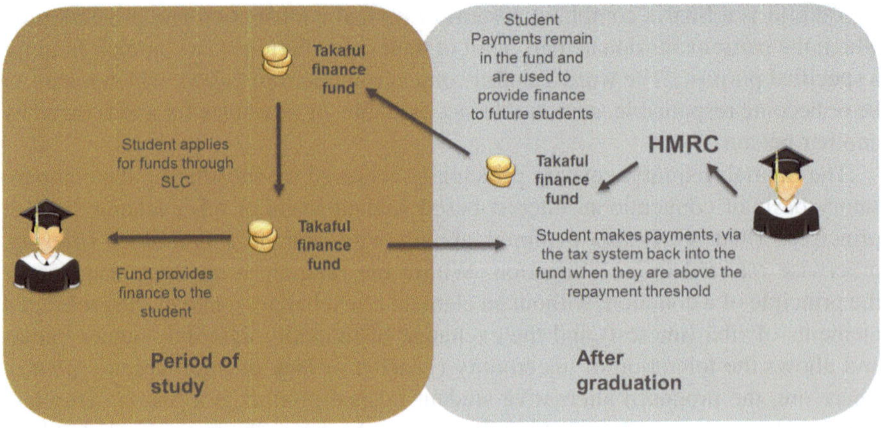

Fig. 12.2 Structure of the takaful alternative student finance

and positivity by the Muslim and non-Muslim communities in the UK on all levels. The work continued since then to address any further details and engineer the required Shariah solution in accordance with the chosen structure. This eventually led to the issuance of the Higher Education and Research Bill that includes a power to enable the Secretary of State to offer alternative student finance (ASF) alongside his current powers to offer grants and loans.[4]

Hence, this is a practical example that had a policy implication, which I wanted to share with the reader of my book.[5] This shows that there is a space for new and robust financial innovation in Islamic finance that meets Shariah requirements and financial considerations. The innovative structure of a takaful-based alternative finance product is a clear example, when the right processes are followed. This new financial innovation addresses a real social problem in the UK that affected many stakeholders in the society, and provided a solution that it is rooted in social and mutual cooperation among various stakeholders in the society.[6]

12.6 Conclusion

By recalling the book objectives that aimed at exploring financial innovation and engineering in Islamic finance, and the existing practices of IFIs in relation to financial innovation and engineering, (Chap. 1, Sect. 1.8) and linking them to the

[4]https://www.gov.uk/government/collections/higher-education-and-research-bill.

[5]http://www.telegraph.co.uk/education/2016/05/17/muslim-students-to-be-given-charitable-sharia-loans/.

[6]http://www.gulf-times.com/story/497246/Al-Rayan-Bank-expert-helps-UK-devise-Shariah-produ.

findings of this book (Chaps. 10, 11 and 12), this book aimed at addressing a gap in the innovation literature. This was achieved by building on the work done by previous research studies in the field of innovation, and seeking to apply those theories to a new field. It also aimed at exploring the process of financial innovation and Shariah compliance implementation in IFIs setting for financial engineering. It also unveiled the absence of clear identified conceptual framework, founding principles, guidelines and Shariah governance of financial innovation in IFIs.

The research attempted to establish and present the theoretical framework and process of enactment of religious rules towards financial innovation and engineering. As a multi-level research study, the book focused more on when and how individual agents are embedded in the philosophical culture and belief of financial institutions with religious perspective. The book also showed that the issue of financial innovation with religious orientation was not explored in the literature prior to this book. The role of religion and its possible positive influence in relation to human interactions and potential reflection of that role on finance, as practiced in the Islamic finance industry, was reflected upon in this book.

The structured framework for analytical process enabled this book to explore both the financial innovation and engineering processes and the level of religious compliance with Shariah rules in IFIs, in that regard. It also examined the institutional purposive action to create, maintain, disseminate financial innovation, the new product development cycle and relevant governance processes in IFIs. Based on the findings of this book, we proposed a conceptual framework for examining the level of Shariah compliance for financial innovation in the Islamic finance industry.

Based on the developed analytical framework, financial innovations in IFIs are driven by a mixture of IFI's religious rules and strategic direction, the formal and informal systems, and the key actors' competencies. The learning philosophy, of the proposed framework, suggests that any work or activities carried out by the IFI should follow clear guidelines for the benefit of all stakeholders in the society, The concept of *Tazkiyah* (growth and purification) requires active participation in the material world, in order to build the earth and innovate to satisfy worldly needs in line with Shariah requirements as the main driver of financial innovation in IFIs.

Business history suggests through different examples that financial innovation in products or in processes alone is not, in most cases, sufficient to create long-term survival or a competitive advantage. There, however, as suggested by the reported findings of this research should be a collective set of understandings and beliefs, pervasively accepted throughout an IFI and likely to occur at all levels and functions, that facilitate continual processes to insure sustainable financial model.

Financial innovations today, even after the severe financial crisis of 2008, are and have been driven by competition among financial institutions, risk shifting, circumventing regulations and legal constraints and profit maximisation, rather than market demands and consumers' needs. This approach ignores society welfare and well-being, ethical financial and banking practices, average consumers and users of financial services and the impact on economic development. It focuses on the benefit of very small group in society in contrast to the benefit of all or at least most stakeholders in the society.

This view of financial innovation diverted the cycle of innovation as developed by the early economists with the objective of addressing particular financial needs in the market. However, as we have seen, it works, currently, in reverse; financial institutions create false financial needs in the market to sell their financial innovations for their sole benefit of profit maximisation, risk shifting and resolving liquidity issues. This practice refers to what some academics (Plosser 2009; Poole 2011; Duska 2009; Jameson 2009) and regulators (Turner (former head of the Financial Services Authority) 2012) called as socially useless or harmful financial innovation.

The reasonable way forward, having diagnosed the disease, is to offer the remedy as painkillers do not make the disease go away and will not solve the problem. This remedy will require a cultural change in the financial system and banking practices that should be based on self-imposed moral and ethical criteria that govern the organisation and the cycle of innovation.

Hence, a religious-based structure and framework for providing financial innovation, as reported from the findings of this book, under which financial practices are structured around intrinsic checks and balances could be the sought after remedy. This is believed to make the ideal banking culture in the Islamic finance industry, to some extent, self-regulating. This is in contrast to the conventional system where the ethical framework has to be imposed and monitored by a regulator, such as the Financial Conduct Authority (FCA) in the UK and other regulatory authorities. This claim about Islamic banking's self-regulation and accountability, and its possible positive impact as a remedy to the traditional banking culture would require further research and closer examination.

Regulations are, thought to be, intrinsic to Islamic finance, Islamic finance is derived from rules and regulations of Shariah, without Shariah there would be no Islamic finance. Whereas, in conventional finance, the rules are an external addition to financial practices and may be hugely variable, depending on economic circumstances, competition, availability of resources, political ideology and many other factors.

This book addresses this considerable gap in the literature by placing past research results into an overall framework that should enhance understanding of religious rules towards financial innovation. The proposed framework in this book would provide a measuring tool, which facilitates the testing and examining of each construct in the overall structure of financial innovation and engineering in the Islamic finance industry.

12.7 Avenues for Future Research

The most appropriate focus of future research is the broader global conceptualisation of religious principles within financial innovation in financial institutions, based on the elements defined in this book. The relative weight of each of the knowledge structure components and the organisational competencies in resources, technology, operations, employees, and markets and their overall influence by the religious-based structure of innovation that an organisation adopts should also be determined for such a measure. Specifically, the effects of financial innovation and engineering with religious view on innovation have yet to be examined empirically.

The view taken here is in accordance with that of Van de Ven et al. (1999) and others (e.g. Siguaw et al. 2006) who highlighted the need for research examining the effects of innovations in areas other than new products and the speed of new product introductions on firm performance. This gap has been addressed to a great extent in this book. Other areas of research include a comparison of religiously-based financial innovation and their counterparts, an analytical study of the influence of religiously-based structure of financial institutions on the stability of financial system. Such relationships have, often, been assumed to hold true without rigorous, empirical research to provide support. This proposed conceptual framework will allow such testing of the difference that religious rules would make to financial innovation.

Glossary

Akhlaq Moralities and ethics.

Amanah Refers to deposits in trust. A person can hold a property in trust for another, sometimes by express contract and sometimes by implication of a contract. Current accounts may be regarded as Amanah (trust).

Bai Sale or exchange.

Bai' al-Dayn A transaction that involves the sale and purchase of securities or debt certificates.

Batil Invalid (contract).

Commutative contract A contract of exchange for value between two parties.

Daman/Dhaman A guarantee or security.

Darura The Shariah principle of necessity which may be applied in extenuating circumstances to achieve approval for a concept.

Fasid Voidable (contract).

Fatwa (pl. Fatawa) A legal pronouncement in Islam provided by an Islamic legal specialist.

Fiqh The science of Islamic jurisprudence or Islamic law.

Fiqh al Muamalat Islamic commercial jurisprudence or the rules of transacting in a Shariah-compliant manner.

Gharar It means any element of uncertainty in any business or a contract which is otherwise preventable or avoidable.

Hadith (pl. Ahadith) Words of the Prophet (SAW), traditions. The narrative record of the sayings and actions of the Prophet Muhammad (PBUH).

Halal Anything permitted by the Shariah. Lawful; one of the five major Shariah categorisations of human acts.

Hanbali One of the Islamic schools of jurisprudence.

Hanafi One of the Islamic schools of jurisprudence.

Haram Anything prohibited by the Shariah. Unlawful; one of the five major Shariah categorisations of human acts.

S. Alamad, *Financial Innovation and Engineering in Islamic Finance*,
Contributions to Management Science, DOI 10.1007/978-3-319-52947-9

Hawala/Hawalah Literally, it means transfer; legally, it is an agreement by which a debtor is freed from a debt by another person accepting to receive a transfer of the obligation, or the transfer of a claim of a debt by shifting the responsibility from one person to another—contract of assignment of debt. It also refers to the document by which the transfer takes place.

Hijra The emigration of the Prophet Muhammad (PBUH) and his followers to Medina.

Ijara/Ijarah Leasing. Sale of a definite usufruct of any non-monetary asset in exchange for definite reward.

Ijara Mawsoofa Bil Thimma A lease agreed upon, perhaps even with a deposit, for delivery and use of an asset in the future.

Ijara Muntahia Bi Tamleek This is a form of leasing contract used by Islamic financial institutions which includes a promise by the lessor to transfer the ownership of the leased property to the lessee, either at the end of the term of the lease period or by stages during the term of the contract. The undertaking or the promise does not become an integral part of the lease contract in order to make it conditional. The rental, as well as the purchase price, is fixed in such a manner that the bank gets back its principal sum along with some profit, which is usually determined in advance.

Ijma/Ijm'a Consensus of all or majority of the leading qualified jurists on a certain Shariah matter in a certain age.

Ijtihad This refers to an endeavour (literally toil) of a qualified jurist to derive or formulate a rule of law to determine the true application of Shariah in a matter on which the Holy Quran and the Sunnah is not explicit.

Illah Underlying rationale.

'Inan (A type of Sharikah) It is a form of partnership in which each partner contributes capital and has a right to work for the business, not necessarily equally.

Istihsan Judicial preference for one legal analogy over another, usually to give preference for the public welfare.

Istijrar A contract between a supplier and a client whereby the supplier supplies a particular item on an ongoing basis on an agreed mode of payment until they terminate the contract. It is also applied between a wholesaler and a retailer for the supply of a number of agreed items.

Istisn'a This is a contractual agreement for manufacturing goods and commodities, allowing cash payment in advance and future delivery or a future payment and future delivery. A manufacturer or builder agrees to produce or build a well-described good or building at a given price on a given date in the future. Price can be paid in instalments, step by step as agreed between the parties. Istisn'a can be used for providing the facility for financing the manufacture or construction of houses, plants, projects and building of bridges, roads and highways.

Manfa'a/Manfaa Usufruct or benefit derived from an asset.

Maqasid A contract which is unenforceable until authorised.

Muamalat Activities which are not explicitly governed by the Shariah with respect to worship.

Mudaraba/Mudarabah/Mudharabah (Trust Financing) This is an agreement made between two parties one of whom provides 100 per cent of the capital for a project and has no control over the management of the project; another party, known as a Mudarib, manages the project using his entrepreneurial skills. Profits arising from the project are distributed according to a predetermined ratio, and financial losses are borne by the provider of capital.

Mudaraba al Muqayyada Restricted Mudaraba—applies when the agreement relates to a specific business or place and it is contractually limited by time, place, partner and deal type.

Mudaraba al Mutlaqa Unrestricted Mudaraba—where the Mudarib is free to act within traditional Shariah parameters.

Mudarib Mudarib manager in a Mudaraba contract. The Mudarib does not invest capital but provides skill and effort. The Mudarib is a co-investor in a bilateral Mudaraba.

Murabaha (cost plus financing) This is a contract sale between the bank and its client for the sale of goods at a price which includes a profit margin agreed by both parties. As a financing technique it involves the purchase of goods by the bank as requested by its client. The goods are sold to the client with an agreed mark-up.

Musawamah Bargaining. A general kind of sale in which the price of the commodity to be traded is bargained between the seller and the purchaser without any reference to the price paid or cost incurred by the former.

Musharaka/Musharakah This Islamic financing technique involves one or more parties who both provide capital towards the financing of a project or business. Both parties share profits on a pre-agreed ratio, but losses are shared on the basis of contributed capital. Management of the project may be carried out by both the parties or by just one party. This is a very flexible arrangement where the sharing of the profits and management can be negotiated and pre-agreed by all parties.

Musharaka Muntahiya Bittamleek/Diminishing Musharaka or Musharaka Mutinaqisa A form of partnership whereby one partner buys out the shares or units of the other according to a specific schedule.

Muwaada/Mua'hida Bilateral promises, two unilateral promises/undertakings extended by two parties on the same subject matter.

Naseeyah Delay.

Parallel Salam A contract taken out to offset the delivery implications of the Salam contract.

Qard Hassan A form of loan identified in the Quran as a means of charity or helping others in need; an interest-free loan that would be paid back on demand or at the agreed time.

Qimar Speculation.

Qiyas Literally, this means measure, example, comparison or analogy. Technically, it means a derivation of a rule on the analogy of an existing law if the basis ('illah) of the two is the same. It is one of the tools of Islamic law.

Quran Text of God, the primary source for jurists. The Book of Divine Revelation that was delivered to humankind by the Prophet Mohammed (PBUH).

Rab al Mal The party providing the finance, the investor.

Riba An excess or increase, interest. Technically, it means an increase over the principal in a loan transaction.

Riba Al-Fadl (Riba al-Quran/Riba al-Jahiliyyah) Riba Al-Fadl (excess) is an exchange of similar commodities, defined as money or certain foods, in unequal amounts. Its prohibition is meant to close the door to riba in lending.

Riba Al Naseeyah/Riba Al-Nasiah (Riba Al-Quran and Riba Al-Jahiliyyah) Riba Al-Nasiah or riba of delay is due to an exchange of money today for more at a later date. Interest, in all modern banking transactions qualifies as Riba Al-Nasiah.

Ribawi Susceptible or containing riba.

Ribawi commodities Gold, silver, wheat, barley, dates, salt; anything which is used as money.

Sadaqat Voluntary charitable donations.

Sahih Valid (contract).

Salaf In its widest application, Salaf is another name for Salam (described below).

Salam A contract for the purchase of a commodity for deferred delivery in exchange for immediate payment according to specified conditions.

Sarf Literally this means exchange. The 'rules of sarf' restrict the methods of exchanging and depositing money in order to prevent riba. These rules are based on the Hadith.

Securitisation The conversion of assets into financial instruments which may be sold in a manner that cuts the asset off from the seller, making it truly the property of the buyer of the financial instrument.

Shariah Islamic canon law derived mainly from the Quran and the Hadith practice and traditions of the Prophet Mohammed (PBUH).

Shirkah An alternative term for Musharakah. A partnership or company.

Shirkat al Aqd Partnership by mutual agreed contract.

Shirkat al Milk Partnership of two or more owners of a property held in common.

Sukuk The is a document or certificate evidencing an undivided pro rata ownership of an underlying asset. Usually referred to as an Islamic bond.

Sunnah/Sunna Custom, habit or way of life. Technically, it refers to the utterances of the Prophet Muhammad (PBUH) other than the Holy Quran known as Hadith, or his personal acts, or sayings of others, tacitly approved by the Prophet.

Ta' Awun Cooperation, an Islamic insurance scheme is based upon cooperation for mutual protection of the members.

Tabarru' A donation/gift the purpose of which is not commercial. Any benefit that is given by a person to another without getting anything in exchange is called Tabarru'. The concept of Tabarru' has been applied within Takaful (Islamic insurance) schemes.

Takaful A Shariah-compliant system of mutual protection, insurance, in which the participants donate part or all of their contributions to a common fund. These may be used to pay claims for damages suffered by some of the participants. The company's role is restricted to managing the insurance operations and investing the insurance contributions.

Tawarruq A form of reverse Murabaha which is tolerated as it involves three sales contracts and three independent parties, frequently used to deliver money to a person wishing to avoid borrowing at interest. Considered objectionable by most Muslim scholars.

Ummah The collective nation of Islamic states. The Islamic universal community.

Underlying asset An asset which is the object of a contract, a specific Sukuk issuance, derivative or guarantee.

Usufruct The right to enjoy the benefit of property which is vested in another person.

Usul al-fiqh Sources of law.

Wa'd Promise, an undertaking by one party regarding future actions.

Wadia/Wadiah Safe custody/resale of goods with a discount on the original stated cost.

Wakala/Wakalah A contract of agency in which one person appoints someone else to perform a certain task on his behalf, usually against a certain fee.

Wakil/Wakeel Agent, representative for commercial purposes with a capacity similar to a power of attorney.

Waqf (pl. Awqaf) Waqf investments or properties are charitable grants with infinite life which may be used to support specific beneficiaries designated by the grantor.

Wujuh Literally, face. This may be interpreted in commercial environments as goodwill or credit for partnership or accounting purposes.

Zakat/Zakah A religious obligation of almsgiving on a Muslim to pay 2.5% of certain kinds of his wealth annually to one of the eight categories of needy Muslims. Literally, it means blessing, purification, increase or cultivation of good deeds. In Shariah, it is an obligation to pay Zakat on wealth above a specified minimum for defined beneficiaries, as noted in the Quran.

References

AAOIFI. (2014). *Shariah standards*. Bahrain: Accounting and Auditing Organization for Islamic Financial Institutions (AAOIFI).

'Aashour, Saead Abdul Fattah. (n.d.). *Maser wa al Shaam fi 'Aser al Ayyoubean wa al Mamaleek*. Lebanon: Dar al Nahdah al 'Arabiyyah.

Abduh, Esa. (1974). *Al Iqtisad al Islami Madkhal wa Manhaj*. Cairo: Dar Nahdat Maser Liltiba'a wa al Nasher.

Abdul Meneam, A. M. (1979). Al Niza al Iqtisadi al Islami, Jeddah: Dar al Mujtama' al'Ilmi.

Abdul Meneam, Afer M. (1979). *Al Niza al Iqtisadi al Islami*. Jeddah: Dar al Mujtama' al 'Ilmi.

Abdul Rahman, Ramadan. (2005). *Mawgef al sharia al Islameyyah mena al Bunook Wa al Mu'amalaat al_Masrifiya wa al_Ta'ameen*. Cairo: Dar al Salaam. (Arabic).

Abdul-Rahman, Yahia. (2010). *The art of Islamic banking and finance, tools and techniques for community-based banking*. New Jersey: Wiley.

Abdullrahim, Najat. (2010). *Service quality of English Islamic banks*. Doctoral thesis, Bournemouth University.

Abernathy, W. J., & Utterback, J. M. (1978). Patterns of industrial innovation. *Technology Review, 80*(7), 40–47.

Abrahamson, E. (1991). Managerial fad and fashions: The diffusion and rejection of innovation. *Academy of Management Review, 16*(3), 586–612.

Abu 'Obaid, al Qasim. Ibn Salaam. (1989). *Kitab al Amwal* (M. 'Amarah, Ed.). Beirut: Dar al Shorouq.

Abu Sulayman, Abd al-Wahab Ibrahhim. (1992). Al-Ikhtiyārāt Dirāsah Fiqhiyya Tahliliyyah Muqāranah. *Majallat al-Buhuth al-Fiqhiyyah al-Muyassarah, 4*(15).

Abu Yousuf, Ya'qoub. Ibn Ibrahim. (1985). *Kitab al Kharaj* (Ihsan Abbas, Ed.). Beirut: Dar al Shorouq.

Abu Zaid, Abdul Azeem. (2004). *Bay' al_Murabaha wa Tatbigatuho al_Mu'asirah fi al-Masaref Al Islameyyah* [Credit sales and its current applications in Islamic banks]. Damascus: Dar al_Fikr. (Arabic).

Abu-Sulayman, A. A. (1976). *The economics of Tawhid and brotherhood, contemporary aspects of economic thinking in Islam*. Indianapolis, IN: American Trust Publications.

Ackermann, J. (2012). *Financial innovation: Too much or too little?* (M. Haliassos, Ed.). Cambridge, MA: MIT Press.

S. Alamad, *Financial Innovation and Engineering in Islamic Finance*, Contributions to Management Science, DOI 10.1007/978-3-319-52947-9

Adam, N. J., & Thomas, A. (2004). *Islamic bonds, your guide to issuing, structuring and investing in Sukuk*. London: Euromoney Books.

Adler, P. S. (2005). The evolving object of software development. *Organization, 12*, 401–435.

Aghion, P., & Tirole, J. (1994). The management of innovation. *The Quarterly Journal of Economics, 109*(4), 1185–1209.

Ahmad, Khurshid. (1971). *Islam: Basic principles and characteristics*. Karachi: University of Karachi.

Ahmad, Ausaf. (1993). Contemporary practices of Islamic financing techniques. *Islamic Research and Training Institute, 20*, 19–59.

Ahmed, Khalid Abdul Rahman. (1976). *Al Tafkeer al Iqtisadi fi el Islam*. Damascus: Dar al Khaffaqeen.

Ahmed, Khurshid. (1980). Economic development in an Islamic framework. In K. Ahmed (Ed.), *Studies in Islamic economics*. Leicester: Islamic Foundation.

Ahmed, Muhyyi Addin. (1995). *Aswāq al-Awrāq al-Maliyya wa 'Aatharuha al-Inma'yya fī al-Iqtisad al-Islamī*. Jeddah: al-Baraka Group.

Ahmed, Shaikh Azmi. (1996). *Islamic investment study group: A report*. Malaysia: Securities Commission.

Ahmed, Habib. (2011). *Product development in Islamic banks*. Edinburgh: Edinburgh University press.

Ahmed, Hasan Azzyyāt, et al. (1990). *Mu'jam Al-Wāsit*. Istanbul: Dār al-Da'wah.

Ahrens, T., & Chapman, C. S. (2006). Doing qualitative field research in management accounting: Positioning data to contribute to theory. *Accounting, Organizations and Society, 31*(8), 819–841.

Al 'Awadi, Rifa'at. (1987). Mena Al Turath al Iqtisadi. *Da'watu el Haqq, 2, 6*(63).

Al Aqla, Ali., Abdul Raheem, W., & Abu Shariah, A. (2004). *Al Nizaam al Mali wa el Iqtisadi fi al Islam*. Riyadh: Al Rushed Publication.

Al Ashqar, Omar Suliman. (1991). *Tareekh al Fiqh al Islami*. Amman: Dar al Nafa'es.

Al Bouti, Saead Ramadan. (1991). *Fiqh al Sirah al Nabawiyyah* (10th ed.). Damascus: Dar al Fikr.

Al Buti, M. Saeed. (2005). *Dawabit al Maslaha*. Damascus: Dar Al Fukr.

Al Dawoudi, Abu Ja'far Ahmed Ibn Naser. (2000). *Al Amwaal*. Kuwait: Bank al Kuwait al Sina'I.

Al Dhabi, Shames al Deen, Muhammad Ibn Ahmed. Ibn Othman. (1996). Ciyar I'laam al Nubalaà, Beirut: al Risalaah Publication.

Al Doori, Abdul Aziz. (1981). *Fi al Tanzeem al Iqtisadi fi Sader al Islam*. Beirut: Dar al Tali'ah.

Al Doori, Abdul Aziz. (1982). *Muqaddimah fi al Tareekh al Iqtisadi* (4th ed.). Beirut: Dar al Talia'a.

Al Doori, Abdul Aziz. (1995). *Tareekh al 'Iraq al Iqtisadi fi al Qarn al Rabe' al Hijri* (3rd ed.). Beirut: Markaz Dirasaat al Wihda al Arabiyyah.

Al Farra', Abu Ya'la Muhammad Ibn al Hussain Al Hanbali. (1973). *Al Ahkaam al Sultaniyyah*. Beirut: Dar al Fikr.

Al Ghazali, Abu Hamid. (1987). *al-Mustasfa min 'illm al Usul*. Karachi: Idarat al Quran.

Al Ghazali, Abi Hamed Muhammad Ibn Muhammad. (n.d.). *Ihya' 'Oloom al Deen*. Beirut: Dar al Ma'rifah.

Al Habishi, Muhammad Ibn Abdul Rahaman Ibn Omar. (1978). *Al Baraka fi Fadel al Sa'I wa al Harakah*. Beirut: Dar al Ma'rifah.

Al Hamshari, Mustafa. (1985). *Al Nizam el Iqtisadi fi el Islam*. Riyadh: Dar al 'Oloom Lltiba'a wa al Nasher.

Al Hanbali, Ibn Rajab. (1988). *Al Istikhraj li Ahkaam al Kharaj*. Kuwait: Bank al Kuwait al Sina'I.

Al Haythami, Ali Ibn Abi Bakr. (1980). *Majma' al Zawa'ed wa Manba' al Fawa'ed*. Syria: Mo'asaset al Ma'aref.

Al-Jawzīyyah, I. Q. (nd). *Ìlam Al-Mūwaqqi'īn*. Beirut: Dar al-Fikr.

Al Jawziyyah, Ib al Qayyem Shames al Deen Muhammad. (1980). *Al Turoq al Hukmiyyah fi al Siyasah al Shar'iyyah*. Beirut: Maktabat al Mu'ayyad.

Al Jazari, Ibn al Atheer. (1978). *Al Kamel fi al Ttareekh*. Beirut: Dar al Fikr.

Al Khun, Mustafa. (1994). *Athar al ikhtilaaf fi al aua'ed al ousoliyya fi ikhtilafi al fuqaha'a*. Beirut: Mua' asaset al Risalah.
Al Mas'oudi, Abi al Hasan. Ali. Ibn al Hussain. (1973). *Murouj al Dhab wa Ma'aden al Jawaher* (Muhammad Muhyi al Deen, Ed., 5th ed.). Beirut: Dar al Fikr.
Al Mawardi, Abu al Hasan Ali Ibn Muhammad Ibn Habib. (1985). *Al Ahkaam al Sultaniyyah wa al Wilayat al Diniyyah*. Beirut: Dar al Kutub al Islamiyyah.
Al Mawardi, Abu al Hasan. (2001). *Al Rutbah fi Talab al Hisbah*. Kuwait: Bank al Kuwait al Sina'I.
Al Muzaini, Khalid Ibn Abdullah. (2007). *Al Fatwa wa Ta'keed al Thawabet al Shar'iyyah*. Saudi: King Fahd University.
Al Mydani, Abdul Rahman Hasan Habanneka. (1996). *La Yasihhu an Yuqal al Insan Khalifatul Allah fi Ardihi Fahiyah Maqulatun Batilah*. Beirut: Alrayyan Publication.
Al-Nawawī, Muhy al-Dīn Abu Zakariyyā, Yahyā. (nd). *Sahīh Muslim Bi Sharh Al-Nawawī*. Cairo: al-Matbaàh al-Mīsriyyah.
Al Nadawi, Ali Ahmed. (1993). *Al Qawa'ed al Fiqhiyyah* (3rd ed.). Damascus: Dar Al Qalam.
Al Najjar, Musleh Abdul Hayy. (2003). *Ta'seel al Iqtisad al Islami*. Riyadh: Al Rushed Publication.
Al Omar, Fouad. (2003). *Muqadimmah fi Tareekh al Iqtisad al Islami wa Tatawroho* [An introduction of Islamic economics history and its development]. Jeddah: Islamic Research and Training Institute.
Al Qalqashandi, Abi al 'Abbas Ahmed Ibn Ali. (1963). *Subeh al A'asha fi Cina'ati al Insha'*. Cairo: Ministry of Education.
Al Qaradaghi, Ali. (2010). *Al Madkhal ila al Igtisad al Islami* (2nd ed.). Beirut: Dar al Basha'er.
Al-Qara Daghī, Ali Muhyi Addin. (1993). *al-Bada'l al-Shar'iyya li Sanadāt al-Khazina al-'Ammah wa al-Khāssah*. Kuwait: Bait al-Ttamūūal-Kuwaitī.
Al Qasimi, Muhammad J. (1976). *Islah al Masajid mena el Bida'ai wal 'awa'ed* (3rd ed.). Beirut: al maktab el Islami (Islamic Publication).
Al Sader, Muhammad. Baqer. (1977). *Iqtisaduna* [Our economy]. Lebanon: Dar al Kitab al Lubnani.
Al Saead, Mustafa Kamel. (1970). *Mabad' 'Elm al Iqtisad*. Beirut: Dar al Nahda al Arabiyyah.
Al Sarkhacey, Shames al Addeen. (1978). *Al Mabsout* (3rd ed.). Lebanon: Dar al Ma'arefah Liltiba'a wa al Nasher.
Al Sawwaf, Ali. (1989). *Dareebat al 'Oshur fi al Dawlah al Islamiyyah al 'oula. Journal of Shariah and Islamic Studies, Kuwait University, 15*, 249–290.
Al Sharbini, Al Khateeb. (1957). *Mughni al Muhtaj 'ala al Minhaj*. Egypt: Matba'at 'esa al Babi al Halabi.
Al Shiraazi, Abdul Rahman Ibn Naser. (1946). *Nihayat al Rutbah fi Talab al Hisbah*. Cairo: Lajnat al Taleef wa al Tarjamah wa al Nasher Publication.
Al Tha'alibi, Abdul Rahman Ibn Muhammad. (1997). *Al Jawahir al Hisan fi Tafseer al Qur'an* (Vol. 2). Beirut: Dar Ihya' al Turath al 'Arabi.
Al Thahabi, Shames al Deen Muhammad Ibn Ahmed Ibn Othman. (1996). *Ciyar I'laam al Nubalaa'*. Beirut: al Risalaah Publication.
Al Zarkashi, Muhammad. (1982). *Al Manthour fi al Qawa'ed*. Kuwait: Ministry of Religious Affairs.
Al Zarqa, Mustafa Ahmed. (1968). *Al Madkhal al Fiqhi al 'Aam*. Damascus: Tarabeen Publication.
Al Zarqa, Mustafa. (1989). *Shareh al Qawa'ed al Fiqhiyyah* (2nd ed.). Damascus: Dar al Fikr.
Al Zarqa, Mustafa Ahmed. (2012). *Al Madkhal al Fiqhi al 'Aaam* (3rd ed.). Damascus: Dar al Qalam.
Al-Amine, Muhammad al-Bashir Muhammad. (2008). *Risk management in Islamic finance: An analysis of derivatives instruments in commodity markets. The Netherlands: Brill.*
Al-Bāhouti, Mansour Bin Younos. (1983). *Kashshaf al-qina'*. Beirut: A'lam al-Kutob.
Al-Barwārī, Sha'bān M. Islām. (2005). *Būrsat al-Awrāq al-Mālīyah min Mnzūr Islāmī* [Bourse Bank notes from an Islamic perspective]. Damascus: Dar al-Fikr.

Al-Bouti, Tawfeeq. (2005). *Al-Boyoa' al-sha'ah* [Common sales] (3rd ed.). Damascus: Dar Al-Fikr. (Arabic).
Al-Bukhai, M. Ibn Ismaī. (1940). *Sahih al-Bukhari*. Beirut: Dār al-Qalam.
Al-Bukhari, M. (1985). *Sahih Al-Bukhari*. Damascus: Dar Al-Fikr.
Al-Bukhari, M. (1993). *Sahih Al-Bukhari*. Damascus: Dar Al-Fikr.
Al-Būtī, M. Sa'eed Ramadān. (2000). *Dawābt al-Maslaha fī al-Sharī'ah Al-īslamiya* (6th ed.). Beirut: Mū'ssast al-Rresala.
Alchaar, Mohamad Nedal, et al. (2009). *Islamic finance qualification* (3rd ed.). London: Securities And Investment Institute.
Al-Dārdeer, Ahmed Abo al-Barakat. (1972). *al-Sharh al-Sagheer Ala Aqrab al-Masalik*. Egypt: Dar al-Kutb al-Elmiyah.
Al-Dhareer, Siddiq M. Al-Ameen. (1997). *Al-Gharar in contracts and its effects on contemporary transactions*. Jeddah: Islamic Research and Training Institute, Islamic Development bank.
Aldrich, H. E., & Martinez, M. A. (2001). May are called but few are chosen: An evolutionary perspective for the study of entrepreneurship. *Entrepreneurship Theory & Practice, 25*(4), 41–56.
Alexakis, C., & Tasikouras, A. (2009). Islamic finance: Regulatory framework—Challenges lying ahead. *International Journal of Islamic and Middle Eastern Finance and Management, 2*(2), 90–104.
Al Farrà, Abu Ya'la Muhammad. Ibn al Hussain. Al Hanbali. (1973). *Al Ahkaam al Sultaniyyah*. Beirut: Dar al Fikr.
Al-Faruqi, I. R. A. (1976). *Foreword contemporary aspects of economic thinking in Islam*. Indianapolis, IN: American Trust Publications.
Ali, Mahfooz. (1968). *Al Ibda' fi Madhar al 'Ibtida'*. Cairo: al Maktabah al Mahmoudiyah al Tijariyah.
Al-Jarihī, Ali Ma'bad. (1989). *al-Idāra al-Maliyya fī al-Islam*. Amman: Mū'ssasat 'Aal al-Bait.
Al-Jawzīyyah, Ibn Qayyim. (n.d.). *I'lam Al-Mūwaqqi'īn*. Beirut: Dar al-Fikr.
Allen, F., & Gale, D. (1988). Optimal securities design. *Review of Financial Studies, 1*, 229–263.
Allen, F., & Gale, D. (1994). *Financial innovation and risk sharing*. Cambridge, MA: MIT Press.
Allen, F., Yago, G., & Barth, J. R. (2012). *Financial innovation (Collection)*. New Jersey: Pearson Education.
Al Mawardi, Abu al Hasan, Ali Ibn Muhammad, Ibn Habib. (1985). Al Ahkaam al Sultaniyyah wa al Wilayat al Diniyyah, Beirut: Dar al Kutub al Islamiyyah.
Al-Māwardi, Ali, Bin Mohammad. (1994). *al-Hawi al-Kabeer*. Beirut: Dar al-Kutb al-Elmiyah.
Almutairi, Humoud. (2010). *A comparison between Islamic and conventional home finance in Kuwait: Client perceptions of the facilities offered by the National Bank of Kuwait and Kuwait Finance House*. Doctoral thesis, Durham University. Retrieved from Durham E-Theses Online http://etheses.dur.ac.uk/543/
Al-Nadawī, Ali Ahmed. (1991). *al-Qūā'd al-Fiqhiya* (2nd ed.). Damascus: Dar al-Qalam.
Al-Nawawī, Muhy al-Dīn Abu Zakariyyā Yahyā. (n.d.). *Sahīh Muslim Bi Sharh Al-Nawawī*. Cairo: al-Matba'ah al-Mīsriyyah.
Al-Qara Daghī, Ali Muhyi Addin. (1993). *al-Bada'l al-Shar'iyya li Sanadāt al-Khazina al-'Ammah wa al-Khāssah*. Kuwait: Bait al-Ttamūūal-Kuwaitī.
Al-Qaradāwī, Yusuf. (1973). *sharī'ah al-Islam Salihah lil-Tatbiq fī Kull Zaman wa Makan* (5th ed.). Cairo: Matba'at al-Madanī.
Al-Qaradāwī, Yusuf. (2003). *The lawful and the prohibited in Islam* (K. El-Helbawy & others, Trans.). London: Al-Birr Foundation.
Al-Salem, Fouad. H. (2009). Islamic financial product innovation. *International Journal of Islamic and Middle Eastern Finance and Management, 2*(3), 187–200.
Al-Shārbini, Muhammad al-Khateeb. (1994). *Mughni al-Muhtāj*. Beirut: Dar al-Fikr.
Al-Zuhaylī, Wahba. (2002). *al-Fiqh al-Islamī wa Adillatuhu* (4th ed.). Damascus: Dar al-Fikr.
Al-Zuhaylī, Wahba. (2003). *Financial transactions in Islamic jurisprudence* (Mahmoud A. - El-Gamal, Trans.). Damascus: Dar Al-Fikr.

Al-Zuhayli, Wahba. (1993). Towards an Islamic stock market. *Islamic Economic Studies, 1*(1), 35–45.

Al-Zuhayli, Wahba. (2002). *Al-Mu'amalaat al Malyyah al Mu'asirah*, Damascus: Dar al-Fikr. (Arabic).

Al-Zuhayli, Wahba. (2007a). *Al-Masaref el Islamiyyah, Hayy'at al Mauso'ah al-'Aarabeyyah.* Damascus. (Arabic).

Al-Zuhayli, Wahbah. (2007b). *Financial transactions in Islamic jurisprudence* (2nd ed.). Damascus: Dar al- Fikr.

Amabile, T. M. (1997). Motivating creativity in organizations: On doing what you love and loving what you do. *California Management Review, 40*(1), 39–58.

Anderloni, L., LIewellyn, T., & Schmidt, R. H. (2009). *Financial innovation in retail and corporate banking*. Cheltenham: Edward Elgar Publishing.

Anderson, P. (1999). Complexity theory and organization science. *Organization Science, 10*(3), 216–232.

Angbazo, L. (1997). Commercial bank net interest margins, default risk, interest rate risk, and off balance sheet banking. *Journal of Banking and Finance, 21*(1), 55–87.

Anwar, Muhammad. (1992). Islamic banking in Iran and Pakistan: A comparative study. *The Pakistan Development Review, 31*(4, Part II), 1089–1097.

Arbrey, P. B., Walthall, A., & Palais, J. B. (2008). *East Asia: A cultural, social, and political history*. Boston, MA: Houghton Mifflin.

Archer, S., & Abdel Karim, R. A. (2007). Specific corporate governance issues in Islamic banks. In S. Archer & R. A. Abdel Karim (Eds.), *Islamic finance: The regulatory challenge*. Singapore: Wiley.

Archer, S., & Abdullah, H. (2007). Operational risk exposure of Islamic banks. In S. Archer & R. A. A. Karim (Eds.), *Islamic finance: The regulatory challenge*. Singapore: Wiley.

Ariff, Mohammad. (1988). Islamic banking. *Asian-Pacific Economic Literature, 2*(2), 46–62.

Ariffin, N. M. (2005). *Enhancing transparency and risk reporting in Islamic banks*. Doctoral thesis, University of Surrey, Surrey.

Arrif, M. (1982). Monetary policy in an interest free Islamic economy: Nature and scope. In M. Arrif (Ed.), *Monetary and fiscal economic of Islam*. Jeddah: International centre for Research in Islamic Economics.

Arrow, K. J. (1962). Economic welfare and the allocation of resources to invention. In R. R. Nelson (Ed.), *The rate and direction of inventive activity: Economic and social factors* (pp. 609–625). Princeton, NJ: Princeton University Press.

Arthur, W. B. (1989). Competing technologies, increasing returns, and lock-in by historical events. *The Economic Journal, 99*(394), 116–131.

Arthur, W. B. (2001). *How growth builds upon growth in high-technology*. Annual Sir Charles Carter Lecture, Northern Ireland Economic Council, Belfast, Northern Ireland.

Asad, M. (1993). *Islam at the crossroads*. Gibraltar: Dar al-Andalus Ltd.

Athanasoglou, P. P., Brissimis, S. N., & Delis, M. D. (2008). Bank specific, industry specific and macroeconomic determinants of bank profitability. *Journal of International Financial Markets, Institutions and Money, 18*(2), 121–136.

Atuahene-Gima, K., & Ko, A. (2001). An empirical investigation of the effect of market orientation and entrepreneurship orientation alignment on product innovation. *Organization Science, 12*(1), 54–74.

Baccaro, L. (2010). Does the global financial crisis mark a turning point for labour? *Socio Economic Review, 8*, 341–376.

Bahattacharyya, S., & Nada, V. (1996). *Client discretion, switching costs and the introduction of new financial products*. Working Paper, University of Michigan.

Balala, Maha-Hanaan. (2010). *Islamic finance and law: Theory and practice in a globalized world*. London: B. Tauris.

Bank for International Settlement. (1986). *Recent innovations in international banking*. Basle: BIS.

Bank Negara Malaysia. (2005). *Money and banking in Malaysia*. Kuala Lumpur: Bank Negara Malaysia.

Barney, J. B. (1991). Firm resources and sustained competitive advantage. *Journal of Management, 17*(1), 99–120.

Barrett, M., & Oborn, E. (2010). Boundary object use in cross-cultural software development teams. *Human Relations, 63*, 1199–1221.

Barry, B. (2005). *Why social justice matters*. Cambridge: Polity.

Bartel, C. A., & Garud, R. (2003). Narrative knowledge in action: Adaptive abduction as a mechanism for knowledge creation and exchange in organizations. In M. Eastery-Smith & M. A. Lyles (Eds.), *Handbook of organizational learning and knowledge management* (pp. 324–342). Malden, MA: Blackwell.

Baumann, U., & Nier, E. (2003, June). Market discipline and financial stability: Some empirical evidence. *Financial Stability Review*, 134–141.

Bechky, B. A. (2003). Sharing meaning across occupational communities: The transformation of understanding on a production floor. *Organization Science, 14*(3), 312–330.

Becker, M. C. (2004). Organizational routines: A review of the literature. *Industrial and Corporate Change, 13*(4), 643–678.

Beekun, R. I., & Badawi, J. A. (2005). Balancing ethical responsibility among multiple organizational stakeholders: The Islamic perspective. *Journal of Business Ethics, 60*, 131–145.

Bentley, J. H. (1993). *Old world encounters: Cross-cultural contacts and exchanges in pre-modern times*. New York: Oxford University Press.

Berger, A. N. (1995). The relationship between capital and earnings in banking. *Journal of Money, Credit and Banking, 27*(2), 432–456.

Berthon, P., Hulbert, J. M., & Pitt, L. F. (1999). To serve or create? Strategic orientations toward customers and innovation. *California Management Review, 42*(1), 37–58.

Bhattacharyya, S., & Nada, V. (2000). Client discretion, switching costs, and financial innovation. *The Review of Financial Studies, 13*(4), 1101–1127.

Black, F. (1975). Fact and fantasy in the use of options. *Financial Analysis Journal*, July/August, 36–72.

Blake, D. (2000). *Financial market analysis* (2nd ed.). Chichester: Wiley.

Blum, J. (2002). Subordinated debt, marker discipline and bank's risk taking. *Journal of Banking and Finance, 26*(7), 1427–1440.

Bødker, S. (1998). Understanding representation in design. *Human–Computer Interaction, 13*(2), 107–125.

Boland Jr., R. J., & Tenkasi, R. V. (1995). Perspective making and perspective taking in communities of knowing. *Organization Science, 6*(4), 350–372.

Boot, A. W. A., & Thakor, A. V. (1997). Banking scope and financial innovation. *The Review of Financial Studies, 10*(4, Winter), 1099–1131.

Bourdieu, P. (1987). The force of law: Toward a sociology of the juridical field. *Hastings Law Journal, 38*, 814.

Bourdieu, P. (1989). Social space and symbolic power. *Sociological Theory, 7*(1), 14–25.

Bourdieu, P. (1990). *In other words, essays towards a reflexive sociology*. Oxford: Polity Press.

Bourdieu, P., with Loic, W. (1992). *Reponses*. Paris: Seuil.

Boyd, J. H., & Smith, B. D. (1996). The co-evolution of the real and financial sectors in the growth process. *World Bank Economic Review, 10*, 371–396.

Boyed, J., & De Nicolo, G. (2005). The theory of bank risk-taking and competition revisited. *Journal of Finance, 60*, 1329–1343.

Boyer, R. (2007). Assessing the impact of fair value upon financial crises. *Socio Economic Review, 5*, 779–807.

Brozen, Y. (1951). Invention, innovation, and imitation. *American Economic Journal, 41*(2), 239–257.

Bruns, H. C. (2013). Working alone together: Coordination in collaboration across domains of expertise. *Academy of Management Journal, 56*, 62–83.

Bryman, A. (2012). *Social research methods* (4th ed.). New York: Oxford University Press.
Buckle, M. J., Buckle, M., & Thompson, J. (2004). *The UK financial system: Fourth edition*. Manchester: Manchester University Press.
Burgelman, R. A. (1983). A process model of internal corporate venturing in the diversified major firm. *Administrative Science Quarterly, 28*(2), 223–244.
Burgelman, R. A., & Sayles, L. R. (1986). *Inside corporate innovation: Strategy, structure, and managerial skills*. New York and London: Free Press and Collier-Macmillan.
Burns, T., & Stalker, G. M. (1961). *The management of innovation*. London: Tavistock.
Burns, T., & Stalker, G. M. (1977). *The management of innovation* (2nd ed.). London: Tavistock.
Cantori, L. J., & Lowrie, A. (1992). Islam, democracy, the state and the West. *Middle East Policy, 1*, 49–61.
Caprio G. Jr., & Levine, R. (2002). *Corporate governance of banks: Concepts and international observations*. Paper Presented at the Conference on Building the pillars of Financial Sector Governance: The Roles of Public and Private Sectors, Organized by the World Bank, IMF, and Brookings Institutions.
Carbo, S., Gardner, E. P. M., & Molyneux, P. (2005). *Financial exclusion*. New York: Palgrave Macmillan.
Carcary, M. (2011). Evidence analysis using CAQDAS: Insights from a qualitative researcher. *The Electronic Journal of Business Research Methods, 9*(1), 10–24.
Carlile, P. R. (2002). A pragmatic view of knowledge and boundaries: Boundary objects in new product development. *Organization Science, 13*(4), 442–455.
Carlile, P. R. (2004). Transferring, translating, and transforming: An integrative framework for managing knowledge across boundaries. *Organization Science, 15*(5), 555–568.
Carlile, P. R., & Rebentisch, E. S. (2003). Into the black box: The knowledge transformation cycle. *Management Science, 49*(9), 1180–1195.
Cassell, C., Bishop, V., Symon, G., Johnson, P., & Buehring, A. (2009). Learning to be a qualitative management researcher. *Management Learning, 40*, 513.
Chandler, A. D. (1962). *Strategy and structure: Chapters in the history of American industrial enterprise*. Cambridge, MA: MIT press.
Chandler, A. D. (1992). Organizational capabilities and the economic history of the industrial enterprise. *The Journal of Economic Perspectives, 6*(3), 79–100.
Chapra, M. U. (1992). *Islam and the economic challenge*. Herndon, VA: International Institute of Islamic Thought.
Chapra, Umar, et al. (1992). The role of the stock exchange in an Islamic economy. In Sheikh Ghazali Abod et al. (Eds.), *An introduction to Islamic finance*. Kuala Lumpur: Quill Publishers.
Charkham, J. (2003). *Guidance for the directors of banks*. Global Corporate Governance Forum, Focus 2, The World Bank.
Chesbrough, H. W. (2003). *Open innovation: The new imperative for creating and profiting from technology*. Boston, MA: Harvard Business School Press.
Chesbrough, H. W., & Teece, D. J. (1996). When is virtual virtuous? Organizing for innovation. *Harvard Business Review, 80*(8), 65–74.
Choudhury, M. Alam. (1986). *Contribution to Islamic economic theory*. Basingstoke and London: Macmillan.
Cohen, W. M., & Levinthal, D. A. (1990). A new perspective on learning and innovation. *Administrative Science Quarterly, 35*(1), 128–152.
Colburn, J. T. (1990). *Trading in options on futures*. New York: New York Institute of Finance.
Cook, M. A. (1970). Introductory remarks. In M. A. Cook (Ed.), *Studies in the economic history of the Middle East*. Oxford: Oxford University Press.
Corbin, J. M., & Strauss, A. (1990). Grounded theory research: Procedures, canons, and evaluative criteria. *Qualitative Sociology, 13*, 3–21.

Corbin, J. M., & Strauss, A. L. (2008). *Basics of qualitative research: Techniques and procedures for developing grounded theory*. Thousand Oaks, CA: Sage.
Cordella, T., & Yeyati, E. L. (1998). *Public disclosure and failure*. CEPR Discussion Paper No. 1886.
Corley, K. G., & Gioia, D. A. (2004). Identity ambiguity and change in the wake of a corporate spin- off. *Administrative Science Quarterly, 49*, 173–208.
Corrocher, N., Malerba, F., & Montobbio, F. (2007). Schumpeterian patterns of innovative activity in the ICT field. *Research Policy, 36*(3), 418–432.
Cresswell, J. W., & Plano Clark, V. L. (2007). *Designing and conducting mixed methods*. London: Sage.
Currier, C. (1987). *The investor's encyclopedia*. New York: Franklin Watts.
Czinkota, M., & Kotabe, M. (2001). *Marketing management* (2nd ed., pp. 118–133). Cincinnati, OH: South-Western College Publishing.
De Young, R., & Rice, T. (2004). Non-interest income and financial performance at US commercial banks. *Financial Review, 39*(1), 101–127.
Delving, J. A. (2005). Detailed study of financial exclusion in the UK. *Journal of Consumer Policy, 28*, 75–108.
Denzin, N. K., & Lincoln, Y. S. (2003). *Collecting and interpreting qualitative materials* (2nd ed.). California: Sage.
Devahuti, D. (1965). *India and ancient Malaya (from the earliest times to circa A.D. 1400)*. Published by D. Moore for Eastern Universities Press. (Its original form was printed by: California: The University of California).
DiVanna, J. A., Sreih, A., & Ainley, M. (2009). *A new financial dawn: The rise of Islamic finance*. Cambridge: Leonardo and Francis Press.
Donaldson, T., & Preston, L. (1995). The stakeholder theory of the corporation: Concepts, evidence, and implications. *Academy of Management Review, 20*, 65–91.
Dosi, G., & Coriat, B. (1998). Learning how to govern and learning how to solve problems: On the co-evolution of competences, conflicts and organizational routines. In J. A. D. Chandler et al. (Eds.), *The dynamic firm: The role of technology, strategy, organization and regions* (pp. 103–133). New York: Oxford University Press.
Drucker, P. F. (1986). *Innovation and entrepreneurship*. Oxford: Elsevier.
Drucker, P. F. (1998). The discipline of innovation. *Harvard Business Review, 63*(3), 3–8.
Duffle, D., & Rahi, R. (1995). Financial market innovation and security design. *Journal of Economic Theory, 65*, 1–42.
Duska, R. F. (2009, March). Corruption financial crises and the financial planner. *Journal of Financial Service Professionals, 63*, 14–16.
Dusuki, A. W., & Mokhtar, S. (2010). *Critical appraisal of Shariah Issues on ownership in asset-based sukuk as implemented in the Islamic debt market*. ISRA Research Paper No. 8/2010.
Dusuki, A. W., et al. (2012). *A framework for Islamic financial institutions to deal with Shariah non-compliant transactions*. ISRA Research Paper No. 42/2012.
Dwabeh, A. M. (2004). *Sanadeeq al Istethmar fi al Bunook al Islameyyah bayna al Nazariyyah wa al Tatbeeq*. Cairo: Dar al Salaam. (Arabic).
Eakins, S. G. (2000). *Financial market and institutions* (3rd ed.). Reading: Addison-Wesley.
Eaton, G. (1994). *Islam and the destiny of man*. Cambridge: The Islamic Texts Society.
Edge, I. (1988). Shariah and commerce in contemporary Egypt. In C. Mallat (Ed.), *Islamic law and finance*. London: Graham and Trotman.
Edmondson, A. C., & McManus, S. E. (2007). Methodological fit in management field research. *Academy of Management Review, 32*(4), 1155–1179.
El Gari, Mohamed A. Bin Eid. (1991). Towards an Islamic stock market. *Journal of Objective Studies, 3*(2), 25–35.
El-Ashker, Ahmed. (1987). *The Islamic business enterprise*. London: Croom Helm.
El-Ashker, A. A. F., & Wilson, R. (2006). *Islamic economics: A short history*. Boston: Brill Academic Publishers.

El-Diwany, T. (Ed.). (2010). *Islamic banking and finance: What it is and what it could be*. UK: 1st Ethical Charitable Trust.
El-Diwany, T. (Ed.). (2010a). *Islamic banking and finance: What it is and what it could be*. Bolton: 1st Ethical Charitable Trust.
El-Diwany, T. (2010b). *The problem with interest* (3rd ed.). London: Kreatoc.
El-Gamal, Mahmoud. (2006). *Islamic finance: Law economics and practice*. New York: Cambridge University Press.
El-Gari, Mohamed Ali. (1993). Towards an Islamic stock market. *Islamic Economic Studies, 1*(1), 1–20.
Euben, R. L. (2002). Contengent borders, syncretic perspectives: Globalisation, political theory and islamizing knowledge. *International Studies Review, 4*(1), 23–48.
Fazlul Karim, Al-Haj M. (1994). *Mishkat al-Masābih*. Karachi: Darul-Ishaat.
Financial Holding Companies. (2006). The dark side of diversification: The case of US financial holding companies. *Journal of Banking and Finance, 30*(8), 2131–2161.
Financial Services Authority. (2007). *Islamic finance in the UK: Regulation and challenges*. FSA Paper. Retrieved October 12, 2013, from http://www.fsa.gov.uk/pages/Library/Communication/Speeches/2007/cb.shtml
Fink, R. E., & Feduniak, R. B. (1988). *Futures trading: Concepts and strategies*. New York: New York Institute of Finance.
Fink, A. (1998). *Conducting research literature reviews: From paper to the internet*. Thousand Oaks: Sage.
Finnerty, J. D. (1992). An overview of corporate securities innovation. *Journal of Applied Corporate Finance, 4*, 23–39.
Fiol, C. M. (2001). Revisiting an identity-based view of sustainable competitive advantage. *Journal of Management, 27*(6), 691–699.
Foss, K., Foss, N., Klein, P., & Klein, S. (2007). The entrepreneurial organization of heterogeneous capital. *Journal of Management Studies, 44*, 1165–1187.
Foster, A. (2010). Initiative March, (2010): A round-up of products, initiatives, mergers and failures. *Business Information Review, 27*(1), 65–80.
Frame, S. W., & White, L. J. (2010). *Technological change, financial innovation, and diffusion in banking*. Working Paper 2009–10, DIANE Publishing.
Freeman, C. (1982). *The economics of industrial innovation* (2nd ed.). London: Frances Pinter.
Freeman, R. E. (1984). *Strategic management: A stakeholder approach*. Boston, MA: Pitman.
Freeman, C. (1991). Networks of innovators: A synthesis of research issues. *Research Policy, 20* (5), 499–514.
Freeman, C. (1994). *Innovation and growth*. In M. Dodgson & R. Rothwell (Eds.), *Handbook of industrial innovation, Part I* (pp. 78–93). Aldershot, UK: Edward Elgar.
Friedman, A., & Miles, S. (2002). Developing stakeholder theory. *Journal of Management Studies, 39*, 1–21.
Gambling, T., & Karim, R. (1991). *Business and accounting ethics in Islam*. London: Mansell.
Garcia, R., & Calantone, R. (2002). A critical look at technological innovation typology and innovativeness terminology: A literature review. *Journal of Product Innovation Management, 19*(2), 110–132.
Gastineau, G. L. (1988). *The option manual*. New York: McGraw Hill.
George, G., McGahan, A. M., & Prabhu, J. (2012). Innovation for inclusive growth: Towards a theoretical framework and a research agenda. *Journal of Management Studies, 49*(4), 1467–6486.
Gharajedaghi, J., & Ackoff, R. L. (1984). Mechanisms, organisms and social systems. *Strategic Management Journal, 5*(3), 289–300.
Ghazanfer, S.M., & Islabi, A. Azim. (1990). Economic thought of an Arab scholastic: Abu Hamid Al Ghazali. *History of Political Economy, 22*(2), 381–403.
Gioia, D. A., & Thomas, J. B. (1996). Identity, image and issue interpretation: Sensemaking during strategic change in academia. *Administrative Science Quarterly, 41*, 370–403.

Goss, B. A., & Yamey, B. S. (1978). *The economic of futures trading*. London: Macmillan Press.

Gough, L. (1994). *How the stock market really works*. London: Pitman Publishing.

Govindarajan, V., & Trimble, C. (2005). Organization DNA for strategic innovation. *California Management Review, 47*(3), 47–76.

Graham, M. B. W., & Shuldiner, A. T. (2001). *Corning and the craft of innovation*. New York: Oxford University Press.

Green, R. M. (1993). Centesimus Annus: A critical Jewish perspective. *Journal of Business Ethics, 12*, 945–954.

Greening, V., & Iqbal, H. (2007). *Risk analysis for Islamic Banks*. Herdon, VA: World Bank Publications.

Van Greuning, H., & Iqbal, Z. (2007). Banking and the risk environment. In A. Simon & R. A. A. Karim (Eds.), *Islamic finance: The regulatory challenge*. Singapore: Wiley.

Van Greuning, H., & Iqbal, Z. (2008). *Risk analysis for Islamic bank*. Washington, DC: The World Bank.

Guba, E. G. (1990). The alternative paradimn dialog. In E. G. Guba (Ed.), *The paradimn dialog* (pp. 17–30). Newbury Park, CA: Sage.

Hadjimanolis, A. (2000). A resource-based view of innovativeness in small firms. *Technology Analysis and Strategic Management, 12*(2), 263–281.

Haleem, Ibrahim. Beak. (1988). *Al Tuhfa al Halimiyah fi Tareakh al Dawlah al 'Othmaniyyah*. Beirut: Mu'ssaset al Kutub al Thaqafiyyah.

Hamed, Mahmoud. H. (2000). *Al Nizam al Mali wa el Iqtisadi fi el Islam*. Riyadh: Dar al Nasher al Daowli.

Hamel, G. (2006). The why, what, and how of management innovation. *Harvard Business Review, 84*(2), 72–84.

Haron, S. (1995). The framework and concept of Islamic interest-free banking. *Journal of Asian Business, 11*, 26–39.

Haron, Abdullah, & Hock, John. Hin. (2007). Inherent risk: Credit and market risks. In S. Archer & R. A. A. Karim (Eds.), *Islamic finance: The regulatory challenge*. Singapore: Wiley.

Hasan, Zulkifli. (2010). Regulatory framework of Shari'ah governance system in Malaysia, GCC countries and the UK. *Kyoto Bulletin of Islamic Area Studies, 3*(2), 82–115.

Hassan, H. H. (1992). The jurisprudence of financial transaction. Discussion. In A. Ahmad & K. R. Awan (Eds.), *Lectures on Islamic economics*. Jeddah: Islamic Research and Training Institute, Islamic Development Bank.

Hersi, Warsame. Mohamed. (2009). *The role of Islamic finance in tackling financial exclusion in the UK*. Doctoral thesis, Durham University. Retrieved from Durham E-Theses http://etheses.dur.ac.uk/23/

Hewson, M. (1985). Computerized futures trading. In G. Roberts (Ed.), *Guide to world commodity markets*. London: Kogan Page.

Hirtle, B. J., & Stiroh, K. J. (2007). The return to retail and the performance of US banks. *Journal of Banking and Finance, 31*(4), 1101–1133.

Hitti, P. K. (1963). *History of the Arabs: From the earliest times to the present* (8th ed.). London: Macmillan.

Homburg, C., Hoyer, W. D., & Fassnacht, M. (2002). Service orientation of a retailer's business strategy: Dimensions, antecedents, and performance outcomes. *Journal of Marketing, 66*(4), 86–101.

Hounshell, D. A. (1992). Continuity and change in the management of industrial research: The Du Pont Company, (1902–1980). In G. Dosi, R. Giannetti, & P. A. Toninelli (Eds.), *Technology and the enterprise in a historical perspective* (pp. 231–259). Oxford: Oxford University Press.

Hounshell, D. A. (1996). The evolution of industrial research in the United States. In R. S. Rosenbloom & W. J. Spencer (Eds.), *Engines of innovation: US industrial research at the end of an era* (pp. 13–85). Boston, MA: Harvard Business School Press.

Hughes, J. R. (1987). The evolution of large technological systems. In W. E. Bijker, J. R. Hughes, & T. R. Pinch (Eds.), *The social construction of technological systems: New directions in the sociology and history of technology* (pp. 51–82). Cambridge, MA: MIT Press.

Hull, J. C. (2002). *Solution manual: Options futures and other derivatives* (5th ed.). New Jersey: Pearson Education.

Hult, G., Tomas, M., Hurley, R. F., & Knight, G. A. (2004). Innovativeness: Its antecedents and impact on business performance. *Industrial Marketing Management, 33*(5), 429–438.

Hurley, R., & Hult, T. (1998). Innovation, market orientation and organizational learning: An integration and empirical examination. *Journal of Marketing, 62*, 42–54.

Hurley, R. F., Hult, G., & Tomas, M. (1998). Innovation, market orientation, and organizational learning: An integration and empirical examination. *Journal of Marketing, 62*(3), 42–54.

Ibn 'Ashur, Muhammad Tahir. (1966). *Maqasid al-Shariah al-Islamiyyah*. Tunis: Matba'at al-Istiqamah.

Ibn al Jawzi, Jamal al Deen. Abi al Faraj. (1995). *Al Muntazam fi Tawareekh al Mulouk wa al Omam* (S. Zakkar, Ed.). Beirut: Dar al Fikr.

Ibn Khaldun, Abdul Rahmaan. Ibn Muhammad. (n.d.). *Muqaddimat Ibn Khaldoon* (Ali Abdul Wahed Wafi, Ed.). Cairo: Dar Nahdat Maser for Publications.

Ibn Mandhur, M. Ibn Makram. (2009). *Lisan Al Arab*. Beirut: DKI.

Ibn Rushd, Al Qadi. (1988). *Al Muqadimaat al Mumahidaat*. Beirut: Dar Al Ghareb al Islami.

Ibn Taymiyyah, Ahmed. (1973). *Al Hisbah Wal Islam*. Kuwait: Dar al Arqam.

Ibn Taymiyyah, Taqyyul Deen Ahmed. (1994). *Al Khilafah wa Al Mulk* (Hammad Salamah, Rev. Ed., 2nd ed.). Jordan: Al Manar Publication.

Ibn-Jazzi, Muhammad Bin Ahmed Bin Yahyia. (1984). *al-Qwaneen al-Fiqhyyah (Juristic Laws)*. Beirut: Dar al-Kitab al-Arabi.

IFSB. (2012, March). *Guiding principles on stress testing for institutions offering Islamic financial services*. IFSB Standard.

Imam, Muslim. (n.d.). *Boughyat Kul Muslim from Shih al-Imam Muslim* (F. Amira Zrein Matraji, Trans.). Beirut: Dar al Fikr.

Iqbal, Zamir. (1999). Financial engineering in Islamic finance. *Proceedings of the Second Harvard University Forum on Islamic Finance: Islamic Finance into the 21st Century*, Centre for Middle Eastern Studies, Harvard University, Cambridge, MA. pp. 229–238.

Iqbal, M., & Khan, T. (2005). *Financial engineering and Islamic contracts*. Hampshire: Palgrave Macmillan.

Iqbal, Zubair and Mirakhor, Abbas. (1987). *Islamic banking*. Washington, DC: International Monetary Fund.

Islamic Fiqh Academy. (1998). *Qarārāt wa Tawṣyāt Majma' al-Fiqh al-Islamī, in Jeddah* (2nd ed., pp. 1–10). Damascus: Dār al-Qalam.

Ismail, Muhammed. Imran. (2010). *Legal stratagems (Hiyal) and usury in Islamic commercial law*. A PhD thesis submitted to Birmingham University in May.

Issawi, C. (1982). *An economic history of the middle east and North Africa*. Columbia: Columbia University Press.

Issawi, C. (1991). *An economic history of the Middle East and North Africa*. Columbia: Columbia University Press.

Ivankova, V. N., et al. (2006). Using mixed methods sequential explanatory design: From theory to practice. *Field Methods, 18*(3), 2–20.

Jameson, D. A. (2009). Economic crises and financial disasters: The role of business communication. *Journal of Business Communication, 46*(4), 499–509.

Jelinek, M. (1979). *Institutionalizing innovation: A study of organizational learning systems*. New York: Praeger.

Jelinek, M., & Markham, S. (2007). Industry-university IP relations: Integrating perspectives and policy solutions. *IEEE Transactions on Engineering Management, 54*(2), 257–267.

Kahf, M. (2004). Islamic banks: The rise of a new power alliance of wealth and Shari'a scholarship. In C. M. Henry & R. Wilson (Eds.), *The politics of Islamic finance* (pp. 17–36). Edinburgh: Edinburgh University Press.

Kamali, M. Hashim. (2000). *Islamic commercial law*. Cambridge: Islamic Text Society.

Kaminsky, G. L., & Reinhart, C. M. (1999). The twin crises: The causes of banking and balance of payments problems. *American Economic Review, 89*, 473–500.

Kaminsky, G. L., & Reinhart, C. M. (2000). On crises, contagion, and confusion. *Journal of International Economics, 51*, 145–168.

Kane, D. (1988). *Principles of international finance*. London: Croom Helm.

Kanter, R. M. (1983). *The masters of change*. New York: Simon and Chuster.

Kanter, R. M. (2002). Strategy as improvisational theatre. *MIT Sloan Management Review, 43*(2), 76–81.

Kanter, R. M. (2008). Makes great companies great? *Computerworld, 42*(2), 36–26.

Katibi, Ghayda. (1994). *Al Kharaj Menzu al Fateh al Islami Hatta Awaset al Qarn al Thaleth al Hijri: al Mumarasaat wa al Nazariyyah*. Beirut: Markaz Dirasaat al Wihda al Arabiyyah.

Katila, R., & Ahuja, G. (2002). Something old something new: A longitudinal study of search behavior and new production. *Academy of Management Journal, 45*, 1183–1194.

Kazem, Muhsen. (1989). *Tareekh al Fikr al Iqtisadi Ibtida'n benasha'tihi wa Intiha'n bel Mareksiyyah*. Kuwait: Kuwait University.

Keller, G., & Warrack, B. (2002). *Statistics for management and economics* (5th ed.). Duxbury: Thompson Learning.

Kerr, M. H. (1971). *The Arab cold war: Gamal Abd Al - Nasir and his rivals, (1958–1970)* (3rd ed.). London: Published for the Royal Institute of International Affairs by Oxford University Press.

Keynes, J. A. M. (1972). *The collected writings of John Maynard Keynes*. London: Macmillan for the Royal Economic Society.

Khaldùn, I. (1958). *The Mùqaddimah: An introduction to history*. Princeton University Press, Complete three volume English translations by Franz Rosenthal. Princeton: An abridged English version by N. J. Dawood for Princeton University Press.

Khallaf, Abdel Wahhab. (1942). *The science of jurisprudence, Ilm Usul al-Fiqh*. Syria: Dar al-Qalam Publication and Distribution.

Khan, Ghulam Ishaq. (1984). Basic issues in Islamic banking. *Journal of Banking and Finance, 1* (2), 24.

Khan, M. Akram. (1988). Commodity exchange and stock exchange in Islamic economy. *The American Journal of Islamic Social Sciences, 5*(1), 98–110.

Khan, Muhammad Akram. (1994). *An introduction to Islamic economics*. Islamabad: The International Institute of Islamic Thought.

Khan, M. Fahim. (1995). *Essay in Islamic economics*. Leicester: The Islamic Foundation.

Khan, Muhammad M. (1996). *Sahih al-Bukari*. Riyadh: Darussalam.

Khir, K., Gupta, L., & Shanmugam, B. (2008). *Longman Islamic banking a practical perspective*. Malaysia: Pearson.

Kimberly, J. (1981). Initiation, innovation and institutionalisation in the creation process. In *The organisational life cycle: Issues in the creation, transformation and decline of organisations*. San Francisco: Jossey-Bass.

King, D. N. (1999). *Financial claims and derivatives*. London: International Thomson Business Press.

King, N. (2004). Using templates in the thematic analysis of text. In C. M. Cassell & G. Symon (Eds.), *Essential guide to qualitative methods in organizational research* (pp. 256–270). Sage: London.

King, A. W., & Zeithaml, C. P. (2003). Measuring organizational knowledge: A conceptual and methodological framework. *Strategic Management Journal, 24*(8), 763–772.

Kling, A. (2010). The financial crisis: Moral failure or cognitive failure? *Harvard Journal of Law & Public Policy, 33*(2), 508–518.

Knorr Cetina, K. (1997). Sociality with objects. *Theory, Culture & Society, 14*, 1–30.
Knorr Cetina, K. (1999). *Epistemic cultures: How the sciences make knowledge*. Cambridge, MA: Harvard University Press.
Knott, G. (1998). *Financial management* (3rd ed.). London: Macmillan Press.
Kokasal, I. (2000). *Taghayur al Ahkaam fi al Shari'ah al Islamiyyah*. Beirut: Dar al Risalah.
Kolb, R. W. (2000). *Futures, options, and swaps* (3rd ed.). Oxford: Blackwell.
Kondratieff, N. D. (1935/51). The long waves in economic life. *Review of Economic Statistics, 17*, 6–105 (1935). Reprinted in Haberler, G. (Ed.). (1951). *Readings in business cycle theory*. Homewood, IL: Richard D. Irwin.
Kosmidou, K., Pasiouras, F., & Tsaklangano, A. (2007). Domestic and multinational determinants of foreign bank profits: The case of Greek banks operating abroad. *Journal of Multinational Financial Management, 17*(1), 1–15.
Kosmidou, K., & Zopounidis, C. (2008). Measurement of bank performance in Greece. *South Eastern Europe Journal of Economics, 1*, 79–95.
Kramer, M., & Porter, M. (2006). Strategy and society: The link between competitive advantage and corporate social responsibility. *Harvard Business Review, 84*, 78–93.
Kumar, S., & Phrommathed, P. (2005). *New product development, an empirical effects of innovation strategy, organisation learning, and market conditions*. New York: Springer Science and Business Media.
Kuran, T. (1986). The economic system in contemporary Islamic thought (Alm-Giving Zakat). *International Journal of Middle East, 18*, 143–149.
Kuran, T. (2011). *The long divergence, how Islamic law held back the Middle East*. New Jersey: Princeton University Press.
Lane, P. J., Koka, B. R., & Pathak, S. (2006). The reification of absorptive capacity: A critical review and rejuvenation of the concept. *The Academy of Management Review, 31*(4), 833–863.
Latour, B. (1996). On inter-objectivity. *Mind, Culture, Activity, 3*(4), 228–245.
Latour, B. (2005). *Reassembling the social: An introduction to actor network theory*. Oxford: Oxford University Press.
Lazonick, W., & Prencipe, A. (2005). Dynamic capabilities and sustained innovation: Strategic control and financial commitment at Rolls-Royce plc. *Industrial and Corporate Change, 14*(3), 501–542.
Lee, R. (1998). *What is an exchange?* New York: Oxford University Press.
Lee, N., & Lings, I. (2008). *Doing business research: A guide to theory and practice*. London: Sage.
Leeuwis, C. (2013). *Communication for rural innovation: Rethinking agricultural extension*. Oxford: Wiley.
Leonardi, P. M. (2011). Innovation blindness: Culture, frames, and cross-boundary problem construction in the development of new technology concepts. *Organization Science, 22*, 347–369.
Levin, R. C., Klevorick, A. K., Nelson, R. R., & Winter, S. G. (1987). Appropriating the returns from industrial research and development. *Brookings Papers on Economic Activity, 3*, 783–831.
Levina, N., & Vaast, E. (2005). The emergence of boundary spanning competence in practice: Implications for implementation and use of information systems. *MIS Quarterly, 29*(2), 335–363.
Levine, R. (2003). *The corporate governance of banks: A concise discussion of concept and evidence* (Discussion Paper No. 3). Paper presented at the Global Corporate Governance Forum, October, Paris.
Lewis, B. (1970). Sources for the economic history in the Middle East. In M. A. Cook (Ed.), *Studies in the economic history of the Middle East*. Oxford: Oxford University Press.
Lewis, B. (1979). Politics and war. In J. Schacht & C. E. Bosworth (Eds.), *The legacy of Islam* (pp. 156–209). Oxford: Oxford University Press.
Lewis, M. K. (2001). Islam and accounting. *Accounting Forum, 25*(2), 103–127.

Li, W. D., Ong, S. K., & Nee, A. Y. C. (2006). *Integrated and collaborative product development environment technologies and implementations*. Singapore: World Scientific Publishing.

Lincoln, Y. S., & Guba, E. G. (1985). *Naturalistic inquiry*. Beverly Hills, CA: Sage.

Lissoni, F., & Metcalfe, J. S. (1993). *Diffusion of innovation ancient and modern: A review of the main themes*. England: University of Manchester.

Lotter, P., & Howladar, K. (2007). *Understanding Moody's approach to unsecured corporate sukuk*. Dubai: Moody's Investors Service.

Lyons, R., Chatman, J., & Joyce, K. (2007). Innovation in services: Corporate culture and investment banking. *California Management Review, 50*(1), 1183–1194.

Maclaurin, W. R. (1953). The sequence from invention to innovation and its relation to economic growth. *Quarterly Journal of Economics, 67*(1), 97–111.

MacMillan, I. C., & McGrath, R. G. (2002). Crafting R&D project portfolios. *Research Technology Management, 45*(5), 48–59.

Macy, J. R., & O'Hara, M. (2003, April). The corporate governance of banks. *FRBNY Economic Policy Review*, 91–107.

Mannan, M. A. (1980). *Islamic economic theory and practice*. Lahore: SH Muhammed Ashraf.

Manu, F. A. (1992). Innovation orientation, environment and performance: A comparison of U.S. and European markets. *Journal of International Business Studies, 23*(2), 333–359.

Manu, F. A., & Sriram, V. (1996). Innovation, marketing strategy, environment, and performance. *Journal of Business Research, 35*(1), 79–91.

March, J. (1990). The technology of foolishness. In D. S. Pugh (Ed.), *Organization theory: Selected readings* (pp. 224–238). Harmondsworth: Penguin Books.

Marshall, C., & Rossman, G. B. (1999). *Designing qualitative research* (3rd ed.). California: Sage.

Martin, X., & Salomon, R. (2003). Knowledge transfer capacity and its implication for the theory of the multinational corporation. *Journal of International Business Studies, 34*(4), 356–373.

Matten, D., & Moon, J. (2008). "Implicit" and "explicit" CSR: A conceptual framework for a comparative understanding of corporate social responsibility. *Academy of Management Review, 33*, 404–424.

McCahery, J., & Picciotto, S. (1995). Creative lawyering and the dynamics of business regulation. In D. Yves & S. David (Eds.), *Professional competition and professional power: Lawyers, accountants and the social construction of markets*. London: Psychology Press.

McGrath, M. E. (Ed.). (1996). *Setting the pace in product development, a guide to product and cycle time excellence*. Burlington, MA: Butterworth Heinemann.

McGrath, R. G., & Nerkar, A. (2004). Real options reasoning and a new look at the R&D investment strategies of pharmaceutical firms. *Strategic Management Journal, 25*(1), 1–21.

McNeil, D. (1996). *Epidemiological research methods*. New York: Wiley.

Merton, R. (1992). Financial innovation and economic performance. *Journal of Applied Corporate Finance, 4*, 12–22.

Mews, C. J., & Abraham, I. (2007, April). Usury and just compensation: Religious and financial ethics in historical perspective. *Journal of Business Ethics, 72*, 1–15.

Miera, D. M., & Repullo, R. (2010). Does competition reduce the risk of bank failure. *The Review of Financial Studies, 23*(10), 3639–3661.

Miles, R. E., & Snow, C. C. (1978). *Organizational strategy, structure, and process*. New York: McGraw Hill.

Miller, D., & Friesen, P. H. (1982). Innovation in conservative and entrepreneurial firms: Two models of strategic momentum. *Strategic Management Journal, 3*(1), 1–25.

Monks, R. A. G., & Minow, N. (2011). *Corporate governance* (5th ed.). Chichester: Wiley.

Moore, N. (2000). *How to do research: The complete guide to designing and managing research projects*. London: Library Association.

Moorman, C., & Slotegraaf, R. J. (1999). The contingency value of complementary capabilities in product development. *Journal of Marketing Research, 36*(2), 239–257.

Mowery, D. C., & Rosenberg, N. (1979). The influence of market demand upon innovation: A critical review of some empirical studies. *Research Policy, 8*(2), 102–153.

Mowery, D. C., & Rosenberg, N. (1998). *Paths of innovation: Technological change in 20th century America*. Cambridge: Cambridge University Press.

Mowery, D. C., & Shane, S. (2002). Introduction to the special issue on university entrepreneurship and technology transfer. *Management Science, 48*(1), v–ix.

Mullineux, A. (1997). Financial innovation, money banking and financial fragility in the UK. In B. Schachter (Ed.), *Derivatives, regulation and banking* (pp. 263–285). North Holland, The Netherlands: Elsevier Science B. V.

Murmann, J. P., & Frenken, K. (2006). Toward a systematic framework for research on dominant designs, technological innovations, and industrial change. *Research Policy, 35*(7), 925–952.

Muslim, Bin al-Hajaj al-Qushiri. (1954). *Sahih Muslim*. Cairo: Dār Iehya' al-Turath al-Arabi.

Muslim, Bin al-Hajaj al-Qushiri. (1976). *Sahih Muslim*. Rendered into English by A. H. Siddiqi. Lahore: Sh. Muhammad Ashraf.

Muslim, Ibn Al-Hajjaj. (1987). *Sahih Muslim*. Damascus: Dar Al-Fikr.

Naqvi, S. (1981). *Ethics and economics: An Islamic thesis*. Leicester: Islamic Foundation.

Nasr, Seyyed Hossein. (2003). *Islam, religion, history and civilisation*. New York: HarperCollins Publisher.

Nelson, R. R. (1959). The simple economics of basic scientific research. *Journal of Political Economy, 67*(3), 297–306.

Nelson, R. R. (1992). What is 'commercial' and what is 'public' about technology, and what should be? In N. Rosenberg, R. Landau, & D. Mowery (Eds.), *Technology and the wealth of nations* (pp. 57–72). Stanford, CA: Stanford University Press.

Nelson, R. R., & Winter, S. G. (1982). *An evolutionary theory of economic change*. Cambridge, MA: Harvard University Press.

Nichols, N. A. (1994). Scientific management at Merck: An interview with CFO Judy Lewent. *Harvard Business Review, 72*(1), 89–99.

Nicolini, D., Mengis, J., & Swan, J. (2012). Understanding the role of objects in cross-disciplinary collaboration. *Organization Science, 23*(3), 612–629.

Nonaka, I. (1994). A dynamic theory of organizational knowledge creation. *Organization Science, 5*(1), 14–37.

Noonan, J. (1957). *The scholastic inquiry into usury*. Cambridge, MA: Harvard University Press.

North, D. C., Davis, L. E., & Calla, S. (1971). *Institutional change and American economic growth*. New York: CUP Archive.

Obaidullah, Mohammad. (1998, November). Financial engineering with Islamic options. *Islamic Economic Studies, 6*(1), 74–98.

Obaidullah, Mohammed. (2005). *Islamic financial services*. Jeddah: Islamic Economics Research Centre, King Abdul Aziz University.

O'Sullivan, M. (2007). Funding new industries: A historical perspective on the financing role of the US stock market in the twentieth century. In N. R. Lamoreaux & K. L. Sokoloff (Eds.), *Financing innovation in the United States, 1870 to the present* (pp. 163–218). Cambridge, MA: MIT Press.

Pasiouras, F., & Kosmidou, K. (2007). Factors influencing the profitability of domestic and foreign commercial banks in the European Union. *Research in International Business and Finance, 21* (2), 222–237.

Patel, P., & Pavitt, K. (2000). How technological competencies help define the core (not the boundaries) of the firm. In G. Dosi, R. Nilson, & S. G. Winter (Eds.), *The nature and dynamices of organisational capabilities* (pp. 313–333). Oxford: Oxford University Press.

Pavitt, K. (1990). What we know about the strategic management of technology. *California Management Review, 32*(3), 17–26.

Pawley, M. (1993). *Financial innovation and monetary policy*. London: Routledge.

Pawlowski, S. D., & Robey, D. (2004). Bridging user organizations: Knowledge brokering and the work of information technology professionals. *MIS Quarterly, 28*(4), 645–672.

Persons, J. C., & Warther, V. A. (1997). Boom and bust patterns in the adoption of financial innovations. *The Review of Financial Studies, 10*(4), 939–967.

Peters, T. J., & Waterman, R. H. (1982). *In search of excellence: Lessons from America's best-run companies*. New York: Harper & Row.

Philippe, J., & Da Silva, M. (1995). *The importance of derivative securities market to modern finance*. Chicago, IL: Catalyst Institute.

Pisano, G. P. (1990). The R&D boundaries of the firm: An empirical analysis. *Administrative Science Quarterly, 35*(1), 153–176.

Plosser, C. I. (2009). Financial econometrics, financial innovation, and financial stability. *Journal of Financial Econometrics, 7*(1), 3–11.

Podolski, T. M. (1986). *Financial innovation and the money supply*. New York: Basil Blackwell Inc.

Poole, W. (2011). Causes and consequences of the financial crisis of (2007–2009). *Harvard Journal of Law & Public Policy, 33*(2), 422–441.

Porter, M. E. (1990). *The competitive advantage of nations*. New York: Free Press.

Prahalad, C. K., & Hamel, G. (1990). The core competence of the corporation. *Harvard Business Review, 68*(3), 79–91.

Qattan, M. A. (2006). Shari'ah supervision: The unique building block of Islamic financial architecture. In T. Khan & D. Muljawan (Eds.), *Islamic financial architecture: Risk management and financial stability* (pp. 273–287). Jeddah: IRTI–IDB.

Quinn, J. B. (1985). Managing innovation: Controlled chaos. *Harvard Business Review, 63*(3), 73–84.

Qur'an. (1995). *Qur'an*. Damascus: Dar Al-Fikr.

Qureshi, D. M. (1988). The role of stock exchange in the Islamic financial system. *Journal of Islamic Banking and Finance, 5*(1), 10.

Qutub, Muhammad. (1974). *Al Tatawour wa al Thabat fi Hayati al Bashar*. Beirut: Dar Al Shorouq.

Radwān, S. A. H. (1996). *Aswaq Al-Awraq Al-Maliyyah* [Financial market]. Cairo: International Institute of Islamic Thought.

Rahman, Y. A. (1994). *Interest free Islamic banking*. Kuala Lumpur: Al-Hilal Publishing.

Rajan, R. G. (2010). *Fault lines*. New Jersey: Princeton University Press.

Ramadan, Tariq. (2009). *Radical reform: Islamic ethics and liberation*. New York: Oxford University Press.

Rammal, H. G. (2006). The importance of *Shari'ah* supervision in IFIs. *Corporate Ownership and Control, 3*(3), 204–208.

Rangapriya (Priya), K.-N. (2014). Organizational ingenuity in nascent innovations: Gaining resources and legitimacy through unconventional actions. *Organization Studies, 35*(4), 483–509.

Rao, K. V. (1994). *Research methodology in commerce and management*. New Delhi: Sterling Publishers Private.

Raquibuz, Zaman M. (1986, September). The operation of the modern financial markets for stocks and bonds and its relevance to an Islamic economy. *American Journal of Social Sciences, 3*(1), 135–138.

Raymond, A. (1981). The economic crisis of Egypt in the eighteenth century. In A. L. Udovitch (Ed.), *The Islamic Middle East, (700–1900): Studies in economic and social history*. Princeton, NJ: The Darwin Press.

Rayner, S. E. (1991). *The theory of contracts in Islamic law*. London: Graham & Trotman.

Reiter, S., Stewart, G., & Bruce, C. (2011). A strategy for delayed research method selection: Deciding between grounded theory and phenomenology. *The Electronic Journal of Business Research Methods, 9*(1), 35–46.

Rendleman Jr., R. J. (2002). *Applied derivatives: Options, futures, and swaps*. Oxford: Blackwell.

Rheinberger, H. J. (1997). *Toward a history of epistemic things: Synthesizing proteins in the test tube*. Palo Alto, CA: Stanford University Press.

Rice, G. (1999). Islamic ethics and the implications for business. *Journal of Business Ethics, 18*, 345–358.

Robson, C. (2002). *Real world research* (2nd ed.). Oxford: Blackwell.

Rogers, E. M. (1976). *Communication and development: Critical perspectives*. London: Sage.

Rogers, E. M. (1983). *Diffusion of innovations*. New York: Free Press.

Rogers, E. M. (2010). *Diffusion of innovations* (4th ed.). New York: The Free Press and Simon and Schuster.

Rosenberg, N. (1990). Why do firms do basic research (with their own money?). *Research Policy, 19*(2), 165–174.

Rosenberg, N., & Nelson, R. R. (1994). American universities and technical advance in industry. *Research Policy, 23*(3), 323–348.

Rosenkopf, L., Metiu, A., & George, V. P. (2001). From the bottom up? Technical committee activity and alliance formation. *Administrative Science Quarterly, 46*(4), 748–772.

Ruttan, V. W. (1959). Usher and Schumpeter on invention, innovation, and technological change. *Quarterly Journal of Economics, 73*(4), 596–606.

Ryan, M. (2009). Mixed methodology approach to place attachment and consumption behaviour: A rural town perspective. *The Electronic Journal of Business Research Methods, 7*(1), 107–116.

Salamon, H. (1998). *Speculation in the stock market from the Islamic perspective* (pp. 27–30). The First International Conference on Islamic Development Management: Management of Economic Development in Islamic Perspective, University Sains Malaysia, Penang, 8–10 December 1998.

Sālih, Nabil A. (1988). *Unlawful gain and legitimate profit in Islamic law*. London: Cambridge Press.

Sandberg, J. (2005). How do we justify knowledge produced within interpretive approaches. *Organisational Research Methods, 8*(1), 41–68. ABI/INFORM Global.

Saunders, M., Lewis, P., & Thornhill, A. (2009). *Research methods for business students* (5th ed.). Essex: Prentice Hall.

Scarbrough, H., et al. (2015). Developing a relational view of the organizing role of objects: A study of the innovation process in computer games. *Organization Studies, 36*(2), 197–220.

Schilling, M. A., & Phelps, C. C. (2007). Interfirm collaboration networks: The impact of large-scale network structure on firm innovation. *Management Science, 53*(7), 1113–1126.

Schumpeter, J. A. (1934). *The theory of economic development*. Boston, MA: Harvard University Press.

Schumpeter, J. A. (1939). *Business cycles*. New York: McGraw-Hill.

Schumpeter, J. A. (1942). *Capitalism, socialism and democracy*. London: Allen and Unwin.

Shalaq, A. F. (1997). Muhammad wa Sharluman wa 'Osoul Awrouppa (Europe) 'Ard wa Mutaba'ah. *Journal of Ijtihad*. Issue: 36, year: 9, 65–83.

Shiller, R. J. (1993). *Macro markets: Creating institutions for managing society's largest economic risks: Creating institutions for managing society's largest economic risks*. New York: Oxford University Press.

Shiller, R. J. (2012). *Financial innovation: Too much or too little?* (M. Haliassos, Ed.). Cambridge, MA: MIT Press.

Siddiqi, M. N. (1981). Muslim economic thinking: A survey of contemporary literature. In K. Ahmad (Ed.), *Studies in Islamic economics*. Leicester: The Islamic Foundation.

Siguaw, J. A., Simpson, P. M., & Enz, C. A. (2006). Conceptualizing innovation orientation: A framework for study and integration of innovation research. *Journal of Product Innovation Management, 23*, 556–574.

Simon, H. (1957). *Administrative behaviour*. New York: Free Press.

Sinclair, P. (2001). *Financial exclusion: An introductory survey*. Edinburgh: Centre for Research into Socially Inclusive Services.

Sinkey, J. F. (1992). Innovation as a diffusion process: Bank technological innovation, the payment system, and information processing. In *The financial services industry* (4th ed., pp. 113–410). New York: Macmillan.

Smith, A. (1789). *An inquiry into the nature and causes of the wealth of nations* (Vol. 3, 5th ed.). England: A. Strahan and T. Cadell.

Smith, A. (1790). *The theory of moral sentiments* (S. M. Soares, Ed., 6th ed.). Brazil: MetaLibri.

Smith, A. (1976). *The wealth of nations* (R. H. Campbell & A. S. Skinner, Eds.). The Glasgow edition of the Works and Correspondence of Adam Smith, Vol. 2b.

Smith, K. (2006). *From petrodollars to Islamic dollars: The strategic construction of Islamic banking in the Arab Gulf.* Cambridge, MA: Harvard University.

Smith, P. G., & Reinertsen, D. G. (1998). *Developing products in half the time: New rules, new tools* (2nd ed.). New York: Wiley.

Sonenshein, S., Decelles, K., & Dutton, J. E. (2014). It's not easy being green: The role of self-evaluations in explaining support of environmental issues. *Academy of Management Journal, 57*(1), 7–37.

Spencer, P. D. (2000). *The structure and regulation of financial markets.* New York: Oxford University Press.

Star, S. L. (2010). This is not a boundary object: Reflections on the origin of a concept. *Science, Technology Human Values, 35*(5), 601–617.

Star, S. L., & Griesemer, J. R. (1989). Institutional ecology, translations and boundary objects: Amateurs and professionals in Berkeley's Museum of Vertebrate Zoology, 1907–1939. *Social Study Science, 19*(3), 389–420.

Stenberg, L. (1996). *The Islamisation of science: Four Muslim positions developing an Islamic modernity.* Lund: Lunds University.

Stoneman, P. (Ed.). (1995). *Handbook of the economics of innovation and technological change.* London: Wiley.

Subramaniam, M., & Venkatraman, N. (2001). Determinants of transnational new product development capability: Testing the influence of transferring and deploying tacit overseas knowledge. *Strategic Management Journal, 22*, 359–378.

Suliman, Abdul Rahaman. (1898). *Majma' al Anhur Shareh Multaqa al Abhur.* Cairo: Dar Ehya' al Turath al Arabi.

Sulyman, Ahmed Yusuf. (1982). *Ra'ī al-Tashree' fī Masa'l al-Boursa, al-Maūsūa'a al-'Ilmiyya wa al-'Amaliyya lil Bunūk al-Islamiyya.* Cairo: al-Ittihad al-Islamī lil Bunūk al-Islamiyya.

Sundararajan, V. (2007). Risk characteristics of Islamic products: Implications for risk measurements and supervision. In S. Archer & R. A. A. Karim (Eds.), *Islamic finance: The regulatory challenge.* Singapore: Wiley.

Sveiby, K.-E., Gripenberg, P., & Segercrantz, B. (Eds.). (2012). *Challenging the innovation paradigm.* New York: Routledge.

Tashakkori, A., & Teddlie, C. (2003). *Handbook on mixed methods in the behavioural and social sciences.* Thousand Oaks, CA: Sage.

Teece, D. J. (1986). Profiting from technological innovation: Implications for integration, collaboration, licensing and public policy. *Research Policy, 15*(6), 285–305.

Teece, D. J. (2006). Reflections on profiting from innovation? *Research Policy, 35*(8), 1131–1146.

Teece, D. J. (2007). Explicating dynamic capabilities: The nature and micro-foundations of (sustainable) enterprise performance. *Strategic Management Journal, 28*(13), 1319–1350.

Teece, D. J., Pisano, G., & Shuen, A. (1997). Dynamic capabilities and strategic management. *Strategic Management Journal, 18*(7), 509–533.

Nik Norzrul Thani. (2001). *Legal aspects of Malaysian Islamic financial systems.* Kuala Lumpur: Sweet and Maxwell Asia.

Thomas, A., Cox, S., Kraty, B., & Euromoney Institutional Investor PLC (Eds.). (2005). *Structuring Islamic finance transactions.* London: Euromoney Books.

Thomsett, M. D. (2001). *Getting started in options* (4th ed.). New York: Wiley.

To, M. H., & Tripe, D. (2002). Factors influencing the perfonricince of foreign owned banks in New Zealand. *Journal of International Financial Markets, Institutions and Money, 12*(4–5), 341–357.

Traxler, M. J. (2008). *Evidence against underspecification in relative clause attachment*. In Poster Presented to the CUNY Sentence Processing Conference, Chapel Hill, NC.

Tripp, C. (2006). *Islam and the moral economy: The challenge of capitalism*. Cambridge: Cambridge University Press.

Trist, E., & Bamforth, K. (1951). Some social and psychological consequences of the long-wall method of coal-getting. *Human Relations, 4*(1), 3–38.

Trott, P. (2008). *Innovation management and new product development* (4th ed.). England: Pearson Education.

Tuan, L. A., et al. (2010). In F. G. Palis (Ed.), *Research to impact: Case studies for natural resource management for irrigated rice in Asia*. Manila: International Rice Research Institute.

Tufano, P. (1989). Financial innovation and first mover advantages. *Journal of Financial Economics, 25*, 213–240.

Turner, A. (2012). *Economic after the crisis, objectives and means*. London: MIT Press.

Tushman, M. L. (1997). Winning through innovation. *Strategy and Leadership, 25*(4), 14–19.

Tzeng, C.-H. (2009). A review of contemporary innovation literature: A Schumpeterian perspective. *Innovation: Management, Policy & Practice, 11*, 373–394.

Ulrich, K. T., & Eppinger, S. D. (2008). *Product development and design*. New York: McGraw Hill.

United Nations Development Program (UNDP). (1994). *Human development report*. Oxford: Oxford University Press.

Usmani, M. Taqi. (1996, June). Options, futures, swaps, and equity investment. *New Horizon*, 10–12.

Usmani, Muhammad. Taqi. (2005). *An introduction to Islamic finance*. Karachi: Maktaba Ma'ariful Qur'an.

Utterback, J. M. (1994). *Mastering the dynamics of innovation: How companies can seize opportunities in the face of technological change*. Boston, MA: Harvard Business School Press.

Van de Ven, A. H. (1999). *The innovation journey*. New York: Oxford University Press.

Van de Ven, A. H., Polley, D. E., Garud, R., & Venkataraman, S. (1999). *The innovation journey*. New York: Oxford University Press.

Visser, H. (2009). *Islamic finance: Principles and practice*. Northampton, MA: Edward Elgar.

Vogel, F. E., & Hayes III, S. L. (1998). *Islamic law and finance: Religion, risk, and return*. London: Kluwer Law International.

Wang, C. L., & Ahmed, P. K. (2007). Dynamic capabilities: A review and research agenda. *International Journal of Management Reviews, 9*(1), 31–51.

Warde, Ibrahim. (2010). *Islamic finance in the global economy* (2nd ed.). Edinburgh: Edinburgh University Press.

Wenger, E. (1998). *Communities of practice: Learning, meaning, and identity*. New York: Cambridge University Press.

Williams, B. (2003). Domestic and international determinants of bank profits: Foreign banks in Australia. *Journal of Banking and Finance, 27*(6), 1185–1210.

Williams, G., & Zinkin, J. (2010). Islam and CSR: A study of the compatibility between the tenets of Islam and the UN global compact. *Journal of Business Ethics, 91*, 519–533.

Wilson, R. (2009). *The development of Islamic finance in the GCC*. Kuwait: The Centre for the Study of Global Governance.

Wilson, R. (2010). Islamic finance: Principles and practices (Book review). *Journal of Islamic Studies*, 1–4.

Wilson, R. (2012). *Legal, regulatory and governance issues in Islamic finance*. Edinburgh: Edinburgh University Press.

Wilson, Rodney, and El-Ashker, Ahmed A. F. (2006). *Islamic economics: A short history*. Boston, MA: Brill Academic Publishers.
Woodward, J. (1965). *Industrial organisation: Theory and practice* (2nd ed.). Oxford: Oxford University Press.
Worren, N., Moore, K., & Cardona, P. (2002). Modularity, strategic flexibility, and firm performance: A study of the home appliance industry. *Strategic Management Journal, 23*(12), 1123–1140.
Yousri, Abdul Rahman. (1987). *Tatawour al Fikr al Iqtisadi* [The development of economic thought] (2nd ed.). Iskandariyyah: Dar al Jami'at al Masriyyah.
Zaltman, G., Duncan, R., & Holbek, J. (1973). *Innovations and organizations*. New York: Wiley.
Zenjawaih, M. (1986). *Al Amwaal* (S. Z. Fayyad, Ed.). Riyadh: Markaz al Malik Faisal lil Bohouth wa el Dirasat al Islamiyyah.
Zidān, Abul Karim. (1974). *al-Wajeez fī 'Usūl al-Fiqh* (5th ed.). Baghdad: Matba'at Salman al-'A'zamī.

Index

S. Alamad, *Financial Innovation and Engineering in Islamic Finance*,
Contributions to Management Science, DOI 10.1007/978-3-319-52947-9